The Emergence of Judaism

The Emergence of Judaism

Jacob Neusner

Westminster John Knox Press
LOUISVILLE • LONDON

© 2004 Jacob Neusner

Most Scripture quotations are the author's translations.

Scripture quotations from the Revised Standard Version of the Bible are copyright © 1946, 1952, 1971, and 1973 by the Division of Christian Education of the National Council of the Churches of Christ in the U.S.A. and are used by permission.

Book design by Sharon Adams
Cover design by Lisa Buckley
Cover illustration: S. Meltzer/PhotoLink

First edition
Published by Westminster John Knox Press
Louisville, Kentucky

This book is printed on acid-free paper that meets the American National Standards Institute Z39.48 standard. ∞

PRINTED IN THE UNITED STATES OF AMERICA

04 05 06 07 08 09 10 11 12 13 — 10 9 8 7 6 5 4 3 2 1

Library of Congress Cataloging-in-Publication Data

Neusner, Jacob, 1932–
    The emergence of Judaism / Jacob Neusner.
        p. cm.
    ISBN 0-664-22780-5 (alk. paper)
    1. Judaism.   I. Title.

    BM45.N38   2004
    296'.09'014—dc22   2004050886

Contents

Part V: Primary Documents

Preface

*J*udaism is the religion that meets God in the Torah—a Hebrew word that means teaching or instruction. In the narrative of Judaism the Torah was given by God to Moses at Mount Sinai. When we follow the way in which the Torah took shape in ancient times, we trace the emergence of Judaism, which took place in the land of Israel (i.e., Palestine). Judaism emerged from the time of Moses, 1200 B.C.E. (Before the Common Era = B.C.) to its full and complete statement in the Talmud of Babylonia, ca. 600 C.E. (Common Era = A.D.)

Of what does the Torah consist? Comprised by writings deemed God-given, the Torah contains the instruction on the way of life and worldview of God's people. It is preserved in writing in the Hebrew Scriptures of ancient Israel (the Old Testament of Christianity) and in oral tradition. Thus the Torah consists of two parts, the written Torah and the oral, or memorized, Torah.

The Torah is in two media, writing and memory. The Torah in Judaism includes writings that are not in the Hebrew Scriptures of ancient Israel. These writings originated in oral tradition, also deriving from God's revelation to Moses at Sinai. Thus Judaism holds that the Torah of Sinai is made up of teachings handed on both in writing and in memory. They are called, respectively, "the Torah that is in writing" and "the Torah that is in memory."

The written part of the Torah (corresponding to Christianity's Old Testament) is divided into three divisions: Torah, Prophets (Hebrew: *Nebi'im*), Writings (Hebrew: *Ketubim*; thus T N K, yielding the acronym, Tanak).

The first division of the Hebrew Scriptures is comprised by the five books of Moses (Pentateuch). These are Genesis, Exodus, Leviticus, Numbers, and Deuteronomy. They tell the story of the creation of the world and of humanity and the formation, within humanity, of God's people, Israel (meaning, the family of Abraham and Sarah and their descendants through Isaac and Rebecca and Jacob [also known as Israel] and Leah and Rachel). That family went down to Egypt and was enslaved there. God brought the Israelites out of

Egypt to Mount Sinai, where they accepted the Torah and were called to form Israel, defined as a kingdom of priests and a holy people.

Second, the prophetic writings are Joshua, Judges, Samuel, Kings, Isaiah, Jeremiah, Ezekiel, and the Twelve Minor Prophets. Joshua through Kings tell the story of how Israel conquered the land of Israel and over centuries formed a monarchy in the family of David and built a temple in Jerusalem for the service of God, but disobeyed God and so lost the land and suffered the destruction of Jerusalem and its temple and went into exile. The prophets Isaiah, Jeremiah, and Ezekiel interpret that story and promise that when Israel keeps God's teaching, it will recover the land.

Third come the Writings (Psalms, Proverbs, Job, Song of Songs, Ruth, Lamentations, Ecclesiastes or Qohelet, Esther, Daniel, Ezra, Nehemiah, Chronicles). The Writings are diverse. Ezra and Nehemiah report how Israel recovered the land and rebuilt the Temple of Jerusalem.

These three large divisions of sacred Scripture form the written part of the Torah.

The memorized part of the Torah consists of oral tradition. That tradition in its principles and contents begins with Moses at Sinai and continues in teachings passed on through the prophets to the sages of later times (called sages or Rabbis). The oral Torah is equal in standing to the written part of the Torah. The oral tradition was preserved through memorization. Generations of masters taught the tradition to their disciples, from Sinai, ca. 1200 B.C.E., to the writing down of the oral tradition, beginning with the Mishnah, a philosophical law code of ca. 200 C.E., continuing with commentaries to the Mishnah and to books of the written Torah. The climax of the writing down of the oral Torah came in 600 C.E., with the Talmud of Babylonia, a commentary to the Mishnah and to Scripture.

Judaism therefore is a religion that took shape in ancient times and has thrived from then to now. First I tell the story (part 1) of how that religion took shape. I tell how its principal writings—the components of the Torah—responded to three crises in the life of the people of Israel, which is comprised by the community of the faithful (not to be confused with the ethnic group, the Jews). Next I define how Judaism emerged in some of its main doctrines and beliefs (part 2). These trace the development, by successive documents, of the doctrine of Israel, the worldview (Torah), the way of life (law), and God. Then I explain why it has flourished for the thousands of years since Sinai, to the present day (part 3). I tell stories about some of the outstanding sages of the Torah, written and oral (part 4). Finally, I introduce Judaism's principal writings of ancient times (part 5). In this way I describe the emergence, in ancient times, of one of the enduring religious traditions of humanity, the Judaism that defines itself out of the Torah in two media, oral and written.

Of course, in antiquity other Judaic religious systems took shape. We know about one of these from the writings of the Dead Sea Scrolls, and about another from the Gospels. The worldview, way of life, and definition of Israel comprising a Judaic religious system set forth here competed with the counterparts portrayed in the Dead Sea Scrolls and in the Christian Gospels. Those communities had their own definitions of Israel, its way of life, and its worldview. They appealed, in part, to the same Scriptures ("Written Torah," "Old Testament"). But each community read those Scriptures in its own distinctive way, and all of them claimed to possess revealed traditions in addition to the Hebrew Scriptures.

Here we address only the Judaism that ultimately defined the norm for the Jewish people, and that is, the Torah as defined by the rabbinic sages of ancient times.

A particular trait of my presentation of the emergence of Judaism requires a brief explanation. I cite verbatim a sizable volume of sources. That is because beyond the Hebrew Scriptures ("Old Testament"), Judaism's writings are not widely known. To make possible a direct encounter between the reader and the religion that is described in these pages, I include ample evidence of how that religion expressed its main ideas.

I write not to advocate a particular religion or religion in general. I seek only to describe a particular religion as it makes itself known in the unfolding of its principal writings in the age in which it emerged. I propose to situate the story of the emergence of Judaism in the historical context of crisis to which that religious system responded. I do not raise questions of truth or meaning. These are best addressed in other settings than the historical one.

I express my thanks to Jack Keller and the entire staff of Westminster John Knox Press for their usual, highly professional production of my book. I have worked with WJK for several decades now, through numerous editors, and the present generation is as good as the best I have ever known.

Jacob Neusner
Bard College
Annandale-on-Hudson, New York 12504
Neusner@webjogger.net

Time Line

ca. 1200 B.C.E.	Exodus from Egypt under Moses; conquest of Canaan under Joshua
1200–1050	Period of the judges
ca. 1050	Samuel
ca. 1013–973	David, king of Judah and then of Israel as well
973–933	Solomon
ca. 930	Kingdom divided into Judah and Israel
ca. 750	Amos
ca. 735	Hosea
ca. 725	Isaiah
722	Assyrians take Samaria; exile ten northern tribes
639–609	Josiah
620	Deuteronomic reforms
ca. 600	Jeremiah
586	Jerusalem Temple destroyed; Judeans exiled to Babylonia
ca. 590	Ezekiel
ca. 550	Second Isaiah
538	First return to Zion under Sheshbazzar
520	Zerubbabel, Haggai lay foundation for Temple
515	Temple completed

ca. 444	The priest Ezra comes from Babylonia, then under Persian rule, with the task assigned to him by the Persian government of taking over Jerusalem and establishing the Torah as the governing document for the Jews of Jerusalem and surrounding Judea
331	Alexander takes the land of Israel (Jerusalem)
168	Judaism prohibited by Antiochus IV; Maccabees revolt
165	Temple regained, purified by Maccabees
ca. 100	Community founded at Dead Sea, produces scrolls
63	Romans conquer Jerusalem, which becomes part of the Roman system
37–4	Herod rules as Roman ally
	Hillel
ca. 40 C.E.	Gamaliel I heads Pharisees
70	Destruction of Jerusalem by Romans
	Yohanan ben Zakkai founds center for legal study and judicial and administrative rule at Yavneh
ca. 80–110	Gamaliel heads academy at Yavneh
	Final canonization of Hebrew Scriptures
	Promulgation of Order of Prayer by Rabbis
115–117	Diaspora Jewries revolt against Trajan
120	Aqiba leads rabbinical movement
132–135	Bar Kokhba leads messianic war against Rome
	Southern part of the land of Israel devastated; Galilee survives and rebuilds
140	Rabbis reassemble in Galilee, restore Jewish government
ca. 200	Judah the Prince, head of Palestinian Jewish community, promulgates Mishnah
ca. 220	Babylonian academy founded at Sura by Rab (R. Abba)
ca. 250	Pact between Jews and Persian king, Shapur I: Jews to keep state law; Persians to permit Jews to govern selves, live by own religion

297	Founding of school at Pumbedita, in Babylonia, by Judah ben Ezekiel
ca. 330	Pumbedita school headed by Abbaye, then Raba, lays foundation of Babylonian Talmud
ca. 400	Talmud of the Land of Israel completed
ca. 450	*Genesis Rabbah,* commentary out of Genesis on the meaning of Israel's history, and *Leviticus Rabbah,* historical laws of Israel's society developed out of the book of Leviticus, are completed
ca. 500	*Pesiqta de Rab Kahana,* set of essays on the salvation of Israel in the messianic time, expected fairly soon, worked out
ca. 400	R. Ashi begins to shape Babylonian Talmud, completed by 600
630–640	Muslim conquest of Middle East
ca. 700	Saboraim complete the final editing of Babylonian Talmud

PART I   The Emergence of Judaism

Chapter 1

Crises, Questions, and Documents

A crisis is a moment of danger and opportunity. Judaism emerged in ancient times in response to three historical crises. Each crisis posed a fundamental question to the Jews. In each case a document recorded the Judaic response to the crisis at hand, answering the question of the age.

The first question was, Who are we that form the community of the faithful? That question became critical in ca. 450 B.C.E. when the Jews rebuilt the Temple of Jerusalem after a period of exile. Then they had to define their community and its vocation.

The second question was, What ought we to do in serving God? That question concerning the way of life of the community of the faithful required an answer in response to the second great crisis. That took place when in 70 C.E. the Temple rebuilt in the fifth century B.C.E. was destroyed. A second defeat, in 135 C.E., made certain that for a long time to come, the Temple would not be rebuilt. With sacrifice in the Temple of Jerusalem shut down, the question of how to serve God became critical.

The third question was, How do we explain ourselves in history and the world round about? That question demanded a response when in the fourth century, Christianity was adopted as the Roman state religion. Competing with Judaism, Christianity argued that its political triumph after three centuries of persecution proved it was the true religion. The crisis was represented by the historical success of Christianity. Then Judaism had to set forth a worldview that from its perspective made sense of history.

The three documents in the emergence of Judaism and the historical questions they answered. Each crisis facing Judaism raised a question answered by an authoritative document. Three writings, named here and defined in a moment, answered the three questions provoked at the specified historical turnings. Thus Judaism took shape in three successive steps.

First came a definition of the group or community of Judaism, which called itself "Israel." This definition was set forth in the Pentateuch.

This was followed by an account of the way of life of that community. The Israelite way of life was defined by the Mishnah.

That way of life was explained by a set of doctrines that portray the worldview of that community. These were spelled out by the Talmud of the Land of Israel.

The three parts of Judaism in the end were joined together in a single statement, which was complete at the end of ancient times. That coherent, systematic statement from then to now has defined the norm of Judaism, thus "normative Judaism."

The three events that marked the emergence of the three fundamental documents of Judaism. The process of reconstruction after a disaster defined the crisis that marked each stage in the emergence of Judaism. Great writings matched great challenges. Large conceptions resolved urgent, important questions.

The date 450 B.C.E. stands for the return to Zion and restoration of the Temple destroyed in 586 B.C.E., with the five books of Moses of the Hebrew Scriptures ("Old Testament"), which we met in the preface, as the outcome.

The date 200 C.E. stands for the promulgation of the Mishnah in response to the restoration of the Jews' self-rule by the Romans in the land of Israel.

The date 400 C.E. refers to the writing of the Talmud of the Land of Israel, a commentary to the Mishnah, which responded to the triumph of Christianity in the preceding century.

These writings take account of what had gone wrong and set forth a design for a restored life for the people of Israel in relationship to God: its definition of itself as a social group, its picture of its way of life, and its account of its worldview.

450 B.C.E.: The Pentateuch and the Definition of Israel

The Pentateuch, the five books of Moses, is completed by the prophetic writings of Joshua, Judges, Samuel, and Kings; these collections tell two stories. They run parallel, one concerning humanity in general represented by Adam and Eve, the other concerning the counterpart, Israel (the holy people, not to be confused with the contemporary state of Israel).

The first is the story of humanity represented by Adam and Eve in the garden of Eden, Genesis 1–3. God created paradise ("the garden of Eden") and then formed Adam and Eve, the first man and the first woman, to live there.

He gave them everything in the garden except the fruit of one tree. That, he commanded them, they were not to eat. They disobeyed God's commandment and were thrown out of paradise. Instead of an easy life for eternity, humanity was given a hard life of work, ending in death.

The story of getting and losing paradise has its parallel in the story of the formation of Israel, children of Abraham and Sarah and their descendants. They became enslaved in Egypt but were freed by God and given the promised land (the land of Israel). They were assigned commandments by God. They disobeyed them. They were thrown out of the land.

Each story tells the story of possession of paradise lost. As Adam and Eve lost Eden by reason of rebellion against God, so Israel lost the land of Israel by reason of rebellion against God—parallel histories.

But there is this difference. Israel lost the land but regained it. And if Israel keeps the rules that God set forth, it would retain the land for all time. So the Pentateuch tells the rules that govern Israel's possession of the land.

How then do Adam and Israel compare and contrast? Adam and Israel had in common possessing and losing paradise. While Adam possessed and lost Eden, Israel possessed and lost the land *but recovered it*. Thus the Pentateuch and Prophets tell the story of exile and return. They underscore the lesson that only by voluntarily submitting humanity's free will to God's wishes can Adam retain Eden, can Israel hold on to the land.

The Torah—God's instruction—contains the lessons that will secure Israel's possession of the land. So the difference between humanity and its loss of Eden and Israel and its loss of the land lay in Israel's possession of the Torah.

This pattern of exile and return responded to a very specific set of historical events. It organized happenings over a period of a century and a half. These happenings thus are formed into the pattern of exile and return. The outcome, the Pentateuch and the prophetic writings that continue its story, defines who and what is Israel. Israel is the people commanded by God in the Torah to love God and worship him.

So much for the story that the Torah tells. It is summarized in Leviticus 26, which says in so many words that when the Israelites obey God, they possess the land, but when they disobey, they are driven out. Now to the historical moment at which this component of Judaism—the definition of the community—emerges. To what crisis of reconstruction does the message of the Pentateuch respond?

The answer to that question lies in the history of the Jews in their land. For Scripture organized and responded to those happenings. In 586 B.C.E., the Judeans of the land of Israel were conquered by the empire of Babylonia. They suffered the destruction of their capital, Jerusalem, their government, and their temple. Some of them were removed from Jerusalem and brought by the victors to their own country, Babylonia, the area around present-day Baghdad in Iraq. For what they called three generations, these Jews lived in Babylonia. Their captors, the Babylonians, lost a war with the Iranians under the emperor Cyrus, who came from Persia, in the southwestern corner of Iran. In the process of inheriting the Babylonians' empire, Cyrus and his successor reversed the policy of the former empire. The Persian rulers of Iran gave permission to go back where they came from ("return home") to diverse groups taken away from their places of origins ("exiled") by the Babylonians.

Some Babylonian Jews after 530 B.C.E. went back to the land of Israel. They began to restore Jerusalem and rebuild the Temple. Not much happened in Judea—the Temple added up to little, so the prophets of the time complained—until, around 450 B.C.E., Ezra, a Jewish viceroy for Jerusalem appointed by the Iranian government, took up his duties and restored the Temple of that city. A small number of the Jews who had settled in Babylonia ("the exiles") went with Ezra and participated in the project of resettling the land. Most Babylonian Jews did not. Whether or not they saw themselves as exiles, they did not then return.

Those who chose to return to the land saw their family history as the story of exile and return. That covered the grandparents, taken away from the land; the parents, brought up in exile; and the grandchildren, the generation of the return to Zion, the mountain on which the Temple was built. That experience defined the norm. The community of the faithful, calling itself "Israel," is defined by the narrative that the Pentateuch sets forth. The story they told themselves concerned those who have possessed the land and lost it, but have been restored to it. That restoration was in order for them to form the community subject to God's rule in the Torah. That is how the Pentateuch would define the community. "Israel" was made up—and would be made up for all time—of those who told about themselves personally the story that the Pentateuch and Prophets set forth about all Israel in general.

The key to that story concerned the task, within humanity, assigned to the holy community of Israel. Israel formed the counterpart to Adam, therefore, in possessing and losing paradise. But Israel was different from Adam in getting a second chance.

What conclusions did Judaism want the Israelites to draw from the narrative of exile and return? The main one is this: Israel could never take its very existence as permanent and unconditional. They had held the land, lost it, and gotten it back. In the Torah they possessed the rules that governed their future relationship to the land, defined by their relationship to God. The story Scripture told was their story, the rules Scripture set forth were the rules God wanted them to keep.

Four lessons followed. The first is the land is not a given, but a gift. Second, the promise to Israel is conditional, and the Torah defines the conditions. Third, the land is there to be lost. Fourth, the people there can lose it and cease to be—all because of what they do or do not do in response to God's commandments in the Torah.

The Pentateuch, read in synagogue worship through the year for all centuries afterward, would retell, week by week, the original story. It would be interpreted as the pattern of the community's life. "Israel," the people of Judaism, was defined as those subject to God's rule.

The Pentateuch thus took the first step in the emergence of Judaism by defining who and what is the community of the faithful. "Israel" is the community in the here and now of which Scripture speaks. It is those subject to God's rule through the Torah.

200 C.E.: The Mishnah and Judaism's Way of Life

The second stage in the emergence of Judaism is signaled by the Mishnah. The Mishnah, a philosophical law code produced in the aftermath of war and reconstruction, is Judaism's most important document after the Torah of 450 B.C.E. Before we consider the crisis and the problem resolved, for Judaism's way of life, by the Mishnah, let us meet the document.

Part of the Oral Torah that we met in the preface, the Mishnah divides the law it sets forth into six principal parts and sixty-three topical expositions or "tractates." It is important because it provides a plan for restoration of a lost paradise, as much as the Pentateuch does. But the plan is set forth only through laws arranged in a system, not through episodic cases set forth within narratives in the manner of the Pentateuch.

The Mishnah was completed in 200 C.E. It contains laws attributed to authorities who flourished from the first century B.C.E. through the end of the second century C.E. It also organizes the laws of the Torah and amplifies them. So the Mishnah contains traditions of earlier times. But its information, some of it originating in most ancient times, was fully organized and systematized only in the last half-century of that period, between 150 and 200 C.E. That was a period of rebuilding after catastrophe, like the age in which the Pentateuch came into being.

What happened to precipitate the crisis of disaster and reconstruction that was resolved by the Mishnah? It was the destruction, in 70 C.E., of the Temple founded in 450 B.C.E. This took place at the height of a war fought by Jews against Rome (66–73 C.E.). Some of the Jewish population of the land of Israel had wished to free the country of subservience to Roman, pagan rule. This first war was followed three generations later by a second great war against Rome (132–135 C.E.), producing a still greater disaster: Jerusalem was closed off to Jews, the Temple Mount was ploughed over, and on its grounds the Romans built a pagan temple.

What was the crisis? People realized that, for a long time to come, the mode of worshiping God through sacrifices in the Temple of Jerusalem would not be restored. Since the Israel defined by the Pentateuch long ago had been defined through holiness deriving from its service to God in the Temple, the issue was raised: Does Israel remain holy even without the Temple, and how is Israel to serve God? So too, the question was raised: Does Israel remain holy if it loses the land or a large part of it? What is the source of Israel's holiness? And what marks Israel as holy?

A single example of how the question of the continuing mode of sanctification was raised is contained in the rule, set forth in Leviticus 22:28, governing the taking of the dam and the fledglings. One may not slaughter the mother and the offspring on the same day. How does that rule apply now that the Temple was destroyed, now that Israelites are loosening the bonds that tie them to the Holy Land? And does it apply only to sacrifices to God or also to animals slaughtered for everyday meat?

> Mishnah tractate *Hullin* 5:1
> [The prohibition against slaughtering on the same day] "it and its young" [Lev. 22:28] applies (1) in the land and outside the land, (2) in the time of the Temple and not in the time of the Temple, (3) in the case of unconsecrated beasts and in the case of consecrated beasts.

The halakah, law, of the Mishnah answers the question of the age. Israel's holiness does not depend on where it is located. It does not depend on when the issue is addressed. It does not depend on whether the activity takes place in the Temple or in the secular world beyond. In all cases, the rule applies wherever Israel is located, whether in the land or abroad. The law pertains whenever Israel thrives, whether the Temple is standing or not. And it applies not only to animals designated for Temple offerings but to those planned for secular use. There is no way of answering the urgent question of the age more clearly: the destruction of the Temple and loss of the land has not removed from Israel its standing as a people consecrated to God and subject to the rules of sanctification originally centered in the Temple.

These represent questions of reconstruction. When Israel's life is being restored without a Temple, outside the land, not in the time of Temple sacrifices, then the way of life of the faith comes up for discussion. Is Israel still holy? How does that holiness come to expression without the Temple? The Mishnah answers that question by saying: in its way of life, the people of God will engage in acts of holiness. That is how the Mishnah is a document of reconstruction and restoration, speaking of hope and not despair.

But Judaism emerged in the Mishnah in dialogue with politics. What made the restoration possible? It was a result of Roman policy. Like the Persians in the time of the Pentateuch, the Romans governed subject peoples by building up local rulers, who could keep the peace. That was the Romans' tolerant policy toward subservient peoples. For the Jews in the land of Israel, the Romans chose an ethnarch, a ruler of the ethnic group. He bore the title *nasi,* translated as "patriarch." And what he did was to respond to the challenge of the restoration by producing a law code, the Mishnah, organized out of ancient traditions and brought to closure in ca. 200 C.E.

As a law code the Mishnah is an odd mixture of practical and theoretical topics. That is because it covered not only topics that fell within the jurisdiction of the Jewish administration of the land, but also topics that the Patriarch could never translate into practice. These concerned the Temple and its procedures, matters of purity, and issues of sanctification in general. Of the six large divisions of the Mishnah, two huge parts, the fifth and the sixth, deal with the Temple and its sacrifices, on the one side, and the rules of purity to protect the holiness of the Temple from uncleanness (for example, deriving from corpses), on the other. It presented the holidays as they were practiced in the Temple. The way the festivals and holy days were kept at home and in the synagogues around the country is mostly ignored by the second division of the Mishnah, where appointed times are treated. Thus three of the six divisions, well over half of the Mishnah in volume, attend to a world that did not exist at the time the document reached closure.

The Mishnah portrayed a world that Israel hoped would come to restoration and preserved the rules to re-create that world. At the same time it emphasized a side of Israel in the here and now: its holiness. The Mishnah's stress on the Temple, priesthood, offerings, and purity rules underscored the sanctity of the people, Israel, from of old. The Mishnah emphasized those aspects of the way of life of the people that preserved and embodied holiness.

Thus the legislation for betrothal and marriage stressed the language of sanctification. A man's betrothal of a woman was called an act of sanctification, for example. As we saw earlier, the food regulations of the Temple, governing what was offered on the altar to God and on the domestic table of the Israelite at home, are explicitly applied to the life of the people even in the age in which the Temple was no longer standing.

The laws that governed the holiness of the land of Israel, requiring that the land be left fallow every seventh year, to enjoy its Sabbath rest just as Israel enjoyed Sabbath repose every seventh day, remained in effect. So the Mishnah in these and other ways reaffirmed the sanctity of Israel and portrayed its way of life as the way of making Israel separate to God.

The spirit of the times that produced the Mishnah is captured in a story told in a later document about the rabbinic sage who escaped from Jerusalem to build a circle of disciples to preserve and hand on the Torah, written and oral.

The Fathers According to Rabbi Nathan IV:V.2

One time [after the destruction of the Temple in August 70] Rabban Yohanan ben Zakkai was going forth from Jerusalem, with R. Joshua following after him. He saw the house of the sanctuary lying in ruins.

R. Joshua said, "Woe is us, for this place that lies in ruins, the place in which the sins of Israel used to come to atonement."

He said to him, "My son, do not be distressed. We have another mode of atonement, which is like [atonement through sacrifice], and what is that? It is deeds of loving-kindness.

"For so it is said, 'For I desire mercy and not sacrifice, and the knowledge of God rather than burnt offerings' (Hos. 6:6)."

The upshot is that the loss of the Temple and its offerings did not mean the end. Israel's way of life, beginning with ethics, would endure. Israel had another way of serving God and atoning for sin, such as the Temple had provided. The people Israel, defined in the Torah's narratives, now possessed in the Mishnah a full account of its way of life, aimed at sanctifying the people in the here and now. But what of history, and where were things heading? The worldview of Judaism would be incomplete until that question found an answer.

400 C.E.: The Talmud and Judaism's Worldview

The third crisis was precipitated by the success of Judaism's competition within the revealed monotheism of Scripture: Christianity. Christianity and Judaism had competed for three hundred years. They shared some of the same holy books, as we saw in the preface. After three centuries of state persecution in the Roman Empire, Christianity suddenly was legalized and then adopted as the state religion.

In Christianity's view, the conversion of the Roman Empire to Christianity, beginning with the legalization by Emperor Constantine in 312, confirmed the claims of Christianity that Christ was really King. The Messiah had come and world history confirmed that fact. Then what was Israel waiting for? A doctrine of history and the Messiah was required to complete Judaism's worldview.

The third crisis thus required explaining great historical events and led to the formulation of Judaism's worldview. This pertained to the meaning and end of history: what happenings matter and where do they indicate we are heading? The document that came into existence at the end of the third critical age was the Talmud of the Land of Israel. It took the form of a commentary to the Mishnah. (Two hundred years later, in 600 C.E., a second such commentary was produced in Babylonia. That was called the Talmud of Babylonia.) Besides explaining the laws, the Talmud of the Land of Israel contained much material of its own. It did not limit itself to explaining the law of the Mishnah. It also contained stories that presented a philosophy of history.

Finished in ca. 400 C.E., the Talmud of the Land of Israel contained the answers to those questions of meaning and order in history and defined an important component of Israel's worldview. Two questions arise. First, what made those questions of history and destiny urgent, and how were they answered in the first Talmud? Second, what marked the task of restoration and renewal?

The question of the historical worldview of Judaism became urgent when Rome first legalized Christianity, then adopted Christianity as the religion of the state. That political process started in the beginning of the fourth century. The age of restoration after a crisis got underway toward the end of the same century, when it had become quite clear that the Jews would remain the stalwart "Israel" that they claimed to be. They would not accept Christianity but would remain loyal to the Torah. After a hundred years, the Talmud of the Land of Israel laid out the worldview that would explain why. It did so when it answered the question, What were the Jews waiting for? And in light of the prophetic promise of a Messiah and the Christians' portrayal of Jesus Christ as Israel's Messiah, the Messiah theme would define the terms of the answer.

The Messiah theme scarcely arises in the Torah of Moses, and it is negligible in the Mishnah. Now, in the setting of Christ's victory in this world, Judaism required a doctrine of the Messiah. It had to show how the sanctification of Israel in the here and now was leading to the success of Israel's faith in the end of days. The first Talmud contained that doctrine.

To understand why, after three hundred years, Christianity presented a crisis for Judaism, we must recall that from the beginning of Christianity in the first century C.E. to the fourth century, Christianity suffered intermittent persecution. Its critics did not regard persecution as validation of its claims. To late-first- and second-century sages are attributed statements dismissive of the Christians' Torah:

Tosefta tractate *Shabbat* 15:3

The books of the Evangelists . . . they do not save from a fire. But they are allowed to burn where they are,

they and the references to the divine name that are in them.

R. Yose the Galilean says, "On ordinary days, one cuts out the references to the divine name that are in them and stores them away, and the rest burns."

Said R. Tarfon, "May I bury my sons, if such things come into my hands and I do not burn them, and even the references to the divine name that are in them.

"And if someone was running after me, I should go into a temple of idolatry, but I should not go into their houses [of worship].

"For idolators do not recognize the Divinity in denying him, but these recognize the Divinity and deny him."

The rabbinic sages tended to dismiss Christianity. They did not engage with it. They thought that Christians knew God but denied him, while the pagans did not know him. That polemic sufficed. But we realize how matters radically changed at the beginning of the fourth century. When the Roman Empire affirmed Jesus Christ as King and Messiah, Christianity could no longer be dismissed or ignored. Christian thinkers claimed that these events proved the truth of Christianity and marked Judaism as no longer a way to God. What was an annoyance to Judaism became a challenge of historical proportions. The Talmud of the Land of Israel contained the response: a doctrine of the Messiah central to the worldview of Judaism.

That meant Judaism had to explain history: the pattern and direction of events. The Christian theologians now rewrote the history of humanity. From creation forward their narratives showed history heading toward Constantine and the climactic moment of the Roman Empire's affirmation.

For its part Judaism had a well-defined way of life, as we saw. Sanctification in the here and now was fully spelled out. But it required a doctrine of history, a worldview about the salvation of Israel at the end of days.

The Talmud of the Land of Israel set forth the Judaic doctrine of the Messiah. The issue was, when will the Messiah come to raise the dead, and what must Israel do to hasten that day? The answers to these questions would form a doctrine of history, specifically, how to position Israel in the pattern of history from the beginning in Eden to the end in the restoration of Eden.

The Talmud of the Land of Israel took up the theme, established from Scripture's time forward, of the Messiah's claim to save Israel. It set forth the doctrine that Israel will be saved through total submission, under the Messiah's gentle rule, to God's yoke and service. In the model of the rabbinic sage, the

Messiah will teach Israel the power of submission. So God is not to be manip-ulated. Keeping the commandments as a mark of submission, loyalty, and humility before God is the rabbinic system of salvation.

So Israel does not save itself. Israel never controls its own destiny, either on earth or in heaven. The only choice is whether to cast one's fate into the hands of cruel, deceitful humans, or to trust in the living God of mercy and love. We now understand the stress on the centrality of hope. Hope signifies patient acceptance of God's rule, and as an attitude of mind and heart, it is something that Israel can sustain on its own as well.

We shall now see how this critical position that Israel's task is humble acceptance of God's rule is spelled out in the setting of teachings about the Messiah in the Talmud of the Land of Israel. Bar Kokhba is the key figure. He had led the second war against Rome, culminating in the defeat of 135. He is represented as the embodiment of arrogance. Since some had thought he was the Messiah, he serves as the figure of the false messiah. Then he weighs in the balance against the sage. The false messiah represents arrogance, the sage, humility. Bar Kokhba, above all, exemplified arrogance against God. He lost the war because of that arrogance. In particular, he ignored the authority of the rabbinic sages, humble as they were.

In part 4 we shall see how the rabbinic sages portrayed Bar Kokhba. In that presentation we find two complementary themes. First, Bar Kokhba treats heaven with arrogance, asking God merely to keep out of the way. Second, he treats an especially revered sage with a parallel arrogance. The sage had the power to preserve Israel. Bar Kokhba destroyed Israel's one protection. The result was inevitable.

The Messiah is transformed into a sage. He is no longer the Messiah embod-ied in the figure of the arrogant Bar Kokhba (in the Talmud's representation of the figure). So the Messiah theme comes to the fore when through advent to power Christianity makes its claim stick. But in the rabbinic sages' hands the Messiah theme reinforced the teaching of the way of life through acts of holi-ness. That is because the climax comes in an explicit statement, cited in a moment, that the conduct required by the Torah will bring the coming Messiah. That explanation of the holy way of life focuses upon the end of time and the advent of the Messiah—both of which therefore depend upon the sanctifica-tion of Israel. So sanctification takes priority, salvation depends on it.

So with their interest in explaining events and accounting for history, the sages invoked what their predecessors had at best found to be of peripheral consequence to their system. The following contains the most striking expres-sion of this viewpoint.

Talmud of the Land of Israel tractate *Ta'anit* 1:1

"The oracle concerning Dumah. One is calling to me from Seir, 'Watchman, what of the night? Watchman, what of the night?' (Isa. 21:11)."

The Israelites said to Isaiah, "O our Rabbi, Isaiah, what will come for us out of this night?"

He said to them, "Wait for me, until I can present the question."

Once he had asked the question, he came back to them.

They said to him, "Watchman, what of the night? What did the Guardian of the ages tell you?"

He said to them, "The watchman says: 'Morning comes; and also the night. If you will inquire, inquire; come back again' (Isa. 21:12)."

They said to him, "Also the night?"

He said to them, "It is not what you are thinking. But there will be morning for the righteous, and night for the wicked, morning for Israel, and night for idolators."

They said to him, "When?"

He said to them, "Whenever you want, He too wants [it to be]—if you want it, he wants it."

They said to him, "What is standing in the way?"

He said to them, "Repentance: 'Come back again' (Isa. 21:12)."

R. Aha in the name of R. Tanhum b. R. Hiyya, "If Israel repents for one day, forthwith the son of David will come.

"What is the scriptural basis? 'O that today you would hearken to his voice!' (Ps. 95:7)."

Said R. Levi, "If Israel would keep a single Sabbath in the proper way, forthwith the son of David will come.

"What is the scriptural basis for this view? 'Moses said, Eat it today, for today is a Sabbath to the Lord; today you will not find it in the field' (Exod. 16:25).

"And it says, 'For thus said the Lord God, the Holy One of Israel, "In returning and rest you shall be saved; in quietness and in trust shall be your strength." And you would not' (Isa. 30:15)."

What is new is the explicit linkage between keeping the law of the Torah and the coming of the Messiah. We must not lose sight of the importance of this passage. What makes it important is its emphasis on repentance, on the one side, and the power of Israel to reform itself, on the other. The Messiah will come any day that Israel makes it possible. Let me underline the most important statement of this large conception:

If all Israel will keep a single Sabbath in the proper (rabbinic) way, the Messiah will come. If all Israel will repent for one day, the Messiah will come. "Whenever you want . . . ," the Messiah will come.

Now, two things are happening here. First, the system of religious obser-vance, including study of Torah, is explicitly described as having salvific power. Second, the persistent hope of the people for the coming of the Mes-siah is linked to the system of rabbinic observance and belief as set forth in the halakah of the Mishnah and related expositions.

In this way, the austere program of the Mishnah develops in a different direc-tion. The Mishnah of 200 C.E. contains no trace of a promise that the Messiah will come if and when the system is fully realized. Here in a document of two hundred years later we find an explicitly messianic statement that the purpose of the law is to attain Israel's salvation: "If you want it, God wants it too."

The law of the Mishnah is now encapsulated within the frame of repen-tance: a change of heart brought about by keeping the covenant with God con-tained in the Torah. The one thing Israel commands is its own heart; the power it yet exercises is the power to repent. These suffice. The entire history of humanity will respond to Israel's will, to what happens in Israel's heart and soul. With the Temple in ruins, repentance can take place only within the heart and mind. That reminds us of what Yohanan ben Zakkai said in response to the same fact: there are actions Israelites can carry out that serve to atone, as sacrifices used to serve.

Israel may contribute to its own salvation, by the right attitude and the right deed. But Israel bears responsibility for its present condition. So what Israel does makes history. Israel makes its own history, therefore shapes its own des-tiny. This lesson, the rabbinic sages maintained, derives from the very condi-tion of Israel even then, its suffering and its despair. (In part 4, we shall encounter a story in which Aqiba says that in so many words.) How so? History taught moral lessons. Israel's own deeds defined the events of history. Rome's role, like Assyria's and Babylonia's, depended upon Israel's own sins. Israel had provoked divine wrath. Then the great empire punished Israel. It was God's agent. Paradoxically, Israel kept Rome in charge.

The Talmud of the Land of Israel's system of history and Messiah presents a paradox. It lies in the fact that Israel can free itself of control by other nations only by humbly agreeing to accept God's rule. The nations—Rome, in the present instance—rest on one side of the balance, while God rests on the other. Israel must then choose between them. There is no such thing for Israel as freedom from both God and the nations, total autonomy and independence. There is only a choice of masters, a ruler on earth or a ruler in heaven.

In the Talmud's theory of salvation, therefore, the framers provided Israel with an account of how to overcome the unsatisfactory circumstances of an unredeemed present, so as to accomplish the movement from here to the much-desired future. When the Talmud's authorities present statements on the promise of the law for those who keep it, therefore, they provide glimpses of the goal of the system as a whole. These invoked the primacy of the rabbi and the legitimating power of the Torah, and in those two components of the system we find the principles of the messianic doctrine. And these bring us back to the argument with Christ triumphant, as the Christians perceived him.

Keeping the law in the right way is represented as not merely right or expedient. It is the way to bring the Messiah, the son of David. Levi states this, as follows:

> Talmud of the Land of Israel tractate *Ta'anit* 1:1.IX
> Said R. Levi, "If Israel would keep a single Sabbath in the proper way, forthwith the son of David will come.
> "What is the scriptural basis for this view? 'Moses said, Eat it today, for today is a Sabbath to the Lord; today you will not find it in the field' (Exod. 16:25).
> "And it says, 'For thus said the Lord God, the Holy One of Israel, "In returning and rest you shall be saved; in quietness and in trust shall be your strength. And you would not"' (Isa. 30:15)."

Here, in a single saying, we find the entire talmudic doctrine set forth concerning Israel's salvation in the coming of the Messiah.

What is most interesting in Talmud of the Land of Israel's picture is that the hope for the Messiah's coming is further joined to the moral condition of each individual Israelite. Hence the messianic fulfillment was made to depend on the repentance of Israel. The coming of the Messiah depended not on historical action in war and in politics but on moral regeneration.

So from a force that moved Israelites to take up weapons on the battlefield, as in the war led by Bar Kokhba, the messianic hope and yearning were transformed into motives for spiritual regeneration and ethical behavior. The energies released in the messianic fervor were then linked to rabbinical government, through which Israel would form the godly society. When we reflect that the message, "If you want it, he [God] too wants it to be," comes in a generation confronting a dreadful disappointment, its full weight and meaning become clear.

Definition of Israel, Its Way of Life and Worldview: Judaism Now Complete

With the provision of a worldview concerning salvation, a way of life concerning sanctification, and a doctrine of the community of the faithful concerning Israel, Judaism emerged whole and complete. By the end of the fourth century, it was clear that Israel, the holy people, had survived the challenge of the Christian triumph in the Roman Empire. There were no massive conversions recorded by the rabbinic sages.

The result of the third response to crisis through a program of restoration was to complete the formation of Judaism. Its definition of the community of the faithful, Israel, and its account of the holy way of life, the halakah, now was complete with the worldview on how Israel would be saved.

The fourth century marks the first century of Christianity as the West would know it: the politically and culturally decisive force in Western civilization. When Rome became Christian, Judaism as it would flourish in Western civilization reached that familiar form and definition that we know today as normative. Judaism was born in the matrix of Christianity triumphant.

PART II

Four Topics in the
Emergence of Judaism

Introduction

*T*he religious system of Judaism emerged in three stages, marked by the Pentateuch for the definition of the community of the faithful called Israel, the Mishnah for the definition of the way of life of that community, and the Talmud of the Land of Israel for the definition of the worldview of that community. Only at the end did all the components come together in a single, coherent system that flourished for fifteen hundred years and still defines the norm. Then the parts fit together into a whole. But how, in the long period of development from the Pentateuch, ca. 450 B.C.E., to the Talmud of the Land of Israel, ca. 400 C.E., did the parts of the system take shape?

Now we take up the three parts and see how each developed. We follow the order of the story told in chapter 1. We follow the development of (1) its theory of what "Israel" is in chapter 2; (2) its way of life, which is set forth in the law of the Mishnah on the foundations of the law of the Torah in chapter 3; and (3) its worldview, contained in the concept of "Torah," with a variety of meanings, in chapter 4. Then we ask what holds the topics all together, which is, (4) the conception of God. That is the topic that forms the center of the religious system, Judaism.

This exposition of the three topics drawn from chapter 1 speaks of development. We address the unfolding of the topics, (1) Israel, (2) law from Scripture to the Mishnah, (3) the Torah, and (4) God. In each topic we follow the emergence of ideas historically. How do we know about the unfolding of a topic over a period of time?

The answer is simple. We follow the sequence of writings ("documents") that as we saw in chapter 1 portray Judaism in its successive stages. We trace the treatment of the principal topics as those books successively portray them. The development of the parts of the system then unfolds book by book.

The three principal topics in their historical emergence therefore are defined in sequence by the dates of completion of those books. As we saw in chapter 1, the books are the Torah (Pentateuch, Prophets, Writings), ca. 450 B.C.E.; the Mishnah, ca. 200 C.E.; and the Talmud of the Land of Israel, ca. 400 C.E. That is how in chapter 1 we traced the emergence of Judaism, stage by stage.

We looked at the Torah (Pentateuch, Prophets, Writings), paying special attention to its narrative picture of Israel. Then we examined the Mishnah for its systematic account of Israel's way of life. Finally, we turned to the Talmud of the Land of Israel to ask about its doctrine of Israel in history and destiny. But we left open the state of other questions: What about "Israel" in the Mishnah and the Talmud of the Land of Israel? What about the way of life of Israel portrayed before the Mishnah, that is, in the Torah? And what about the doctrine of the meaning of history in the writings prior to the Talmud of the Land of Israel?

To answer these questions we double back to the same writings, Pentateuch, Mishnah, Talmud of the Land of Israel. But now it is with a different purpose. We want to follow the development of our topics over time. First, we ask about the conception of Israel in the Mishnah and the Talmud, that is, the later books, as they treat the received doctrine. Second, we ask how the way of life put forth in law by the Mishnah fits together with the narrative of Scripture. Third, we ask about the conception of "Torah." As we saw in chapter 1, the worldview of Judaism ultimately focused on keeping the Torah as a means of sanctifying Israel to attain salvation in the end of days. So "Torah" forms the foundations of the worldview put forth by the successive documents of Judaism.

In this way we trace the development of the topics introduced, book by book, in chapter 1. To those topics we add the climax of Judaism, its doctrine of God.

Our interest is in history. What kind of history now emerges? It is an account of the development of a topic stage by stage, book by book, of principal topics of Judaism. The holy books tell us what the important authorities of Judaism were thinking when those books were completed. We therefore follow the unfolding of our main topics, as the successive writings expounded those topics.

That means we want to know about how ideas unfolded from one book to the next. That is why, varying our questions somewhat, we repeat the sequence of the principal parts as they emerged in chapter 1.

Let us form an overview of what is to follow in chapters 2, 3, and 4.

Israel. What about "Israel," the name of the social group formed by the community of Judaism? We found in chapter 1 that the Torah told the story of the formation and calling of the community of Judaism. Members of the community took the story personally, and the community as a whole found its narrative in that story as well. In this topical presentation we ask what happened to that same narrative in the unfolding emergence of Judaism. We ask how in the Mishnah and in the Talmud of the Land of Israel the concept of Israel unfolds. Chapter 2 shows how the idea of "Israel" developed from the Torah to the Mishnah and finally to the Talmud of the Land of Israel. That is a step-by-step, book-by-book, account of the development of the topic, "Israel."

The way of life, the Law. The second topic to emerge called for an account of the way of life of the community of Judaism. We found that the Mishnah organized and regularized the rules. These formed a way of life meant to mark Israel as a holy community, set apart to serve God. In chapter 3, we look backward from the Mishnah to the written Torah (Pentateuch). We ask how the laws of the Mishnah take up the story of the Israel told in the Torah by the community of Judaism. We want to know how the laws of the Mishnah correspond to the narrative of Scripture. We see a striking fact. The community of Judaism in the laws of the Mishnah acts out in everyday life the teachings implicit in the rules and stories told by the Torah. To see exactly what that means, we take up some specific sets of rules. We examine the interplay between the Torah's story and the way in which the Mishnah sets forth rules for proper conduct.

The worldview. The third topic is the conception of the Torah as that is defined in the successive books of Judaism. The concept of "Torah" bears a number of meanings, as it is used in the holy books. Tracing the unfolding of those meanings shows us how Judaism ultimately emerged.

That is how, in chapters 2, 3, and 4, we follow the emergence of principal parts of Judaism topic by topic, book by book.

God, just and merciful. That brings us to the system's climactic topic. In chapter 5 we see how the system as a whole holds together. It is through the belief in God. The way of life, the worldview, the definition of Israel—all respond to the will and word of that one God. Judaism is a monotheistic religion, meaning it knows God as one, unique, above nature and governing history. Furthermore, it is called "ethical monotheism," meaning, the one God is merciful, patient, and just. Thus all things that are and that happen come about by God's loving will, to which Israel responds: "You will love the Lord your God with all your heart, with all your soul, and with all your might" (Deut. 6:5).

Judaism's ethical monotheism is not phrased as philosophical propositions in systematic theological language. Rather, it emerges from the Torah's narrative. The Torah tells that the world was made by a single Creator. The Creator is governed by principles of justice and mercy that he himself has revealed. The Torah given by God to Moses defines God's way of telling humanity about that one God. That is the keystone of the system, which makes the parts cohere.

Ethical monotheism raises the question, How does Judaism match the condition of the world with the conviction of God's justice? The answer to that question shows the picture as a whole. It sets forth how the theory of "Israel," the community of Judaism, its way of life (law) and worldview (Torah), all come together in a single coherent statement about the foundations of human existence. These are set forth by the one God's benevolent, beneficent will.

Chapter 2

The Definition of Israel

Israel in Judaism, and What about the Gentiles?

Today when people speak of "Israel," they refer only to the state of Israel. But that usage is very recent. It began in 1948, when the State of Israel was proclaimed. From that time the meaning of "Israel" has varied, sometimes referring to a place, sometimes to the community of Judaism as it did until 1948.

The point is that in Judaism from Scripture forward the word *Israel* has had a different meaning. In the Torah and in prayers "Israel" refers to the holy people of God: the children of Abraham, Isaac, and Jacob who stood at Sinai. "Israel" refers to those who receive the Torah—God's revealed will—and enter the covenant with God. "Israel" then encompasses those born into the people and those that join the people by choice.

What difference does it make to be part of Israel? When people call themselves "Israel," they adopt for themselves and take personally the narrative of the Torah. They regard themselves as part of that group of which the Torah speaks. That is an act of religious faith and theological affirmation. It is not a mere genealogical description, let alone a political platform.

If to be Israel is to take personally the stories Scripture tells, then what narratives in particular define Israel? As we saw in chapter 1, the Torah selected as normative the story of two experiences that stories tell. The one is the story of the exile from Jerusalem and destruction of the Temple, the other, the story of the return to Zion and rebuilding of the Temple. These together marked the life of Israel.

The chosen narrative defined the pattern of Israel's life. The story of how the group had had a home and lost it but got it back is unsettling. Then the life of Israel is subject to stipulations and conditions, for example, a covenant with God. If you do this, I will do that, and if you do not do this, I will not do that—these are the terms set forth in Leviticus 26, Deuteronomy 32, and other passages of the Torah. The terms of the covenant involved a holy way of life on the land endowed with moral traits. The story stressed the uncertainty of the ongoing existence of the group unless certain conditions were met. It set forth the notion that the group came from somewhere and was en route to some further destination. These terms highlighted the issue of who is an Israelite, and what Israel is.

But a great many questions were left open. The one that immediately demands an answer is, what about the gentiles, those who are not Israel? If Israel are those who know God through his self-revelation in the Torah, can gentiles share in that knowledge? Gentiles can enter the status of Israel. In that case they join Israel in the world to come. This the gentiles will do in exactly the way that Israel does: by accepting God's rule as set forth in the Torah. If a gentile keeps the Torah, he or she is saved from death. But by keeping the Torah, the gentile has ceased to be gentile and become Israelite, worthy even of the high priesthood.

Here is an explicit statement on the subject. Gentiles can know God too. But, when they do, they become part of Israel. For in Judaism, as defined by the Torah, "Israel" means, those who know God. First comes the definition of how Israel becomes Israel, which is by accepting God's dominion in the Torah. The passage comes from a commentary to the book of Leviticus that came to closure in the century after the Mishnah, in ca. 300 C.E.:

Sifra CXCIV:II.1
"The Lord spoke to Moses saying, 'Speak to the Israelite people and say to them, I am the Lord your God':"

R. Simeon b. Yohai says, "That is in line with what is said elsewhere: 'I am the Lord your God [who brought you out of the land of Egypt, out of the house of bondage]' (Exod. 20:2).

"'Am I the Lord, whose sovereignty you took upon yourself in Egypt?'
"They said to him, 'Indeed.'
"'Indeed, you have accepted my dominion.'
"'They accepted my decrees: "You will have no other gods before me."'"

"That is what is said here: 'I am the Lord your God,' meaning, 'Am I the one whose dominion you accepted at Sinai?'
"They said to him, 'Indeed.'
"'Indeed you have accepted my dominion.'
"'They accepted my decrees: "You shall not copy the practices of the land of Egypt where you dwelt, or of the land of Canaan to which I am taking you; nor shall you follow their laws."'"

So much for the definition of Israel in the time of the Mishnah.

How are the gentiles defined in that same development? The same definition is explicitly brought to bear upon the gentiles. That yields the clear inference that gentiles have the power to join themselves to Israel as fully naturalized

Israelites. The Torah that defines their status also constitutes the ticket of admission to the world to come that Israel will enter in due course. Sages could not be more explicit than they are when they insist that the gentiles cease to be in the status of gentiles when they accept God's rule in the Torah:

Sifra CXCIV:II.15

". . . by the pursuit of which man shall live":

R. Jeremiah says, "How do I know that even a gentile who keeps the Torah, lo, he is like the high priest?

"Scripture says, 'by the pursuit of which man shall live.'"

And so it says, "'And this is the Torah of the priests, Levites, and Israelites,' is not what is said here,

"but rather, 'This is the Torah of the man, O Lord God' (2 Sam. 7:19)."

And so it says, "'open the gates and let priests, Levites, and Israelites enter it' is not what is said,

"but rather, 'Open the gates and let the righteous nation, who keeps faith, enter it' (Isa. 26:2)."

And so it says, "'This is the gate of the Lord. Priests, Levites, and Israelites . . .' is not what is said,

"but rather, 'the righteous shall enter into it' (Ps. 118:20)."

And so it says, "'What is said is not, 'Rejoice, priests, Levites, and Israelites,'

"but rather, 'Rejoice, O righteous, in the Lord' (Ps. 33:1)."

And so it says, "It is not, 'Do good, O Lord, to the priests, Levites, and Israelites,'

"but rather, 'Do good, O Lord, to the good, to the upright in heart' (Ps. 125:4)."

"Thus, even a gentile who keeps the Torah, lo, he is like the high priest."

That is not to suggest that God does not rule the gentiles. He does—whether they like it or not, whether they acknowledge him or not. God responds, also, to the acts of merit taken by gentiles, as much as to those of Israel. The upshot is, God rules. God cares for all humanity. Israel through accepting the Torah enters into a special relationship with him. All humanity have the option of entering into that same relationship, defined by the Torah.

Israel in the Mishnah

What is at stake in forming Israel, and why does it matter? The Mishnah explicitly answers that question.

"Israel" in the law of the Mishnah bears two identical meanings. It refers to (1) the Israelite community consisting of (all) the Jews—persons born of a Jewish mother—now and here, dead and alive and destined to be born. "Israel" further refers to (2) the Israel of which the Torah speaks. And they are one and the same.

Not only so, but in the Mishnah the concept of Israel may refer to an individual male Jew or to "all Jews," that is, the Jews viewed as a whole community. The individual woman is nearly always called *bat yisrael,* daughter of an Israelite.

What about Israel as the extended family of Abraham and Sarah? Earlier in the Torah the narrative stressed the genealogical definition. Later on in the Talmud of the Land of Israel and related writings, emphasis is placed on Israel as extended family. But the Mishnah rarely makes use of the category "family/children of Israel." The concept of Israel serves a different purpose.

How does the concept of Israel work in the Mishnah? In the law of the Mishnah the concept of Israel defines boundaries, distinguishing Israel from something else, depending on context. First, it sets out who is outside, thus Israel versus non-Israel—the frontiers on the outside of society. Second, it also indicates the social boundaries within. In the Mishnah, Israel refers to a caste, on an upward progression leading to Levite and priest (Hebrew *kohen*). Thus it is Israel-not-priest. The Levite was a temple assistant, and the priest was the temple official.

The Mishnah thus uses Israel to distinguish among Israelites, the holy priesthood from the ordinary Israelite. By contrast, the gentiles represent an undifferentiated mass. To the system of the Mishnah, whether a gentile is a Roman or an Aramaean or a Syrian or a Briton does not matter. That is because distinctions among gentiles rarely, if ever, make a difference. "Gentile" is then an abstraction, standing for outsider, "everybody else."

How Does the Mishnah Mark a Stage in the Development of the Topic of Israel?

The Mishnah's law emphasized making Israel holy. It stressed that in the people of Israel the holiness that had formerly centered on the temple now endured. Israel's holiness survived the physical destruction of the holy building and the cessation of its sacrifices. God's stake in the world was not limited to his abode in the Temple of Jerusalem. That is because he dwelt among the people, Israel, whether in the Holy Land or abroad.

What is the point of Israel's being holy? The answer is given in a passage of the Mishnah that says, "All Israelites have a portion in the world to come." That is, they are destined to rise from the dead and after judgment be restored to Eden. So at stake in being holy is eternal life. "Israel" stands for those that will live forever.

> Mishnah tractate *Sanhedrin* 10:1
> All Israelites have a share in the world to come,
> as it is said, "your people also shall be all righteous, they shall inherit the land forever; the branch of my planting, the work of my hands, that I may be glorified" (Isa. 60:21).
> And these are the ones who have no portion in the world to come:
> He who says, the resurrection of the dead is a teaching that does not derive from the Torah, or that the Torah does not come from Heaven; or an Epicurean (hedonist).

In this passage of the Mishnah Israel is defined inclusively. To be Israel is to have a share in the world to come. Israel then is a social entity that is made up of those who share a common conviction. That Israel bears an otherworldly destiny. Israel is a social group that endows its individual members with life in the world to come; an Israelite is one who enjoys the world to come. Excluded from this Israel are Israelites who exclude themselves. This law of the Mishnah extends "Israel" to encompass all those born of a Jewish mother or who accept the rule of God in the Torah.

Israel in the Talmud of the Land of Israel

We turn now to the formulations in the Talmud of the Land of Israel, which, we recall, came to closure in the century after the conversion of the Roman Empire to Christianity. We find ourselves in a quite different world, one in which, as we saw in chapter 1, history figured, and destiny mattered. And that affected the representation of Israel.

When the rabbinic sages wished to know what Israel was, they found the answer not only in abstract definitions such as the Mishnah presents. In addition, in commentaries to Genesis and to Leviticus that were produced at the end of the fourth century C.E., they reread the Torah's story of Israel's origins for the answer. To begin with, as Scripture told them the story, Israel was a man, also called Jacob, and his children are "the children of Jacob" or "the children of Israel." So "the children of Israel" comprised the extended family of that man. By extension, Israel formed the family of Abraham and Sarah, Isaac and Rebecca, Jacob and Leah and Rachel.

But precisely what did that mean for the Israel of the fifth century C.E., facing a triumphant Christianity? Defining Israel as a family produced two consequences. First, children in general are admonished to follow the good example of their parents. The deeds of the patriarchs and matriarchs therefore taught lessons on how the children were to act. Second, the stories of the family were carefully reread to provide a picture of the meaning of the latter-day events of the descendants of that same family. Accordingly, the lives of the patriarchs signaled the future history of Israel.

Why did the narrative of Israel as a family serve an especially important purpose for the Talmud of the Land of Israel and related writings? As before, the advent of Christianity defines the context. It led the Israelites to emphasize doctrines of the Torah that answered the Christians' position. The Christian church now claimed to constitute the true Israel. So the rabbinic sages answered in kind: "You claim to form 'Israel after the spirit.' Fine, and *we* are Israel after the flesh." Then genealogy forms the link.

Converts to Judaism did not present an anomaly as the passage of *Sifra,* cited above, has shown. Within the theory of Israel as the extended family of the patriarchs and matriarchs, they were held to be children of Abraham and Sarah, who had "made souls," that is, converts, in Haran, a point repeated in the documents of the period. So Israelites by choice appealed to Abraham and Sarah as their father and their mother in Israel.

That genealogical continuity formed of all Israel a single family. If Israelites form a family, then they know full well what links them. It was the common ancestry. It encompassed also the obligations imposed by common ancestry upon the cousins who make up the family.

The Metaphor of the Family:
"Israel's Children" in *Genesis Rabbah*

Alongside the Talmud of the Land of Israel, a commentary to the book of Genesis, called *Genesis Rabbah,* ca. 400, translates the narrative of Scripture into a systematic picture of the Israel of the fifth century in its competition with Christianity. The sages found in the stories of Genesis the meaning of events in their own times.

The rabbinic sages who produced *Genesis Rabbah* took the Torah personally. So they regarded the book of Genesis as a letter written that morning to them by God. They brought their concerns to the Torah and found in the Torah messages in response to their anguish. Families have histories. Israel viewed as family found in the record of its family history events formed into meaningful patterns. That is why the sages searched in the deeds of the patriarchs and matriarchs for messages concerning the future history of the children. They looked in the facts of biography for the laws of history. They proposed to generalize. Genesis provided facts concerning the family. Careful sifting of those facts would yield the laws that dictated why to that family things happened one way, rather than some other.

Among these social laws of the family history, one took priority. It concerned Israel's situation among the gentiles. The rabbinic sages wanted to discover the laws of history. That is because, in their own time, world-shaking historical events had taken place in the character of the Roman Empire. These laws would then explain the movement of empires upward and downward. The stories of Genesis would point toward the ultimate end of it all.

The conclusion they reached matched their query. Scripture provided the model for the ages of empires. Its narrative yielded a picture of four monarchies, to be followed by Israel as the fifth and final one.

In reading Genesis, in particular, the rabbinic sages found that time and again events in the lives of the patriarchs prefigured the four monarchies, among which, of course, the fourth, last, and most intolerable was Rome. As in the time of the patriarchs and the prophets, so now Israel's history falls under God's dominion. Whatever will happen carries out God's plan, and that plan for the future has been laid out in the account of the origins supplied by Genesis.

The fourth kingdom, Rome, is part of that plan, which we can discover by carefully studying Abraham's life and God's word to him.

Genesis Rabbah XLIV:XVIII
"Then the Lord said to Abram, 'Know of a surety [that your descendants will be sojourners in a land that is not theirs, and they will be slaves there, and they will be oppressed for four hundred years; but I will bring judgment on the nation that they serve, and afterward they shall come out with great possessions']" (Gen. 15:13–14):
"Know" that I shall scatter them.
"Of a certainty" that I shall bring them back together again.
"Know" that I shall put them out as a pledge [in expiation of their sins].
"Of a certainty" that I shall redeem them.
"Know" that I shall make them slaves.
"Of a certainty" that I shall free them.

Here is that pattern of exile and return that we encountered in chapter 1. Only now the pattern is made particular to a given verse of Genesis. The interpretation of Genesis 15:13–14 parses the cited verse and joins within its simple formula the entire history of Israel, punishment and forgiveness alike.

The conduct of the patriarchs determined the future history of their descendants. Here is how sages take up the detail of Abraham's provision of a bit of water, showing what that act had to do with the history of Israel later on. The intricate working out of the whole then encompasses the merit of the patriarchs, the way in which the deeds of the patriarchs provide a sign for proper conduct for their children, the history and salvation of Israel. The pattern we shall meet is simple. First we identify an act of the patriarchs and matriarchs. Then we ask where God responded to that act through an act of grace to their children, in the wilderness, for example. Then, what about the land of Israel? Finally, we ask how that same act will produce a result for the age to come, that is, when the Messiah comes and raises the dead and brings Israel back to the land, restoring humanity to Eden.

Genesis Rabbah XLVIII:X
"Let a little water be brought" (Gen. 18:4):
Said to him the Holy One, blessed be he, "You have said, 'Let a little water be brought' (Gen. 18:4). By your life, I shall pay your descendants back for this: 'Then sang Israel this song, "spring up O well, sing you to it"' (Num. 21:7)."
That recompense took place in the wilderness. Where do we find that it took place in the land of Israel as well?
"A land of brooks of water" (Deut. 8:7).
And where do we find that it will take place in the age to come?
"And it shall come to pass in that day that living waters shall go out of Jerusalem" (Zech. 14:8).
["And wash your feet" (Gen. 18:4)]: [Said to him the Holy One, blessed be he,] "You have said, 'And wash your feet.' By your life, I shall pay your descendants back for this: 'Then I washed you in water' (Ezek. 16:9)."
That recompense took place in the wilderness. Where do we find that it took place in the land of Israel as well?
"Wash you, make you clean" (Isa. 1:16).
And where do we find that it will take place in the age to come?
"When the Lord will have washed away the filth of the daughters of Zion" (Isa. 4:4).

Abraham showed hospitality to the angels who came to meet him. God promises to pay back his descendants. And this takes place in the wilderness, in the land of Israel, and in the age to come. In the wilderness, God provided water for Israel (Num. 21:7). In the land of Israel, he did the same (Deut. 8:7). And in the age to come, the same will happen. So too Abraham washes the feet of the guests, and God did the same for Abraham's children in the wilderness, in the land,

and in the age to come. The passage proceeds to take each gesture of Abraham as a model of what would happen to his descendants in the future: in the wilderness, in the land, and in the age to come. Each detail is linked to this same pattern.

> [Said to him the Holy One, blessed be he,] "You have said, 'And rest yourselves under the tree' (Gen. 18:4). By your life, I shall pay your descendants back for this: 'He spread a cloud for a screen' (Ps. 105:39)."
>
> That recompense took place in the wilderness. Where do we find that it took place in the land of Israel as well?
>
> "You shall dwell in booths for seven days" (Lev. 23:42).
>
> And where do we find that it will take place in the age to come?
>
> "And there shall be a pavilion for a shadow in the daytime from the heat" (Isa. 4:6).

"Rest yourselves under the tree" yields the provision of a shelter for Israel in the wilderness, in the land, and in the age to come. The same pattern extends to nourishment in those three stages, first for bread, then for meat:

> [Said to him the Holy One, blessed be he,] "You have said, 'While I fetch a morsel of bread that you may refresh yourself' (Gen. 18:5). By your life, I shall pay your descendants back for this: 'Behold I will cause to rain bread from heaven for you' (Exod. 16:45)."
>
> That recompense took place in the wilderness. Where do we find that it took place in the land of Israel as well?
>
> "A land of wheat and barley" (Deut. 8:8).
>
> And where do we find that it will take place in the age to come?
>
> "He will be as a rich grain field in the land" (Ps. 82:16).
>
> [Said to him the Holy One, blessed be he,] "You ran after the herd ['And Abraham ran to the herd' (Gen. 18:7)]. By your life, I shall pay your descendants back for this: 'And there went forth a wind from the Lord and brought across quails from the sea' (Num. 11:27)."
>
> That recompense took place in the wilderness. Where do we find that it took place in the land of Israel as well?
>
> "Now the children of Reuben and the children of Gad had a very great multitude of cattle" (Num. 32:1).
>
> And where do we find that it will take place in the age to come?
>
> "And it will come to pass in that day that a man shall rear a young cow and two sheep" (Isa. 7:21).

Finally, Abraham stood guard over his guests, and God would do the same for Abraham's children and heirs:

[Said to him the Holy One, blessed be he,] "You stood by them: 'And he stood by them under the tree while they ate' (Gen. 18:8). By your life, I shall pay your descendants back for this: 'And the Lord went before them' (Exod. 13:21)."

That recompense took place in the wilderness. Where do we find that it took place in the land of Israel as well?

"God stands in the congregation of God" (Ps. 82:1).

And where do we find that it will take place in the age to come?

"The breaker is gone up before them . . . and the Lord at the head of them" (Mic. 2:13).

Everything that Abraham did thus brought a reward to his descendants. In this world and in the age to come, Israel enjoys the benefit of Abraham's meritorious actions. Each detail of Abraham's deeds prefigured the history of Israel—in the wilderness, in the Land, and, finally, in the age to come. All this is systematic and orderly. We note that there are five statements of the same proposition, each drawing upon a clause in the verse that is spelled out. Obviously, it is the merit of the ancestors that connects the living Israel to the lives of the patriarchs and matriarchs of old.

The historical life of Israel, the nation, continued the individual lives of the patriarchs. The theory of who is Israel, therefore, is seen once more to rest on genealogy: Israel is one extended family, all being children of the patriarchs and matriarchs of Genesis. This theory of Israelite society, and of the Jewish people in the time of the sages of *Genesis Rabbah,* made of the people a family, and of genealogy a kind of theology. The importance of that proposition in countering the Christian claim to form the new Israel cannot escape notice. Israel, sages maintained, is Israel after the flesh, and that in a most literal sense.

Jacob's contribution to knowledge of the meaning and end of Israel's history, as the rabbinic sages uncovered it in the book of Genesis, is exemplified in the following:

Genesis Rabbah LXX:VI

". . . so that I come again to my father's house in peace, then the Lord shall be my God" (Gen. 28:20–22):

R. Joshua of Sikhnin in the name of R. Levi: "The Holy One, blessed be he, took the language used by the patriarchs and turned it into a key to the redemption of their descendants.

"Said the Holy One, blessed be he, to Jacob, 'You have said, "*Then* the Lord shall be my God." By your life, all of the acts of goodness, blessing, and consolation which I am going to carry out for your descendants I shall bestow only by using the same language:

""Then in that day, living waters shall go out from Jerusalem" (Zech. 14:8).

"Then in that day a man shall rear a young cow and two sheep" (Isa. 7:21).

"Then, in that day, the Lord will set his hand again the second time to recover the remnant of his people" (Isa. 11:11).

"Then, in that day, the mountains shall drop down sweet wine" (Joel 4:18).

"Then, in that day, a great horn shall be blown and they shall come who were lost in the land of Assyria" (Isa. 27:13).'"

Jacob's word choice is echoed in the prophetic passages that deal with Israel's redemption. His "then" matched the prophets' "then." The union of Jacob's biography and Israel's history yields the passage at hand. It is important only because it says once again what we have now heard throughout our survey of *Genesis Rabbah*—but makes the statement as explicit as one can imagine.

Israel as Unique among Nations in *Leviticus Rabbah*

Genesis is not the only biblical book that the fifth-century C.E. rabbinic sages reread in light of the events of the fourth century. Leviticus, which is devoted to the sanctification of Israel, is another. A cogent and propositional commentary to the book of Leviticus, *Leviticus Rabbah,* ca. 450, treats the laws of the ongoing sanctification of the life of Israel as an account of the rules of the one-time salvation of Israel. It is a companion of *Genesis Rabbah* and addresses questions dealt with there.

To the framers of *Leviticus Rabbah,* the Israel of their time remains the Israel of which the prophets prophesied—Israel after the flesh and Israel after the spirit, both in one community. And that is not only because Israel today continues the family begun by Abraham, Isaac, Jacob, Joseph, and the other tribal founders, and bears the heritage bequeathed by them. Israel is what it is also because of its character as a holy nation. It is unique among nations.

Here again, in *Leviticus Rabbah* Rome is the penultimate empire on earth. Israel will constitute the ultimate one. That message sees the shifts in world history in a pattern and places at the apex of the shift Israel itself. The view takes up the issue made urgent by the advent of the Christian emperors. Rome, among the successive empires, bears special traits, most of which derive from its distinctively Christian character. We realize that we have moved very far from the genealogical theory of Israel.

Here is how *Leviticus Rabbah* portrays Israel among the nations. What the passage does is compare the various world empires to animals that are forbidden for Israelites to eat. Each has traits that mark it as distinct, and the traits are formed by historical events. Babylonia conquered and destroyed the First Temple of Jerusalem. Media produced the wicked Haman of the book of Esther. Greece, which produced Alexander the Great, the conqueror of the whole world, is treated affirmatively, because Alexander honored the Israelite high priest, Simeon the Righteous. By contrast, Rome is represented as the worst.

Leviticus Rabbah XIII:V

Moses foresaw what the evil kingdoms would do [to Israel] [when he said,] "The camel, rock badger, and hare" (Deut. 14:7). [Compare: "Nevertheless, among those that chew the cud or part the hoof, you shall not eat these: the camel, because it chews the cud but does not part the hoof, is unclean to you. The rock badger, because it chews the cud but does not part the hoof, is unclean to you. And the hare, because it chews the cud but does not part the hoof, is unclean to you, and the pig, because it parts the hoof and is cloven-footed, but does not chew the cud, is unclean to you" (Lev. 11:4–8).]

The verse about the animals Israel may not eat now yields a series of plays on the words that describe the forbidden animals, which stand for the four empires. The play starts with *grh*, the Hebrew word for "chew the cud." Those letters include *gr*, which means "stranger." So the interpretation will speak of how the great world empires treat strangers, that is, Israel:

"The camel" (Lev. 11:4)—this refers to Babylonia.
"For it chews the cud" [now meaning: Babylonia brings up the stranger]—for it exalts righteous men: "And Daniel was in the gate of the [Babylonian] king" (Dan. 2:49).
"The rock badger" (Lev. 11:5)—this refers to Media.
"For it chews the cud—For it brings up the stranger"—for it exalts righteous men: "Mordecai sat at the gate of the king [of Media]" (Est. 2:19).
"The hare" (Lev. 11:6)—this refers to Greece.
"For it chews the cud—For it brings up the stranger"—for it exalts the righteous.
"The pig" (Lev. 11:7)—this refers to Rome.
"But it does not chew the cud—it does not bring up the stranger"—for it does not exalt the righteous.
And it is not enough that it does not exalt them, but it kills them.

Babylonia honored Daniel, Media (Persia) honored Mordecai, whom we meet in connection with Queen Esther in part 4, and Greece honored the righteous man in the person of the Jerusalem high priest, Simeon the Righteous. But Rome does not exalt the righteous but kills them, as we shall see in part 4.

The last reading of the phrase "bring up the cud" forms a play on the word for "bring along in its train," because the letters of the latter coincide with those of the former. It makes the point that each of the world empires brought along in its train a successor: Babylonia was followed by Media, Media by Greece, Greece by Rome. But Rome will be succeeded only by Israel, with no further world empire contemplated. Rome rather restores the crown to the one to whom it belongs.

> Another interpretation [now treating "bring up the cud" (*gr*) as "bring along in its train" (*grr*)]:
>
> "The camel" (Lev. 11:4)—this refers to Babylonia.
>
> "Which brings along in its train"—for it brought along another kingdom after it.
>
> "The rock badger" (Lev. 11:5)—this refers to Media.
>
> "Which brings along in its train"—for it brought along another kingdom after it.
>
> "The hare" (Lev. 11:6)—this refers to Greece.
>
> "Which brings along in its train"—for it brought along another kingdom after it.
>
> "The pig" (Lev. 11:7)—this refers to Rome.
>
> "Which does not bring along in its train"—for it did not bring along another kingdom after it.
>
> And why is it then called "pig" (*hzyr*)? For it restores (*mhzrt*) the crown to the one who truly should have it [namely, Israel, whose dominion will begin when the rule of Rome ends].
>
> That is in line with the following verse of Scripture: "And saviors will come up on Mount Zion to judge the mountain of Esau [Rome], and the kingdom will then belong to the Lord" (Obad. 21).

The animals Israel is not to eat therefore stand for historical periods and events and bring a message concerning world empires in relationship to Israel. In the interpretations of the animals of Leviticus 11:4–8/Deuteronomy 14:7, the camel, rock badger, hare, and pig, the pig, standing for Rome, again emerges as different from the others and more threatening than the rest.

The doctrine of Israel thus encompasses Rome. Rome, which is descended from Esau or from Israel's relation, Edom, does not pretend to praise God but only blasphemes. It does not exalt the righteous but kills them. Of greatest importance, while all the other beasts bring further ones in their wake, the pig does not: "It does not bring another kingdom after it." It will restore the crown to the one who will truly deserve it, Israel. "Esau will be judged by Zion," so Obadiah 21.

This is a compelling way of saying that the now-Christian empire requires differentiation from its pagan predecessors: matters have gotten worse. But beyond Rome, standing in a straight line with the others, lies the true shift in history, the rule of Israel and the cessation of the dominion of the (pagan) nations. Rome in the fourth century became Christian. Sages responded by facing that fact quite squarely and saying, "Indeed, it is as you say, a kind of Israel, an heir of Abraham as your texts explicitly claim. But we remain the sole legitimate Israel, the bearer of the birthright—we and not you. So you are our brother: like Esau to Jacob, like Ishmael to Isaac."

Jacob and Esau, Israel and Rome: The Reason Why

The doctrine of Israel therefore emerges as acutely relevant to the religious conflict of the fourth century. Christian Rome is like and not like Israel. In Esau, Rome is given a position in Israelite genealogy. It is like Israel in a way in which no other state or nation is like Israel, and, consequently, in the odd metaphors of Rome as an animal unlike other animals or Rome as an empire unlike other empires, we have to appeal to a special relationship between Rome and Israel. And that special relationship, already prepared, can only be genealogical.

The doctrine of Israel in the Talmud of the Land of Israel, and related writings contained two important points about the gentiles, both of them centered on Rome in particular.

First, Rome is like Israel but not like Israel at all. In *Leviticus Rabbah* Esau is compared to a pig. The reason for the aptness of the analogy is simple. The pig exhibits public traits expected of a suitable beast, in that it shows a cloven hoof, such as the laws of acceptable beasts require. But the pig does not exhibit the inner traits of a suitable beast, in that it does not chew the cud. Accordingly, the pig confuses and deceives. The polemic against Esau = Rome is simple. Rome claims to be Israel in that it adheres to "the Old Testament," that is, the written Torah of Sinai. Specifically, Rome is represented as only Christian Rome can have been represented: it superficially looks kosher but it is not kosher.

Second, just as Israel had survived Babylonia, Media, Greece, so would they endure to see the end of Rome.

To deliver their message the rabbinic sages read Scripture in a new way. Scripture is no longer read as a history book, concerning things that happened one time only and long, long ago. True, it can be seen as a sequence of one-time and linear events. But that is not how the sages saw the Torah. Rather, the sages treated everything that happened as a repetition of known and already experienced patterns.

The sages of Judaism relived the written Torah's world in their own times and terms. That is what we see when we follow the emergence of the topic of Israel, from its origins in the written Torah to its development in the successive writings, the Mishnah, Talmud, and Midrash.

Chapter 3

The Torah's Story and the Mishnah's Law: The Way of Life of Judaism

How the Law Turns Stories into Actions

The Mishnah in ca. 200 C.E. formed of diverse laws and stories of the Torah a pattern of actions meant to regulate Israel's social order. Scripture's laws in Exodus, Leviticus, Numbers, and Deuteronomy present cases in the setting of narratives. These are not well organized and sometimes they contain contradictions. The Mishnah organizes the cases into generalizations. It systematizes details into a cogent whole. It thus reworks the laws and narratives of Scripture into a systematic statement. That statement defines Israel's way of life. It sets forth in a coherent way the rules of practical conduct. For that reason Israel's way of life is defined by the Torah's cases and stories.

The Mishnah's laws thus make sense best when we see how they relate to the Torah's stories. Then we grasp how narrative details are translated into normative rules. In the Mishnah's exposition of the laws that convey the rules of conduct that are implicit in stories, two master narratives of the Torah take priority. First is the story of the creation of the world, Genesis 1–3. Second is the narrative of Israel's liberation from Egyptian slavery, escape through the sea, advent at Mount Sinai, where Moses gave the Torah that conveyed God's teaching, and then the generation of wandering in the wilderness en route to the promised land.

Precisely how the laws of the Mishnah translate into practical actions of everyday life the stories and rules that Scripture sets forth is illustrated in three examples given here, two expositions of laws that concern creation and one of laws that act out the wandering in the wilderness.

The Torah's Story of Creation and Adam and Eve in Eden and the Mishnah's Law on Israel in the Land of Israel

The Torah identifies the land of Israel as the location of Israel's meeting with God. The story narrated by the Pentateuch makes clear that Israel's possession of the land indicates Israel's standing with him. This conviction comes to expression not only in the narrative of the Torah but in the normative law of the Mishnah.

The story the Torah tells is now familiar. Adam and Eve possessed Eden, rebelled against God, and lost Eden. Consequently humanity had to work for its living and ended up in the grave. Along these same lines, Israel was freed from Egyptian slavery and wandered in the wilderness for forty years, until the rebellious generation that left Egypt had died out. Their children then entered the promised land. In this pattern, at what point does Israel compare with Adam and Eve in Eden? Israel's moment of entering the land of Israel corresponded to Adam and Eve's entering Eden. But like Adam and Eve in Eden, Israel in the land rebelled and sinned and lost the land.

The stories of Adam and Eve and Israel diverge: Israel got a second chance. That is where the Mishnah's law takes over. God in the Torah defines the conditions in which Israel is to work that particular land. The law of the Mishnah responds to that definition, building on the implications of the Torah's laws. Specifically, the Mishnah's laws express in rules the conviction that God owns the land and Israel lives from its bounty as sharecroppers of God's land. The land is comparable to the garden of Eden, and it is to be farmed in accord with the procedures guiding the creation of heaven and earth. We now follow the way in which two Mishnah tractates translate into laws the implications of the story of Eden and the land.

Everything in Order and in Place. *Kil'ayim:* Mixed Seeds

Creation takes place when chaos is brought under control and ordered, that is, when the world is made perfect. God created the world out of chaos and emptiness. Creation was orderly. The law of the Mishnah tractate *Kil'ayim*, "mixed seeds," responds to that narrative. It holds that Israel in farming the Holy Land is to restore the orderly appearance of the land to conform to the condition of creation.

The Torah makes clear that God is concerned not only with the use of the land but with its good order. That is in line with the account of creation, which stresses that each species was created in its own framework. Species were not mixed together, but each had its place in the order of creation. The story of Genesis 1 expresses this idea when it speaks of each species of creation subject to its own "name," that is, kept in its own category or classification. The land must resemble Eden.

How is the land made orderly and well organized? It is to be sown in such a way that species—wheat and grapevines, for example—are kept distinct. And that applies to all the produce of the land, whether vegetable or animal. The law of Mishnah tractate *Kil'ayim,* which means, mixed species, elaborates upon the law of Leviticus 19:19: "You shall not let your cattle mate with a different kind; you shall not sow your field with two kinds of seed; you shall not put on cloth from a mixture of two kinds of material." It further elaborates on the law of Deuteronomy 22:9–11: "You shall not sow your vineyard with a second kind of seed, otherwise the crop from the seed you have sown and the produce of the vineyard may not be used; you shall not plow with an ox and an ass together; you shall not wear cloth that combines wool and linen."

A mark of how God blessed creation comes about when all things were ordered, properly in place, each according to its kind. This means not mixing classes or species of flora or fauna—plants, animals, fibers, thus, whether plants, crops in a vineyard, kinds of animals, or diverse sources of fabrics, linen from the earth and wool from animals. Mixing them violates the principles of order established in creation, when each species was set forth in its own category ("according to its name").

But who defines a class? The law of the Mishnah takes the view that it is the human being who does. It is the human being's definition of species and perception of their mixtures that governs. What in human eyes *appears* orderly is deemed in good order. That explains the stress of the law of tractate *Kil'ayim* on appearances. If plants look alike, they are considered to belong to the same kind. The *appearance* of confusion, not the actual sowing together of two kinds, imposes liability for violating the law.

Take, for example, the issue of growing two or more crops in the same field. The Torah supplies only the rule that this may not be done. But the law of the Mishnah goes further. It holds that if the field would *appear* to contain more than a single crop, then the law is invoked; but if the field would appear to contain one crop only, with other crops growing adjacent to, but not within, the main crop, then appearance takes over and the field does not violate the law. If different kinds of crops appear to be planted in an orderly way, they are deemed sown separately, even within the same field. But if someone cannot with the naked eye distinguish them from one another, they are deemed as mixed in kind.

The upshot is clear. If in a person's view the field contains mixed crops, it is forbidden. But if from the human perspective it does not, then the law is not violated. If properly distinguished, therefore, wheat and barley may grow in the same field if they are kept separate within the field, and so on. It follows that if items when mingled together do not appear to confuse diverse species, they may be planted together.

When it comes to adjacent spaces, the rule is the same. Sufficient distance to set off one species from another prevents violating the law. How things look, not how they actually are, defines the governing standard. Consequently, the Israelite bears responsibility for preventing the mixing of species in the land. If diverse kinds grow without the owner's intent, the crops do not have to be destroyed—for instance, if they are growing among vines—but once the householder finds out, he has to remove the diverse kinds.

From one viewpoint *Kil'ayim* takes God's perspective on the land, imagining the landscape as seen from on high. God wants to see in the land an orderly and regular landscape, each species in its proper place. So too God wants to see Israel clothed in garments that preserve the distinction between animal (wool) and vegetable (linen) exactly where that distinction operates for fabrics. God wants to see animals ordered by their species, just as they were when Noah brought them into the ark (Gen. 7:14). What that means is that grapes and wheat are not to grow together, oxen and asses are not to be yoked together, and wool and linen are not to be woven together in a single garment.

But who bears responsibility for restoring the perfection of creation? The Mishnah's law empowers humanity to impose order upon the world. The Israelite householder has the power to do in the land of Israel what God did in creating the world at Eden, that is, establish order, overcome chaos, perfect the world for the occasion of sanctification. The law of the Mishnah treats the Israelite as God's partner in overcoming chaos and establishing order. It is the Israelite's perspective that governs and that identifies chaos or affirms order.

Acting Out Eden's Drama, with a Difference. *'Orlah:* The Produce of an Orchard in the Fourth Year after It Is Planted

Scripture's parallel stories show that Israel is to the land of Israel as Adam and Eve are to Eden. It got the land and lost it but can return, just as Adam and Eve were given Eden but lost it through disobedience. Israel and Adam and Eve share in common responsibility for their condition. Each party rebelled and so lost paradise.

Then the law of the Mishnah has a task. It is to show that Israel has learned its lesson. Judaism holds that the Torah makes the difference. Keeping the Torah, the covenant between God and Israel, teaches Israel to love God and to want to do his will. Then what Israel does, how it conducts itself, takes the measure of how Israel is overcoming the sin of disobedience.

The law of the Torah is God's remedy for the condition of Adam. It gives Israel the occasion to sin as Adam and Eve sinned, but to refrain from doing so. That is a spiritual exercise of repentance.

How is this done? Adam and Eve sinned by disobeying God's prohibition against their eating the fruit of a specific tree. So Israel is placed into temptation to do the same. It has the chance to show it has learned the lesson of Eden.

That establishes the context in which we read a particular law, the law that governs the disposition of fruit of a fruit tree in the first three years after it is planted and in the fourth year of the same cycle. We shall now see how in the exposition of the Mishnah and its companion writing, which we shall meet in a moment, the rule relates to the creation story. It tells us the way in which by keeping the law the Israelite once more acts out the creation narrative.

The Mishnah tractate *'Orlah* elaborates on the Torah's commandment at Leviticus 19:23–25: "When you come to the land and plant any kind of tree for food, you shall treat it as forbidden. For three years it shall be forbidden, it shall not be eaten. In the fourth year all its fruit shall be set aside for jubilation before the Lord, and only in the fifth year may you use its fruit, that its yield to you may be increased: I am the Lord your God."

The law of the Torah thus holds that produce of a fruit tree is forbidden for the first three years after the tree is planted. In the fourth year it is brought to Jerusalem, the Holy City, and eaten in the Holy Place. From the fifth year after planting onward, the fruit is available for ordinary use.

The rule before us seems arbitrary and pointless. What, specifically, is the purpose for the prohibition of using the fruit for three years and having the Israelites present themselves with it to Jerusalem in the fourth?

The specificities of the law turn out to define with some precision a message on the relationship of Israel to the land of Israel and to God.

The first is that the prohibition of *'Orlah* fruit applies solely within the land of Israel and not to the neighboring territories occupied by Israelites, which means that it is the union of Israel with the land of Israel that invokes the prohibition. This is the sense of Scripture as derived by *Sifra,* ca. 300 C.E., a rabbinic commentary to the book of Leviticus that complements the Mishnah's treatment of the law:

Sifra CCII:I.1

"When you come [into the land and plant all kinds of trees for food, then you shall count their fruit as forbidden; three years it shall be forbidden to you, it must not be eaten. And in the fourth year all their fruit shall be holy, an offering of praise to the Lord. But in the fifth year you may eat of their fruit, that they may yield more richly for you: I am the Lord your God" (Lev. 19:23–25)].

Might one suppose that the law applied once they came to Transjordan? Scripture says, ". . . into the land,"
the particular land [of Israel].

Here, some trait deemed to inhere in the land of Israel and in no other territory must define the law, and a particular message ought to inhere in this law. This same point is reached once more: it is only trees that *Israelites* plant in the land that are subject to the prohibition, not those that gentiles planted before the Israelites inherited the land:

Sifra CCII:I.2
"When *you* come into the land and plant":
excluding those that gentiles have planted prior to the Israelites' coming into the land.
Or should I then exclude those that gentiles planted even after the Israelites came into the land?
Scripture says, "all kinds of trees."

A further point of special interest requires that the Israelite plant the tree as a deliberate act; if the tree merely grows up on its own, it is not subject to the prohibition. So Israelite action joined to intention is required; that is what activates the system:

Sifra CCII:I.4
". . . and [deliberately] plant . . .":
excluding one that grows up on its own.
". . . and plant . . .":
excluding one that grows out of a grafting or sinking a root.

The several points on which *Sifra*'s reading of the law of the Mishnah and the verses of the Torah that pertain alert us to the narrative that is embedded in the law of Mishnah tractate '*Orlah*.

First, the law takes effect only from the point at which Israel enters the land. That is to say, Israel's entry into the land marks the beginning of the time at which the trees produce fruit that are subject to God's concern. To understand, we must know that, elsewhere, the law of the Mishnah treats the entry of Israel into the land as counterpart to the restoration of Eden.

A rabbinic sage maintains that if the Israelites had not sinned upon entering the land, the entire narrative of Scripture would consist of the five books of Moses and the book of Joshua, which describes the conquest of the land. Israel would have had no further history, just as if Adam and Eve had not rebelled against God's will, the Torah would have been complete with the creation story, Genesis 1:1–2:3.

So there is no missing the essential message. The law of the Mishnah has no better way of comparing the entry of Israel into the land with the moment at which the creation of Eden took place. Israel's entry into the land marks a new beginning for humanity, comparable to the very creation of the world.

Second, according to the law of the Mishnah, the attitude of the Israelite in planting the tree counts. If the Israelite plants the tree for its fruit, his intention is what subjects the tree to the 'Orlah rule. If an Israelite does not plant the tree with the plan of producing fruit, then the tree is not subject to the rule. If the tree grows up on its own, not by the act and precipitating intentionality of the Israelite, the 'Orlah rule does not apply. If an Israelite does not plant the tree to produce fruit, the 'Orlah rule does not apply. And the tree must be planted in the ordinary way; if grafted or sunk as a root, the law does not apply. In a moment, this heavy emphasis upon Israelite intentionality will produce a critical result.

But, before reaching that juncture, let us ask some fundamental questions.

First, what is the counterpart in the story of Adam and Eve in the garden to Israelite observance of the restraint of three years? Second, why should Israelite intentionality play so critical a role?

The answer becomes obvious when we ask a third question: Can we think of any other commandments concerning fruit trees in the land that—the sages say time and again—is Eden? Of course we can: "Of every tree of the garden you are free to eat; but as for the tree of knowledge of good and evil, you must not eat of it" (Gen. 2:16).

The story of creation and the law of produce in the fourth year compare. But there is this difference: the law of Mishnah tractate 'Orlah imposes upon Israel a more demanding commandment than God's imperative to Adam and Eve. Of the fruit of *no* tree in the new Eden may Israel eat for three years. That demands considerable restraint.

Not only so, but it is Israel's own intentionality—not God's—that imposes upon every fruit-bearing tree the prohibition of use of the produce for three years. That applies to not only the one tree of Eden but all fruit trees planted in the land. So once Israel wants the fruit, it must show that it can restrain its desire and wait for three years.

By its act of will, Israel imposes upon itself the requirement of restraint. When Israelites plant fruit trees in the Land, it is as if they have taken the Land for the first time, so they must repeat that same exercise of self-restraint. That is, when planting fruit trees they are to act as though, for the case at hand, they have just come into the Land. How do these laws in detail respond to the story of the loss of paradise?

The Details of the Law of Mishnah Tractate *'Orlah* and the Statement That They Make about Creation

The first detail of the law that captures our attention is the basic rule: why *three years* in particular? The narrative of creation answers the question. Fruit trees were created on the third day of creation. Then, when Israel by intention and action designates a tree—any tree—as fruit bearing, Israel must wait for three years, corresponding to how in creation the world waited for three days for the advent of the fruit-bearing tree.

Second, why *fruit trees* in particular? Once more the narrative of creation gives a self-evident answer: it is a fruit-bearing tree that was the object of a particular commandment, a prohibition recapitulated now. But there is this difference. It is not one tree alone, but fruit trees in general: those that nourish humanity. So the planting of every tree imposes upon Israel the challenge God set in the garden to Adam and Eve. It is the occasion to meet once more the temptation that the first Adam could not overcome.

Israel now recapitulates the temptation of Adam and Eve then, but Israel, the new Adam, possesses, and is possessed by, the Torah. And that makes all the difference. So by its own action and intention in planting fruit trees, Israel finds itself in a veritable orchard of trees like the tree of knowledge of good and evil. The difference between Adam and Israel is that, permitted to eat all fruit but one, Adam ate the forbidden fruit. By contrast Israel refrains for a specified span of time from fruit from *all* trees. This restraint marks what has taken place, the regeneration of humanity. So Israel waits for three years—as long as God waited in creating fruit trees.

Third, what about the disposition of the produce of the tree in the fourth year after planting? Even after three years, Israel may not eat the fruit wherever it chooses. Rather, in the fourth year from planting, Israel will still show restraint, bringing the fruit only "for jubilation before the Lord" in Jerusalem.

That signals a striking contrast between Israel in the land and Adam and Eve in Eden. When Adam ate, he shamefully hid from God for having eaten the fruit. But when Israel eats the fruit, it does so proudly, joyfully, in God's very presence. So the once-forbidden fruit is now eaten in public, not in secret, before God, as a moment of celebration.

That detail too recalls the fall. After eating the forbidden fruit, Adam and Eve hid out; they did not want to be seen by God. But then the contrast is clear. Faithful Israel refrains when it is supposed to. Therefore it has every reason to show itself to the Lord, which is what people do when they bring produce to Jerusalem to eat it there. Then eating "before the Lord," Israel has nothing to hide, and everything to show.

Fourth, what happens then? In the fifth year Israel may eat on its own, the time of any restraint from enjoying the fruit tree having ended. The days of the week correspond to the seven days of creation as the rabbinic sages read them. Then why release all prohibitions of the fruit of the tree in the fifth year after it is planted?

The fifth year corresponds to Thursday of the week of creation. How does that work? Creation—as the creation narrative portrays matters—began on Sunday and was complete on Friday and then sanctified by Sabbath repose on the seventh day, Saturday, the Sabbath. So we find that Adam and Eve, having spent the first Sabbath in the garden, sinned on Sunday, the first day of the second week of creation.

With these details of the narrative in hand, we return to the law. Placing Adam's sin on the first day after the first Sabbath, thus Sunday, we may calculate that the three forbidden years during which the tree's fruit may not be used correspond to Sunday, Monday, and Tuesday. Then Wednesday of the second week of creation, the fourth day corresponds to the fourth year when the fruit is to be brought to Jerusalem. Thursday (the fifth year) and Friday provide the equivalent of a double portion for the Sabbath—the second Sabbath of creation.

So now the three prohibited years allow Israel to show its true character, fully regenerate, wholly and humbly accepting God's commandment, the one Adam broke. And the rest follows.

The story that the laws embody in actions of commission or omission is then complete. The laws of mixed seeds, *Kil'ayim,* and produce of a fruit tree in the first three years after it is planted, *'Orlah,* translate details of Scripture's narratives of Creation into concrete activities. Israel then acts out its own story.

What is the point of the law of the Mishnah? It is to show that, by its own act of restraint, the new Adam, Israel, displays its repentance in respect to the very sin that the old Adam committed, the sin of disobedience and rebellion. Facing the same opportunity to sin, Israel again and again over time refrains from the sin that cost Adam Eden. So by Israel's manner of cultivation of the land and its orchards, Israel manifests what in the very condition of humanity has changed by the giving of the Torah. The Torah then represents humanity's second chance, through Israel.

Only in the land that succeeds Eden can Israel, succeeding Adam, carry out the acts of repentance and rebirth that the Torah makes possible.

The Torah's Narrative of Israel's Dwelling in the Wilderness and Mishnah Tractate *Sukkah*

The story of creation forms only one of the two master narratives of the human condition that the law of the Mishnah makes concrete in everyday conduct. The other ever-present story concerns the beginning of Israel in the wilderness of Sinai.

The details are simple and familiar. The Israelites, children of Abraham and Sarah and their children and grandchildren, went down to Egypt by reason of years of drought in the land and were enslaved there. God sent Moses to free them from Egyptian bondage. Moses led them through the Sea of Reeds ("Red Sea"), which parted to allow them to cross but closed and prevented their pursuers from following. After that miracle the Israelites were brought to Mount Sinai, in the wilderness. There they were offered, and accepted, the Torah. Approaching the land after the revelation of the Torah at Mount Sinai, the freed slaves did not have confidence in God's promises. They turned away. Consequently, God condemned the generation of freed slaves to wander for forty years in the wilderness. There they would die out. Only their children would be worthy of entering the promised land.

How the wandering in the wilderness is translated from story to law comes to the surface in the laws of the observance of the Festival of Sukkot, the Festival of Tabernacles (huts). The festival begins on the first full moon after the autumnal equinox of September 21. (Its counterpart in the spring, Passover, commemorating the liberation from Egypt, begins on the first full moon after the vernal equinox, March 21.)

To understand the context of the festival, we have to know that Judaism tells time with a lunar calendar, adjusted regularly to correlate with the solar seasons. The fifteenth day of the lunar month marks the full moon. Now the first day of the lunar month in which Sukkot falls, the lunar month of Tishre, is the New Year. In Judaism that is the judgment day. Then God sits in judgment on all the world and decides the fate of nations and individuals for the coming year. The tenth day following the New Year is the Day of Atonement, which atones for sin and brings forgiveness for sin. In Hebrew, the New Year is called Rosh Hashanah and the Day of Atonement is called Yom Kippur.

Then the Festival of Tabernacles follows in sequence. It is the third part of the season of judgment and atonement marked by the New Year and Day of

Atonement. We realize that these fall on the first and the tenth days of the lunar month of Tishre. Sukkot comes on the fifteenth through the twenty-second days of that same month. The Festival of Tabernacles therefore is integral to the penitential season of judgment, atonement, and forgiveness of sin. It marks the happy outcome.

Scripture supplies nearly all of the pertinent facts of Sukkot, the Feast of Booths or Tabernacles (Lev. 23:33–43). It explicitly links the Festival of Tabernacles to Israel's dwelling in the wilderness for forty years. But the narrative leaves to the Mishnah the work of defining details: "You shall dwell in booths [sukkot] for seven days; all that are native in Israel shall dwell in booths, that your generations may know that I made the people of Israel dwell in booths when I brought them out of the land of Egypt; I am the Lord your God."

In reverting to the wilderness, Israel is to take shelter in any random, ramshackle hut, covered with what in form and in purpose one otherwise does not value. Israel's dwelling in the wilderness is fragile, random, and transient—like Israel in the wilderness.

Numbers 29:12–38 specifies the offerings on the occasion of the Festival of Sukkot, and Deuteronomy 16:13–15 assigns the feast to Jerusalem, at the same time arranging for rejoicing in the towns elsewhere.

The Torah thus has the Festival of Tabernacles commemorate Israel's condition in the wilderness. During the festival, for a week's time, Israel moves from its permanent houses to impermanent huts, reenacting the fragility of its life in the wilderness. The details of the Mishnah's laws bear a message that the story conveys in narrative form.

Once more we recall how sages maintain that had Israel not sinned, the Torah would have contained only the Pentateuch and the book of Joshua. That is a neat way of stating in a few words the conviction that permeates the narrative reading of the land as counterpart to Eden, Israel as counterpart to Adam. It is on that basis that the wilderness marks the interval between slavery in Egypt and eternal life in the land.

How do details of the Mishnah's presentation translate the story into law? It is at the sukkah—the hut—itself that we find the center of the Mishnaic legal repertoire concerning the festival. The interim, temporary abode of Israel in between Egypt and the land is the house that is not a house. Not only so, but it is protected by a roof that is open to the elements but serves somewhat.

How does the law pertain? The Mishnah now defines details to make concrete the message that Israel in the wilderness lived in houses open to the rain and affording protection only from the harsh sunlight, shade but not protection such as a roof provides. Their abode was constructed of what was insusceptible to uncleanness. Only what is useful is susceptible to uncleanness.

That is, the materials that were used had to be otherwise useless, bits and pieces of this and that.

First comes the statement that the roofing for the sukkah must be insusceptible to uncleanness:

> Mishnah tractate *Sukkah* 1:4
>
> This is the general rule: Whatever is susceptible to uncleanness and does not grow from the ground—they do not make sukkah roofing with it. And whatever is not susceptible to uncleanness, but does grow from the ground [and has been cut off]—they do make sukkah roofing with it.

Second is the law that the covering of the sukkah must provide shade but not complete protection from rain or sun:

> Mishnah tractate *Sukkah* 2:2
>
> A sukkah [the roofing of which] is loosely put together, but the shade of which is greater than the light, is valid. The [sukkah] [the roofing of which] is tightly knit like that of a house, even though the stars cannot be seen from inside it, is valid.

Third comes the requirement that one treat the sukkah as home for the holiday:

> Mishnah tractate *Sukkah* 2:9
>
> All seven days a person treats his sukkah as his regular dwelling and his house as his sometime dwelling. [If] it began to rain, at what point is it permitted to empty out [the sukkah]? From the point at which the porridge will spoil. They made a parable: To what is the matter comparable? To a slave who came to mix a cup of wine for his master, and his master threw the flagon into his face.

Fourth is the issue of building the sukkah fresh, year to year, which is debated by the Mishnah's initial authorities, the disciples of the masters Hillel and Shammai, who flourished in the beginning of the first century C.E.

> Mishnah tractate *Sukkah* 1:1
>
> A superannuated sukkah—the House of Shammai declare it invalid. And the House of Hillel declare it valid. And what exactly is a superannuated sukkah? One made thirty days [or more] before the Festival [of Sukkot]. But if one made it for the sake of the festival [intending the hut to serve as the sukkah for the festival], even at the beginning of the year, it is valid.

Israel then is instructed to live in a temporary shack just when the seasons turn in the autumn. How, in the land of Israel, does the weather change? The dry summer ends, the autumnal rains start. The odd timing should not be missed. It is not with the coming of the spring and the dry season, when the booth serves a useful purpose of shelter against the sun, but at the advent of the autumn and the rainy season. For by definition, the sukkah does not protect against the rain. Now it is an abode that cannot serve in the season that is coming, announced by the new moon that occasions the festival.

The home is abandoned altogether, a hut being constructed for the occasion. During the festival the Israelite moves out of his or her home altogether, eating meals and (where possible) sleeping in the sukkah, making the sukkah into his or her regular home, and the home into the random shelter. In the wilderness God's abode shifted along with Israel from place to place. The Festival of Sukkot confronts the Israelite with the impermanence of the human condition, which is represented by death in the wilderness, before the promised land is reached.

The Meaning of the Details of Mishnah Tractate *Sukkah* and the Statement That They Make about Israel in the Wilderness

In Scripture's narrative, we recall, the generation of the wilderness is condemned to live in huts as they wander for forty years. That lasts until the entire generation that left Egypt has died out. That is because the generation that left Egypt rejected the land when it had the opportunity to enter it. Then the generation born in the wilderness may enter the land. The sukkah, the temporary abode of the wandering Israelite, is random and fragile. In its transience it matches Israel's condition in the wilderness, wandering between Egypt and the land.

How do the details call to mind the Torah's presentation of the sukkot in the setting of wandering in the wilderness?

Now, after the season of repentance, Israel has atoned and lived. But that is only in the condition of the wilderness, like the generation that, after all, had to die out before Israel could enter the land and its intended eternal life.

All seven days a person treats his or her sukkah with the flimsy roof made of useless material as the regular dwelling and the house as the sometime dwelling. Scripture's story of Sukkot reminds Israel annually by putting the Israelites into huts (tabernacles) that Israel now lives like the generation of the wilderness then. In the penitential season Israel is reminded that it is sinful and meant to die. The law of the Mishnah underscores not only transience. It emphasizes the immediacy of the wilderness condition. The Mishnah's law requires that the sukkah be constructed fresh. Every year Israel is directed to replicate the wilderness generation.

The message is not to be missed. We recall the Mishnah's definition of Israel: all those destined to rise from the grave, stand in judgment, and enter into Eden. So in this life Israel is en route to the land that stands for Eden. But even beyond the penitential season Israel bears its sin and all will die. But in death Israelites enjoy the certainty of resurrection, judgment, and eternal life to come.

On the occasion of Sukkot, Israel reenters the wilderness and its situation of death on the near term. But wandering in the wilderness ended in the entry into the land. What is the point? Only in the context of the New Year and the Day of Atonement does the Festival of Tabernacles make sense—it is only as the final act in the penitential season and its intense drama.

Sukkot celebrates the advent of the rainy season with prayers and activities meant to encourage the now-conciliated God to give ample rain to sustain the life of the land and its people. So the message of the laws of the Mishnah in the story told by Scripture cannot be missed. Israel has rebelled and sinned, but Israel has also atoned and repented.

Why stress the fragility of the sukkah, its roof with holes, its insubstantial quality? Because in the wilderness, en route to the land, still-sinful Israel depended wholly and completely on God's mercy. They relied on his infinite capacity to forgive in response to repentance and atonement. Israel in the wilderness depends for all things on God. There, the narrative tells, they eat food he sends down from heaven, drink water he divines in rocks.

So too they live in fragile huts (tabernacles) constructed of worthless shards and remnants of this and that. Even Israel's shelter now is made to depend upon divine grace: the wind can blow it down, the rain prevent its very use. Returning to these huts (tabernacles), built specifically for the occasion (not last year's), the Israelite here and now lives in total dependence upon God's mercy.

The law of the Mishnah transforms remembering into reliving the condition of the wilderness. The law of the sukkah makes the statement that Israel of the here and now is sinful like the Israel that dwelt in the wilderness. Israel depends on and looks only to God. And God has just now forgiven last year's sin. God kept Israel alive in the wilderness. The law of the Mishnah turns Israel in the sukkah into the people that is en route to the land, which is Eden. True, Israel is en route, it is not yet there. A generation comes, a generation goes, but Israel will get there, all together at the end.

So we see that the law of the Mishnah in its way makes exactly the same statement about the same matters that the narrative does in its terms. But the narrative speaks in large and general terms to the world at large. For its part the law of the Mishnah through small and particular rules speaks to the everyday concerns of ordinary Israelites.

Chapter 4

Torah: The Worldview of Judaism

Definitions of the Word *Torah* in Judaism

*O*ur survey of how the word *Torah* is used in the successive writings of Judaism in ancient times begins with an overview. Only then do we ask the Mishnah, the Talmud of the Land of Israel, and the later Talmud of Babylonia to show us how they defined and used the word.

The Hebrew word *torah* means "teaching." In Judaism it is the teaching that God revealed to Moses at Mount Sinai. We recall from the preface the most familiar meaning of the word: "Torah = the five books of Moses," the Pentateuch, which are Genesis, Exodus, Leviticus, Numbers, Deuteronomy. The Torah may also refer to the entirety of the Hebrew Scriptures (called by Christianity the "Old Testament"). The Torah furthermore covers instruction in two media, writing and memory. The written part corresponds to the Pentateuch. The oral part covers the teachings ultimately written down by the sages of the Torah in ancient times. It is contained, in part, in the Mishnah, Talmud, and midrash compilations. But there is more: what the world calls "Judaism" the faithful know as "the Torah."

Seven Meanings of the Word *Torah*

As Judaism emerged in ancient times, the word *Torah* carried seven distinct meanings. Here are the meanings assigned to the word *Torah* in the classical writings:

1. When the Torah refers to a particular thing, it is to a scroll containing divinely revealed words.

2. The Torah may further refer to revelation, not as an object but as a corpus of doctrine: God's instruction to Moses at Sinai.
3. When one "does Torah" the disciple "studies" or "learns," and the master "teaches," Torah. Hence while the word *Torah* never appears as a verb, it does refer to an act.
4. The word also bears a quite separate sense, torah as "category or classification or corpus of rules." For example, "the torah of driving a car" is a usage entirely acceptable to some documents. This generic usage of the word does occur.
5. The word *Torah* commonly refers to a status, distinct from and above another status, as "teachings of Torah" as against "teachings of scribes." For the two Talmuds that distinction is absolutely critical to the entire hermeneutic enterprise. But it is important even in the Mishnah.
6. Obviously, no account of the meaning of the word *Torah* can ignore the distinction between the two Torahs, written and oral.
7. Finally, the word *Torah* refers to a source of salvation, often fully worked out in stories about how the individual and the nation will be saved "through Torah." This can refer to the rabbinic sage, viewed as a living Torah when his actions are treated as models of behavior that realizes the Torah. In general, the sense of the word *salvation* is not complicated. Kings who do what God wants win battles, those who do not, lose. So too here, people who study and do Torah are saved from sickness and death. The way Israel can save itself from its condition of degradation also is through Torah.

These seven meanings did not appear at the same time. If we ask the principal holy books of Judaism what they mean by the word *Torah,* we follow the emergence of the full sense of the word. We proceed from the meaning of "Torah" in the Mishnah (200 C.E.) to tractate *'Abot* (250 C.E.), then to the Talmud of the Land of Israel (400 C.E.), finally to the Talmud of Babylonia (600 C.E.), which makes the fullest statement.

The Mishnah and the Torah

The written Torah leaves no doubt as to the origins of its laws. It portrays through a narrative the circumstances in which its laws were revealed by God to Moses. The Mishnah thus lays no claim to the power of prophecy in behalf of its authorities. The framers of the Mishnah gave no hint of the nature of their book.

Unlike biblical law codes, the Mishnah contains no story of its own origin, like the one contained in the repeated phrase of the Pentateuch, "The Lord spoke to Moses saying, speak to the children of Israel and say to them. . . ."

The Mishnah does not make reference to God's giving the laws to a named sage. Nor does the code speak of itself as the Torah.

But the question required attention. Upon coming to closure the Mishnah gained political status as the constitution of Jewish government of the land of Israel. Judah the Patriarch, Rome's recognized ruler of the Jews in the land of Israel, sponsored it. The rabbinic sages applied it in the country's courts and administration. Accordingly, the clerks who knew and applied its law had to explain the standing of that law. In the context of Israel's life and Scripture that meant its relationship to the law of the Torah. But from the Mishnah's own testimony we do not know whether the Mishnah was supposed to be part of the Torah or whether it stood in some clearly defined relationship to the existing Torah.

But we do know what the Mishnah understood by the word *Torah*. Apart from the conventional meanings—God's revelation to Moses at Sinai—the word *Torah* was an indicator of status. The Mishnah places a high value upon studying the Torah and upon the status of the sage.

> Mishnah tractate *Horayot* 3:8
> A priest takes precedence over a Levite, a Levite over an Israelite, an Israelite over a *mamzer* [one whose parents cannot legally marry by reason of consanguinity], a *mamzer* over a *netin* [descendant of a temple slave], a *netin* over a proselyte, a proselyte over a freed slave.
>   Under what circumstances?
>   When all of them are equivalent.
>   But if the *mamzer* was a disciple of a sage and a high priest was an '*am ha'arets* [a person ignorant of the Torah], the *mamzer* who is a disciple of a sage takes precedence over a high priest who is an '*am ha'arets*.

So Torah study was meritorious, signifying supernatural status. But what was studied beyond the written Torah is not specified by the Mishnah. Besides the Pentateuch, Prophets, and Writings, not only did no physical scroll deserve veneration, but no corpus of writings demanded obedience.

The issue is whether we find in the Mishnah the assertion that whatever the sage has on the authority of his master goes back to Sinai. We do not. No one claims to find the Torah of Sinai in the Mishnah, and in the Mishnah, the Mishnah is not explicitly signified as part of the Torah.

"Torah" in Tractate *'Abot*

At issue in *'Abot* is not the Torah, but the authority of the sage. It is that standing that transforms a saying into a Torah saying. It places a saying into the classification of the Torah.

Tractate *'Abot* says a great deal about Torah study. It regards "study of Torah" as what a sage does. What is striking is that the substance of Torah is what a sage says. That is so whether or not the saying of the sage cites Scripture and so relates to scriptural revelation. The content of the sayings attributed to sages endows those sayings with a certain status—*because sages have said them.*

To define that status, we notice several facts. First, in tractate *'Abot* the sages usually do not quote verses of Scripture and explain them, nor do they speak in God's name. They rarely cite a verse of Scripture to prove that what they say is so. Yet the tractate explicitly claims that sages talk Torah. It follows is that if a sage says something, what he says may fall into the classification of a teaching of the Torah.

How do the authors of tractate *'Abot* present proof for the claim that their teachings form part of the Torah? They represent themselves as links in a chain of tradition beginning with God's handing the Torah over to Moses at Sinai. To show what they mean, the rabbinic sages list their names in a sequence of sages extending backward to Moses at Sinai. So they place themselves into a chain of tradition extending from God's teaching of Moses to the latest sage's teaching given to his disciple.

The simple formula that is repeated throughout bears the burden of that claim: "Rabbi X says. . . ." The formula is the one thing the framers of the document never omit and always emphasize: (1) the name of the authority behind a saying, from Simeon the Righteous on downward, and (2) the word *says.*

So what is important to the redactors is what they never have to tell us. Because a recognized sage makes a statement, what he says constitutes, in and of itself, a statement in the status of Torah: part of God's teaching to Moses at Sinai. Since that part is not written down, what is implicit is that an oral tradition forms part of the Torah.

Let us consider the opening statements of tractate *'Abot,* so we shall see what "receiving" and "handing on" Torah consists of—that is, the contents of "Torah."

Tractate *'Abot* 1:1–9
    1:1 Moses received Torah at Sinai and handed it on to Joshua, Joshua to elders, and elders to prophets.
        And prophets handed it on to the men of the great assembly.
        They said three things:
        "Be prudent in judgment.
        "Raise up many disciples.
        "Make a fence for the Torah."

1:2 Simeon the Righteous was one of the last survivors of the great assembly.

He would say: "On three things does the world stand:

"On the Torah,

"and on the Temple service,

"and on deeds of loving-kindness."

1:3 Antigonos of Sokho received [the Torah] from Simeon the Righteous.

He would say,

"Do not be like servants who serve the master on condition of receiving a reward,

"but [be] like servants who serve the master not on condition of receiving a reward.

"And let the fear of Heaven be upon you."

1:4 Yose b. Yoezer of Seredah and Yose b. Yohanan of Jerusalem received [it] from them.

Yose b. Yoezer says,

"Let your house be a gathering place for sages.

"And wallow in the dust of their feet.

"And drink in their words with gusto."

1:5 Yose b. Yohanan of Jerusalem says,

(1) "Let your house be wide open.

(2) "And seat the poor at your table ['make them members of your household'].

(3) "And don't talk too much with women."

1:6 Joshua b. Perahiah and Nittai the Arbelite received [it] from them.

Joshua b. Perahiah says,

"Set up a master for yourself.

"And get yourself a fellow disciple.

"And give everybody the benefit of the doubt."

1:7 Nittai the Arbelite says,

"Keep away from a bad neighbor.

"And don't get involved with a wicked man.

"And don't give up hope of retribution."

1:8 Judah b. Tabbai and Simeon b. Shatah received [it] from them.

Judah b. Tabbai says,

"Don't make yourself like one of those who make advocacy before judges [while you yourself are judging a case].

"And when the litigants stand before you, regard them as guilty.

"And when they leave you, regard them as acquitted (when they have accepted your judgment)."

1:9 Simeon b. Shatah says,

"Examine the witnesses with great care.

"And watch what you say,
"lest they learn from what you say how to lie."

To spell out what this means, let us look at the opening sentences. "Moses received Torah," and it reached "the men of the great assembly." "The three things" those men said bear no resemblance to anything we find in the written Torah, in Scripture. They focus upon the life of sagacity—prudence, discipleship, a fence around the Torah. As we proceed, we find time and again that, while the word *Torah* stands for two things, divine revelation and the act of study of divine revelation, it produces a single effect, the transformation of unformed human into sage.

One definition of what it means to participate in the formulation and transmission of the Torah takes shape in Yohanan ben Zakkai's assertion that the purpose for which a man (an Israelite) was created was to study Torah, followed by his disciples' specifications of the most important things to be learned in the Torah. All of these pertain to the conduct of the wise person, the sage.

Tractate *'Abot* 2:8–9
2:8 Rabban Yohanan b. Zakkai received [it] from Hillel and Shammai.
He would say,
"(1) If you have learned much Torah, (2) do not puff yourself up on that account, (3) for it was for that purpose that you were created."
He had five disciples, and these are they: R. Eliezer b. Hyrcanus, R. Joshua b. Hananiah, R. Yose the priest, R. Simeon b. Netanel, and R. Eleazar b. Arakh.
He would list their good qualities:
R. Eliezer b. Hyrcanus: A plastered well, which does not lose a drop of water.
R. Joshua: Happy is the one who gave birth to him.
R. Yose: A pious man.
R. Simeon b. Netanel: A man who fears sin.
And R. Eleazar b. Arakh: A surging spring.
He would say, "If all the sages of Israel were on one side of the scale, and R. Eliezer b. Hyrcanus were on the other, he would outweigh all of them."
Abba Saul says in his name, "If all of the sages of Israel were on one side of the scale, and R. Eliezer b. Hyrcanus was also with them, and R. Eleazar [b. Arakh] were on the other side, he would outweigh all of them."
2:9 He said to them, "Go and see what is the straight path to which someone should stick."
R. Eliezer says, "A generous spirit."

R. Joshua says, "A good friend."

R. Yose says, "A good neighbor."

R. Simeon says, "Foresight."

R. Eleazar says, "Good will [generosity of spirit]."

He said to them, "I prefer the opinion of R. Eleazar b. Arakh, because in what he says is included everything you say."

He said to them, "Go out and see what is the bad road, which someone should avoid."

R. Eliezer says, "Envy."

R. Joshua says, "A bad friend."

R. Yose says, "A bad neighbor."

R. Simeon says, "Defaulting on a loan."

(All the same is a loan owed to a human being and a loan owed to the Omnipresent, blessed be he, as it is said, The wicked borrows and does not pay back, but the righteous person deals graciously and hands over [what he owes] (Ps. 37:21.)

R. Eleazar says, "Bad will [envy]."

He said to them, "I prefer the opinion of R. Eleazar b. Arakh, because in what he says is included everything you say."

Now, in light of these statements, we ask: what defines and delimits Torah? It is the sage himself. Torah is what a sage learns. And since authorities listed in tractate 'Abot occur also in the Mishnah, what follows? It is that the Mishnah contains teachings of the Torah. That is because authorities whose sayings are found in the Mishnah possess Torah from Sinai. *What they say forms part of the Torah of Sinai.*

But the issue of tractate 'Abot is not the status of the Mishnah. It is the status of the teachings of the rabbinic sages, which happen to fill up the Mishnah too. The real point is the claim that through study of the Torah sages enter God's presence. It is an act that we should therefore compare with the act of prayer: of talking and listening to God. Tractate 'Abot contains the allegation in so many words that, in the encounter with the actual words of the Torah, as much as in reciting Psalms or declaiming Scripture or saying prayers, faithful Israel encounters God's word.

Given the place within the Torah that is attributed to the Mishnah teachings as just now defined—oral tradition of Sinai—we should not find surprising that tractate 'Abot will frame the matter in terms of "words of the Torah" encompassing the Mishnah and much more. But we also should not miss the implicit allegation that the Mishnah's teaching is part of the Torah of Sinai.

What follows is simple: encountering God's words in the Mishnah as much as in Scripture, one meets God in the Torah. Here is the explicit allegation:

Tractate *'Abot* 3:6
Rabbi Halafta of Kefar Hananiah says, "Among ten who sit and work hard on the Torah study the Presence of God comes to rest, as it is said, 'God stands in the congregation of God' (Ps. 82:1) [and 'congregation' involves ten persons].

"And how do we know that the same is so even of five? For it is said, 'And he has founded his vault upon the earth' (Amos 9:6).

"And how do we know that this is so even of three? Since it is said, 'And he judges among the judges' [a court being made up of three judges] (Ps. 82:1).

"And how do we know that this is so even of two? Because it is said, 'Then they that feared the Lord spoke with one another, and the Lord hearkened and heard' (Mal. 3:16).

"And how do we know that this is so even of one? Since it is said, 'In every place where I record my name I will come to you and I will bless you' (Exod. 20:24) [and it is in the Torah that God has recorded his name]."

Had the rabbinic sage not said that God is present among those who labor at the study of the Torah, we should have found it difficult to say so. But here is an explicit claim of direct encounter with God in the words of the Torah. That God is present when Israelites pray and invoke the holy name of God in supplication is easily grasped. Then there is a "you," referring to God, in what is said. But why studying the Torah, which includes the teachings of sages who set forth the laws of the Mishnah, should impel a response of divine attendance is not self-evident.

But there is, as yet, no narrative that explicitly sets forth the story of the dual Torah, one in writing and the other in memory. That narrative would come in the Talmud of the Land of Israel and be fully exposed in the later Talmud of Babylonia.

The Oral Torah: The Dual Torah in the Talmud of the Land of Israel

The framers of the Mishnah nowhere claimed that what they had written forms part of the Torah. They did not say in so many words that their law enjoys the status of God's revelation to Moses at Sinai. Later on, two hundred years beyond the closure of the Mishnah, times had changed. The Christians would claim that the Jews had misrepresented the revelation of Sinai, that they falsified the Torah. So arose the need to explain the standing and origin of the Mishnah. That led some to posit two things. First, God's revelation of the Torah at Sinai encompassed the Mishnah as much as Scripture. Second, the

Mishnah was handed on through oral formulation and oral transmission from Sinai to the framers of the document as we have it.

These two convictions are, I think, implicit in tractate *'Abot.* But they emerge in so many words from the references of the Talmud of the Land of Israel to the dual Torah, part in writing, part handed on in oral tradition and now in the Mishnah. Once the teachings of sages in the Mishnah had entered the status of tradition received from Sinai, it would take but a short step to a theory of the Mishnah as part of the revelation at Sinai.

But the matter goes further. The relationship of the Mishnah to Scripture is not a mere generality. It is made specific. Verses of Scripture are cited as proof of laws of the Mishnah. Thus a passage of the Mishnah will be quoted. Then in the Tosefta sometimes, and routinely in the Talmud of the Land of Israel and its successor, the question is asked, "What is the origin of this statement?" And the answer is given, "As it is written . . . ," followed by a specific verse of Scripture.

This is occasional in the Tosefta. In the Talmud of the Land of Israel we find the first sustained and systematic effort to explain how specific teachings of the Mishnah relate to specific teachings of Scripture: through citing statements of law in Scripture as proof for the validity of statements of law in the Mishnah.

We ask, then, about the conception of the Torah that underlies such initiatives. How do the Talmud of the Land of Israel's sages propose to explain the Mishnah viewed as a whole?

The answer is that these sages explicitly distinguished between the Torah in writing and the Torah in the medium of memory. They further presented the implication that the Mishnah formed part of that other Torah, the oral one. The context of the Talmud's statement is the following passage of the Mishnah, which asks about the basis, in Scripture, of the Mishnah's laws:

Mishnah tractate *Hagigah* 1:8
    The absolution of vows hovers in the air, for it has nothing [in the Torah] upon which to depend. [There are no verses in Scripture that validate the procedure of absolving vows that sages endorse.]
    The laws of the Sabbath, festal offerings, and sacrilege—lo, they are like mountains hanging by a string,
    for they have little Scripture for many laws.
    Laws concerning civil litigations, the sacrificial cult, things to be kept cultically clean, sources of cultic uncleanness, and prohibited consanguineous marriages have much on which to depend.
    And both these and those [equally] are the essentials of the Torah.

The point is, there are laws of the Mishnah that rest on Scripture, and laws that while valid have no scriptural foundation. The Mishnah does not explore that fact or draw any conclusions from it.

The Talmud of the Land of Israel examines this allegation in the Mishnah. The following passage refers to the assertion that the laws on cultic cleanness presented in the Mishnah rest on deep and solid foundations in Scripture.

Talmud of the Land of Israel tractate *Hagigah* 1:7
The laws of the Sabbath, festal offerings, and sacrilege—lo, they are like mountains hanging by a string:

R. Jonah said R. Hama bar Uqba raised the question in reference to the view that there are many verses of Scripture on cleanness, "And lo, it is written only, 'Nevertheless a spring or a cistern holding water shall be clean; but whatever touches their carcass shall be unclean' (Lev. 11:36). [That is the only verse of Scripture that deals with the immersion pool, which effects the decontamination of objects or persons that have become unclean.] And from this one verse you derive many laws. [So how can the Mishnah passage say what it does about many verses for laws of cultic cleanness?]"

R. Zeira in the name of R. Yohanan: "If a law comes to hand and you do not know its nature, do not discard it for another one, *for lo, many laws were stated to Moses at Sinai, and all of them have been embedded in the Mishnah.*"

The truly striking assertion appears when in this very context the Mishnah is claimed to contain statements made by God to Moses. The passage proceeds to a further, and far more consequential, proposition. It asserts that part of the Torah was written down, and part was preserved in memory and transmitted orally. That view accounts for the passages of the Mishnah that do not rest on statements of Scripture.

In context, moreover, that distinction between writing down and memorizing laws must encompass the Mishnah, thus explaining its origin as part of the Torah. Here is a clear and unmistakable expression of the distinction between two forms in which a single Torah was revealed and handed on at Mount Sinai, part in writing, part orally.

Which takes priority, the teachings of the written Torah or those of the oral Torah? That question is raised in so many words in this same context of the explication of the Mishnah statement in tractate *Hagigah* 1:7 that some passages of the Mishnah have little foundation in the written part of the Torah:

Talmud of the Land of Israel tractate *Hagigah* 1:7
R. Zeirah in the name of R. Eleazar: "'Were I to write for him my laws by ten thousands, they would be regarded as a strange thing' (Hos. 8:12). Now

is the greater part of the Torah written down? [Surely not. The oral part is much greater.] But more abundant are the matters that are derived by exegesis from the written [Torah] than those derived by exegesis from the oral [Torah]."

And is that so?

But more cherished are those matters that rest upon the written [Torah] than those that rest upon the oral [Torah]. . . .

R. Haggai in the name of R. Samuel bar Nahman, "Some teachings were handed on orally, and some things were handed on in writing, and we do not know which of them is the more precious. But on the basis of that which is written, 'And the Lord said to Moses, "Write these words; in accordance with these words I have made a covenant with you and with Israel"' (Exod. 34:27), [we conclude] that the ones that are handed on orally are the more precious."

All that is lacking is an explicit reference to the Mishnah. But the context suffices to make the point. Once more, the fact that a tradition is handed on orally is a mark of priority. Now the Mishnah and other rabbinic writings are explicitly included within the oral tradition of Sinai, so the picture is complete. Once more, the truly remarkable, extreme claim is given in italics.

Talmud of the Land of Israel tractate *Hagigah* 1:7
R. Yohanan and R. Yudan b. R. Simeon—
    One [of the named authorities] said, "If you have kept what is preserved orally and also kept what is in writing, I shall make a covenant with you, and if not, I shall not make a covenant with you."
    The other said, "If you have kept what is preserved orally and you have kept what is preserved in writing, you shall receive a reward, and if not, you shall not receive a reward."
    [With reference to Deut. 9:10: "And on them was written according to all the words that the Lord spoke with you in the mount,"] said R. Joshua b. Levi, "He could have written, 'On them,' but wrote, 'And on them.' He could have written, 'All,' but wrote, 'According to all.' He could have written, 'Words,' but wrote 'The words.' [These then serve as three encompassing clauses, serving to include] Scripture, Mishnah, Talmud, laws, and lore. Even what an experienced student in the future is going to teach before his master already has been stated to Moses at Sinai."
    What is the scriptural basis for this view?
    "There is no remembrance of former things, nor will there be any remembrance of later things yet to happen among those who come after" (Qoh. 1:11).
    If someone says, "See, this is a new thing," his fellow will answer him, saying to him, "this has been around before us for a long time."

Here we have absolutely explicit evidence that people believed part of the Torah had been preserved not in writing but orally. Linking that part to the Mishnah remains a matter of implication. But it surely comes fairly close to the surface when we are told that the Mishnah contains Torah traditions revealed at Sinai. From that view it requires only a small step to the allegation that the Mishnah is part of the Torah, the oral part.

How Was the Mishnah Formulated?
The Theory of the Talmud of Babylonia

We find that claim in so many words in the Talmud of Babylonia, in which in general Judaism emerged fully spelled out. We saw how tractate 'Abot implicitly states that the Mishnah's laws originate at Sinai, meaning, with God. This claim is made explicit in the Talmud of Babylonia, which speaks of an oral tradition of Sinai ultimately written down in the Mishnah in particular.

This story makes explicit that a specific, verbal revelation at Sinai comes down through the generations in an unbroken chain of memorization—an oral tradition ending up in the Mishnah:

Talmud of Babylonia tractate 'Erubin 54b/5:1.I.43
What is the order of Mishnah teaching? Moses learned it from the mouth of the All-Powerful. Aaron came in, and Moses repeated his chapter to him, and Aaron went forth and sat at the left hand of Moses. His sons came in and Moses repeated their chapter to them, and his sons went forth. Eleazar sat at the right of Moses, and Ithamar at the left of Aaron.

Rabbi Judah says, "At all times Aaron was at the right hand of Moses."

Then the elders entered, and Moses repeated for them their Mishnah chapter. The elders went out. Then the whole people came in, and Moses repeated for them their Mishnah chapter. So it came about that Aaron repeated the lesson four times, his sons three times, the elders two times, and all the people once.

Then Moses went out, and Aaron repeated his chapter for them. Aaron went out. His sons repeated their chapter. His sons went out. The elders repeated their chapter. So it turned out that everybody repeated the same chapter four times.

Here is an explicit account of verbal revelation of the Mishnah, word for word. It tells how the Mishnah originated at Sinai when Moses received the Torah from God. In that model the disciples received the Torah from their masters, in that same chain of tradition. The Torah that is under discussion is orally formulated and then orally transmitted. It is not written down on tablets. It is recorded in the word-for-word dictation of God to Moses, Moses to Aaron, Aaron to his sons Eleazar and Ithamar, then to the whole people, to the elders, and so on down. And the orally formulated and orally transmitted teaching is called "the Mishnah." The root of the word is the Hebrew letters *sh-n-y,* meaning "repeat," hence, generically, *mishnah* with a small *m* would mean, "that which is repeated," meaning, from memory.

So in this story the Mishnah is defined as the outcome of a chain of tradition beginning at Sinai and transmitted in a process of discipleship, memorizing the words of the master and handing them on to a new generation of disciples. When God gave the Torah at Sinai, then, included was the oral tradition ultimately embodied in the Mishnah, and, by extension, in other teachings of the rabbinic sages who form links in the chain of tradition from Sinai.

It was at this point that the doctrine of the dual Torah reached its definitive statement, in the famous story with which we conclude this chapter. It involves the first-century B.C.E. authorities, Shammai and Hillel, but first surfaces in the Talmud of Babylonia. The story then articulates the view of matters held at the end of the emergence of Judaism. Some would claim, with justification, that the main point—the duality of the Torah of Sinai—was implicitly present all along.

Talmud of Babylonia tractate *Shabbat* 31a
There was the incident of a certain gentile who came before Shammai. He said to him, ""How many Torahs do you have?"

He said to him, "Two, one in writing, one memorized."

He said to him, "As to the one in writing, I believe you. As to the memorized one, I do not believe you. Convert me on condition that you will teach me only the Torah that is in writing."

He rebuked him and threw him out.

He came before Hillel. He said to him, "Convert me.

"My lord, how many Torahs were given?"

He said to him, "Two, one in writing, one memorized."

He said to him, "As to the one in writing, I believe you. As to the memorized one, I do not believe you."

He said to him, "My son, sit."

He wrote for him, aleph, beth.

He said to him, "What is this?" He said to him, "An aleph."

He said to him, "This is not an aleph but a beth."

He said to him, "What is this?"

He said to him, "Beth."

He said to him, "This is not a beth but a gimel."

He said to him, ""How do you know that this is an aleph and this a beth and this a gimel? But that is what our ancestors have handed over to us— the tradition that this is an aleph, this a beth, this a gimel. Just as you have accepted this teaching in good faith, so accept the other in good faith."

That claim of a revelation in two media is the point at which the Mishnah was fully absorbed into the Torah as a whole.

In the same context in the Talmud of Babylonia, namely, the story about Hillel and the oral Torah, the Mishnah was given its rightful place even in the prophetic heritage, as its laws were correlated with the virtues of the moral life:

> Talmud of Babylonia tractate *Shabbat* 31a
> Said R. Simeon b. Laqish, "What is the meaning of the verse of Scripture, 'And there shall be faith in your times, strength, salvation, wisdom, and knowledge' (Isa. 33:6)?
>   "'faith': this refers to the Mishnah division of Agriculture (Seeds).
>   "'in your times': this refers to the Mishnah division of Holy Seasons.
>   "'strength': this refers to the Mishnah division of Women.
>   "'salvation': this refers to the Mishnah division of Damages.
>   "'wisdom': this refers to the Mishnah division of Holy Things.
>   "'and knowledge': this refers to the Mishnah division of Purities.
>   "Nonetheless: '. . . the fear of the Lord is his treasure' (Isa. 33:6)."

Now the message of Isaiah provides a categorical structure to encompass the six divisions of the Mishnah's laws of Judah the Patriarch, and the Torah is made whole. No wonder that the sage, in his person, could stand for the unity of the Torah in two media.

The Sage as the Torah Incarnate

"Torah" bore yet another meaning: a source of salvation. That surfaces in the Talmud of the Land of Israel, but it is implicit in tractate *'Abot* when the sage says that God joins groups of disciples when they study the Torah. The act of "study of Torah" imparts supernatural power. Mastery of Torah transformed the man engaged in Torah learning into a supernatural figure, who could do things ordinary folk could not do.

> Talmud of the Land of Israel tractate *Ta'anit* 3:4.I
> There was a pestilence in Sepphoris, but it did not come into the neighborhood in which R. Haninah was living. And the Sepphoreans said, "How is

it possible that that elder lives among you, he and his entire neighborhood, in peace, while the town goes to ruin?"

[Haninah] went in and said before them, "There was only a single Zimri in his generation, but on his account, twenty-four thousand people died. And in our time, how many Zimris are there in our generation? And yet you are raising a clamor!"

One time they had to call a fast, but it did not rain. R. Joshua carried out a fast in the south, and it rained. The Sepphoreans said, "R. Joshua b. Levi brings down rain for the people in the south, but R. Haninah holds back rain for us in Sepphoris."

They found it necessary to declare a second time of fasting, and sent and summoned R. Joshua b. Levi. [Haninah] said to him, "Let my lord go forth with us to fast." The two of them went out to fast, but it did not rain.

He went in and preached to them as follows: "It was not R. Joshua b. Levi who brought down rain for the people of the south, nor was it R. Haninah who held back rain from the people of Sepphoris. But as to the southerners, their hearts are open, and when they listen to a teaching of Light [Torah] they submit [to accept it], while as to the Sepphoreans, their hearts are hard, and when they hear a teaching of Light, they do not submit [or accept it]."

When he went in, he looked up and saw that the [cloudless] air was pure. He said, "Is this how it still is? [Is there no change in the weather?]"

Forthwith, it rained. He took a vow for himself that he would never do the same thing again. He said, "How shall I say to the creditor [God] not to collect what is owing to him."

The tale about Joshua and Haninah is striking. The particular power of the sage was in knowing the law. The sage now embodies the Torah of Sinai. He exercises the supernatural power of the Torah. He serves like the Torah itself to reveal God's will.

With the sage now treated as the embodiment of the Torah, the Torah ceased to denote only a concrete and material thing—a scroll and its contents. 'Abot stands at the beginning of this process. What sages said formed a chain of tradition extending back to Sinai. Hence it was equivalent to the Torah. The upshot is that words of sages enjoyed the status of the Torah. The small step beyond was to claim that what sages said was Torah, as much as what Scripture said was Torah. Then what the sage said was in the status of the Torah, because the sage was understood as the Torah incarnate.

Chapter 5

God

Monotheism: There Is Only One God

*J*udaism emerged in ancient times as a self-validating system of ideas. The way of life, the worldview, the definition of the social group that embodies the way of life and the worldview—these hold together in the doctrine of God that animates the entire structure. Judaism knows God through the Torah. The Torah tells the story of God's self-revelation to humanity through Adam, unsuccessfully, and then through Israel, beginning with Abraham and Sarah. It is because God wants to be known and makes himself known that Israel claims to know God. The Torah contains that knowledge of God that God wishes to impart to humanity. For Judaism the encounter with God therefore takes place in the Torah, hence, in the study of the Torah. Israel's worldview and way of life therefore are set forth by the Torah that God set forth at Sinai: a closed and complete construction.

The most important thing that the Torah teaches about God is that God is one and unique. The creed of Judaism maintains: "Hear, Israel, the Lord our God, the Lord is one" (Deut. 6:4). The belief that God is one and unique is called "monotheism." The opposite, the belief that there are many gods, is called "polytheism."

What difference does it make whether there is one God alone or many? The difference is that a religion of numerous gods finds many solutions to one problem; a religion of only one God presents one solution to many problems. People try to explain why things happen as they do. They assume that the world is reasonable, so they look to supernatural power(s) for reasons.

Life, however, is seldom fair. Rules rarely work. To explain the reason why, polytheisms adduce multiple causes of chaos, a god per anomaly. Diverse gods do various things, so, it stands to reason, ordinarily outcomes conflict. Monotheism by nature explains many things in a single way. One God rules.

Life is meant to be fair, and just rules are supposed to describe what is ordinary, all in the name of that one and only God. So in monotheism a simple logic governs to limit ways of making sense of things.

But that presents a problem. If one true God has done everything, then, since he is the one and only God, all-powerful and all-knowing, all things are credited to, and blamed on, him. In that case he can be either good or bad, just or unjust—but not both.

Ethical Monotheism: The One and Only God Is Good

Judaism as it emerged in the ancient world systematically reveals the justice of the one and only God of all creation. God is not only God but also good. The rabbinic sages turned to the Torah, written and oral, to expose the justice of God. In their system the world order is based on God's justice and equity. They told the story of the struggle between God's plan for creation—to create a perfect world of justice—and human will.

The Four Principles of Judaic Ethical Monotheism

The theology of Judaism sets forth four basic principles. They are as follows:

1. *Creation, the Torah as the plan.* God formed creation in accord with a plan, which the Torah reveals. World order can be shown by the facts of nature and society set forth in that plan to conform to a pattern of reason based upon justice. Those who possess the Torah—Israel—know God, and those who do not—the gentiles—reject him in favor of idols. What happens to each of the two sectors of humanity, respectively, responds to their relationship with God. But why do the gentiles presently prevail? Israel in the present age is subordinate to the nations, because God has designated the gentiles as the medium for penalizing Israel's rebellion. God means through Israel's subordination and exile to provoke Israel to repent. Private life as much as the public order conforms to the principle that God rules justly in a creation of perfection and stability.

2. *The perfection of creation and justice.* The perfection of creation, realized in the rule of exact justice, is signified by the timelessness of the world of human affairs. A few enduring patterns impose order upon multiple signs of change. No present, past, or future marks time, but only the repetition of those patterns.

3. *God's will and humanity's will in conflict.* Israel's condition, public and personal, therefore marks flaws in creation. And what is the cause of those

flaws? What disrupts perfection is the sole power capable of standing on its own against God's power, and that is humanity's will. What humanity controls and God cannot coerce is humanity's capacity to form intention. He or she can therefore choose either arrogantly to defy or humbly to love God. Because humanity defies God, the sin that results from humanity's rebellion flaws creation and disrupts world order. The pattern of the rebellion of Adam in Eden governs. The act of arrogant rebellion caused the exile from Eden. That narrative accounts for the condition of humanity. God retains the power to encourage repentance through punishing humanity's arrogance. In mercy, moreover, God exercises the power to respond to repentance with forgiveness. Thus a change of humanity's attitude evokes a corresponding change in God's. So humanity has the power to initiate the process of reconciliation with God. That is done through repentance. By means of an act of humility humanity may restore the perfection of the order that through arrogance has been marred.

4. *Restoration of perfection.* God ultimately will restore the perfection that embodied his plan for creation. In the work of restoration death, which comes about by reason of sin, will die. The dead will be raised and judged for their deeds in this life. Most of them, now justified, will go on to eternal life in the world to come. The pattern of man restored to Eden is realized in Israel's return to the land of Israel. In that age to come, however, that sector of humanity that through the Torah knows God will encompass all of humanity. Idolators lose out on eternal life. But in the end of days all humanity will know the one, true God.

Each of the four parts—(1) the perfectly just character of world order, (2) indications of its perfection, (3) sources of its imperfection, and (4) media for the restoration of world order—and their results stand in logical order. Each belongs in its place. Set in any other sequence the four principles become incomprehensible.

The four principles tell a single continuous story. Further, each element in order forms part of an unfolding story. And the story is heading toward a climax and an end: judgment and the restoration of humanity to Eden, embodied by Israel in the land, as we saw in the law of the Torah set forth in chapter three.

Is the God of Judaism a God of Vengeance?

Does that stress on God's justice mean that God is the "angry and vengeful God of the Old Testament," as some suppose? That is not how the rabbinic sages of the oral part of the Torah present matters at all. In that one, whole Torah God is called "the Merciful One." He appears as infinitely loving. Justice without mercy destroys the world, mercy without justice corrupts it. God is made manifest to Israel in many ways, but is always one and the same: the God who is both just and merciful.

The Many Faces of God in the Torah

God shows not one but many faces in the Torah, oral and written. The context and circumstance determine the matter: God's purpose at a given moment of self-revelation. Certainly one of the most memorable characterizations presents God as a warrior when Israel crossed the Reed Sea pursued by the Egyptian army of Pharaoh, but the following passage shows that that presentation is only partial:

> *Mekilta Attributed to R. Ishmael Shirata* Chapter 1 = XXIX:2
> "The Lord is a man of war, the Lord is his name" (Exod. 15:3):
>   Why is this stated?
>   Since when he appeared at the sea, it was in the form of a mighty soldier making war, as it is said, "The Lord is a man of war,"
>   and when he appeared to them at Sinai, it was as an elder, full of mercy, as it is said, "And they saw the God of Israel" (Exod. 24:10),
>   and when they were redeemed, what does Scripture say? "And the like of the very heaven for clearness" (Exod. 24:10); "I beheld until thrones were placed and one that was ancient of days sat" (Dan. 7:9); "A fiery stream issued" (Dan. 7:10)—
>   [so God took on many forms.] It was, therefore, not to provide the nations of the world with an occasion to claim that there are two dominions [one ruled by a good God, the other by an evil God] in heaven [but that the same God acts in different ways and appears in different forms]
>   that Scripture says, "The Lord is a man of war, the Lord is his name."
>   [This then bears the message:] The one in Egypt is the one at the sea, the one in the past is the one in the age to come, the one in this age is the one in the world to come: "See now that I, even I, am he" (Deut. 32:39); "Who has wrought and done it? He who called the generations from the beginning. I the Lord who am the first and with the last I am the same" (Isa. 41:4).

The main point then is clear: however we know God, in whatever form or aspect, it is always one and the same God. That is the essence of monotheism. So faithful Israel knows God as intimate friend and companion and never wanders far from God's sight or God's love.

God as Premise, Presence, Person, and Personality

Among the infinite possibilities for the encounter with God, the rabbinic sages know God in four aspects: (1) as a philosophical principle or premise of reality, that is, the one who created the world and gave the Torah; (2) as a living presence, for example, supernatural being resident in the Temple and present where two or more persons seek him in study of the Torah; (3) as a sentient person, for example, the one to whom prayer is addressed; and (4) as a distinctive personality, the God we can know and make our model.

Let me now spell these out in some detail.

1. God as premise occurs in passages of the oral part of the Torah in which an author reaches a particular decision because that author believes God created the world and has revealed the Torah to Israel. That is the given of the Mishnah's conception of God. The purpose of the Mishnah is to show, in the here and now of the social and natural world, what it means that God is one.

2. God as presence stands for yet another consideration. It involves an author's referring to God as part of a situation in the here and now. When an author (e.g., of a passage in the Mishnah) speaks of an ox goring another ox, he or she does not appeal to God to reach a decision and does not suggest that God in particular has witnessed the event and plans to intervene. But the Torah (Numbers 5) also expects that God will intervene in a particular case. God is not only premise but very present in making a decision.

3. One may readily envisage God as premise and presence without invoking a notion of the particular traits or personality of God. But there is a setting in which God is held always to know and pay attention to specific cases, and that involves God as a "you," that is, as a presence. For example God hears prayer, hence is not only a presence but a person, a "you," responding to what is said.

4. In the Torah God emerges also as a vivid and highly distinctive personality. In references to God as a personality, God is given corporeal traits. Not only so, but in matters of heart and mind and spirit, individual traits of personality endow God with that particularity that identifies every individual.

A definitive statement of the proposition that in diverse forms God appears to humanity is in the following, which represents the state of opinion of the fully exposed religious system of Judaism, at the time of the Talmud of the Land of Israel:

Pesiqta de Rab Kahana XII:XXV
    Another interpretation of "I am the Lord your God [who brought you out of the land of Egypt]" (Exod. 20:2):

Said R. Hinena bar Papa, "The Holy One, blessed be he, had made his appearance to them with a stern face, with a neutral face, with a friendly face, with a happy face.

"With a stern face: in Scripture. When a man teaches his son Torah, he has to teach him in a spirit of awe.

"With a neutral face: in the Mishnah.

"With a friendly face: in the Talmud.

"With a happy face: in lore.

"Said to them the Holy One, blessed be he, 'Even though you may see all of these diverse faces of mine, nonetheless: "I am the Lord your God who brought you out of the land of Egypt" (Exod. 20:2).'"

So far we deal with attitudes. As to the representation of God in concrete ways, through artistic media, the following is explicit:

Pesiqta de Rab Kahana XII:XXV

Said R. Levi, "The Holy One, blessed be he, had appeared to them like an icon that has faces in all directions, so that if a thousand people look at it, it appears to look at them as well.

"So too when the Holy One, blessed be he, when he was speaking, each Israelite would say, 'With me in particular the Word speaks.'

"What is written here is not, 'I am the Lord, your [plural] God,' but rather, 'I am the Lord your [singular] God who brought you out of the land of Egypt' (Exod. 20:2)."

That God may show diverse faces to various people is now established. The reason for God's variety is made explicit. People differ, and God, in the image of whom all mortals are made, must therefore sustain diverse images—all of them formed in the model of human beings:

Pesiqta de Rab Kahana XII:XXV

Said R. Yose bar Hanina, "And it was in accord with the capacity of each one of them to listen and understand what the Word spoke with him.

"And do not be surprised at this matter, for when the manna came down to Israel, all would find its taste appropriate to their circumstance, infants in accord with their capacity, young people in accord with their capacity, old people in accord with their capacity.

"Infants in accord with their capacity: just as an infant sucks from the teat of his mother, so was its flavor, as it is said, 'Its taste was like the taste of rich cream' (Num. 11:8).

"Young people in accord with their capacity: as it is said, 'My bread also which I gave you, bread and oil and honey' (Ezek. 16:19).

"Old people in accord with their capacity: as it is said, 'The taste of it was like wafers made with honey' (Exod. 16:31).

"Now if in the case of manna, each one would find its taste appropriate to his capacity, so in the matter of the Word, each one understood in accord with capacity.

"Said David, 'The voice of the Lord is in [accord with one's] strength' (Ps. 29:4).

"What is written is not, 'in accord with his strength in particular,' but rather, in accord with one's strength, meaning, in accord with the capacity of each one.

"Said to them the Holy One, blessed be he, 'It is not in accord with the fact that you hear a great many voices, but you should know that it is I who [speaks to all of you individually]: 'I am the Lord your God who brought you out of the land of Egypt' (Exod. 20:2).''

The individuality and particularity of God rest upon the diversity of humanity. It must follow, the model of humanity—"in our image"—dictates how we are to envisage the face of God. And that is the starting point of our inquiry. The Torah defines what we know about God—but the Torah also tells us that we find God in the face of the other: "in our image, after our likeness," means everyone is in God's image, so if we want to know God, we had best look closely into the face of all humanity, one by one.

The Mishnah: God as Premise

For the philosophers who wrote the Mishnah the most important thing they wished to demonstrate about God is that God is one. And this they proposed to prove by showing, in a vast array of everyday circumstances, the fundamental order and unity of all things, and the unity of all things in a ladder, a hierarchy, ascending upward to God. So all things through their unity and order lead to one thing, and all being derives from the one God.

In the Mishnah many things are placed into sequence and order, and the order of all things is shown to have a purpose, so that the order is purposive. The Mishnah time and again demonstrates these two contrary propositions: many things join together by their nature into one thing, and one thing yields many things.

So things are not only orderly, but are so ordered that many things fall into one classification, and one thing may hold together many things of a single classification. At the apex of that ordering of all things is God, creator of the world.

The Talmud of the Land of Israel: God as Person

When we come to the Talmud of the Land of Israel we meet God in familiar but also fresh representation. The context in which this Talmud took shape—the legitimation, then state-sponsorship, of Christianity—requires mention. The representation of God in man, God incarnate, in Jesus Christ, as the Christians saw him, found a powerful reply in sages' re-presentation of God as person, individual and active. God is no longer only, or mainly, the premise of all being, as in the Mishnah, nor is God only or mainly the one who makes the rules and enforces them. God is now presented in the additional form of the one who makes decisions in the here and now of everyday life, responding to the individual and his or her actions.

As portrayed in the Talmud of the Land of Israel God forms a living presence in the world. God in his very Presence intervened in Israel's history, for example, at the Sea of Reeds:

> Talmud of the Land of Israel tractate *Sanhedrin* 2:1.III
> When the All-Merciful came forth to redeem Israel from Egypt, he did not send a messenger or an angel, but the Holy One, blessed be he, himself came forth, as it is said, "For I will pass through the land of Egypt that night" (Exod. 12:12)—and not only so, but it was he and his entire retinue.

The story that God's Presence went into exile with Israel recurs. God was encountered as a very real presence, actively listening to prayers, as in the following:

> Talmud of the Land of Israel tractate *Berakot* 9:1.VII
> See how high the Holy One, blessed be he, is above his world. Yet a person can enter a synagogue, stand behind a pillar, and pray in an undertone, and the Holy One, blessed be he, hears his prayers, as it says, "Hannah was speaking in her heart; only her lips moved, and her voice was not heard" (1 Sam. 1:13). Yet the Holy One, blessed be he, heard her prayer.

God as "you" who hears prayer presents a fine example of how God is represented as a person.

Genesis Rabbah and the Talmud of Babylonia: God's Personality

For sages God and humanity are indistinguishable in their physical traits. They are distinguished in other, important ways, as *Genesis Rabbah* shows.

Scripture has God create Adam and Eve "in our image, after our likeness" (Gen. 1:26). This was understood as a physical resemblance. God and the human being are mirror images of one another. In *Genesis Rabbah* we find the simple claim that the angels could not discern any physical difference whatever between Adam and God:

Genesis Rabbah VIII:X
Said R. Hoshaiah, "When the Holy One, blessed be he, came to create the first man, the ministering angels mistook him [for God, since man was in God's image,] and wanted to say before the latter, 'Holy, [holy, holy is the Lord of hosts].'

"To what may the matter be compared? To the case of a king and a governor who were set in a chariot, and the provincials wanted to greet the king, 'Sovereign!' But they did not know which one of them was which. What did the king do? He turned the governor out and put him away from the chariot, so that people would know who was king.

"So too when the Holy One, blessed be he, created the first man, the angels mistook him [for God]. What did the Holy One, blessed be he, do? He put him to sleep, so everyone knew that he was a mere man.

"That is in line with the following verse of Scripture: 'Cease you from man, in whose nostrils is a breath, for how little is he to be accounted' (Isa. 2:22)."

But that does not tell the whole story. It was in the Talmud of Babylonia in particular that God would be represented as a fully exposed personality, like a human. There we see the full characterization of God as a personality that humanity can know and love.

God is portrayed as engaged in conversation with human beings because God and humanity can understand one another within the same rules of discourse. When we speak of the personality of God, traits of a corporeal, emotional, and social character define matters. The following story shows us the movement from the abstract and theological to the concrete and narrative way of talking about God:

Talmud of Babylonia tractate *Sanhedrin* 111a-b
"And Moses made haste and bowed his head toward the earth and worshiped" (Exod. 34:8):
  What did Moses see?
  Hanina b. Gamula said, "He saw [God's attribute of] being long-suffering (Exod. 34:7)."
  Rabbis say, "He saw [the attribute of] truth (Exod. 34:7)."
  It has been taught on Tannaite authority in accord with him who has said, "He saw God's attribute of being long-suffering."

For it has been taught on Tannaite authority:

When Moses went up on high, he found the Holy One, blessed be he, sitting and writing, "Long-suffering."

He said before him, "Lord of the world, 'Long-suffering for the righteous?'"

He said to him, "Also for the wicked."

[Moses] said to him, "Let the wicked perish."

He said to him, "Now you will see what you want."

When the Israelites sinned, he said to him, "Did I not say to you, 'Long-suffering for the righteous'?"

[Moses] said to him, "Lord of the world, did I not say to you, 'Also for the wicked'?"

That is in line with what is written, "And now I beseech you, let the power of my Lord be great, according as you have spoken, saying" (Num. 14:17).

Once we are told that God is long-suffering, then in narrative form that trait is given definition. God thus emerges as a personality, specifically because Moses engages in argument with God. He reproaches God, questions God's actions and judgments, holds God to a standard of consistency—and receives appropriate responses. God in heaven does not argue with humanity on earth. God in heaven issues decrees, forms the premise of the earthly rules, constitutes a presence, may even take the form of a "you" for hearing and answering prayers.

When God argues, discusses, defends, and explains actions, then God gains the traits of a personality like a human being. It is in particular through narrative that that transformation of God from person to personality takes place.

Scripture knows that God has a face, upon which human beings are not permitted to gaze. But was that face understood in a physical way, and did God enjoy other physical characteristics? An affirmative answer emerges in the following, which settles the question:

Talmud of Babylonia tractate *Berakot* 7a

"And he said, 'You cannot see my face'" (Exod. 33:20).

It was taught on Tannaite authority in the name of R. Joshua b. Qorha, "This is what the Holy One, blessed be he, said to Moses:

"'When I wanted [you to see my face], you did not want to, now that you want to see my face, I do not want you to.'"

This differs from what R. Samuel bar Nahmani said R. Jonathan said.

For R. Samuel bar Nahmani said R. Jonathan said, "As a reward for three things he received the merit of three things.

"As a reward for: 'And Moses hid his face' (Exod. 3:6), he had the merit of having a glistening face.

"As a reward for: 'Because he was afraid to' (Exod. 3:6), he had the merit that 'They were afraid to come near him' (Exod. 34:30).

"As a reward for: 'To look upon God' (Exod. 3:6), he had the merit: 'The similitude of the Lord does he behold' (Num. 12:8)."

"And I shall remove my hand and you shall see my back" (Exod. 33:23).

Said R. Hana bar Bizna that R. Simeon the Pious said, "This teaches that the Holy One, blessed be he, showed Moses [how to tie] the knot of the phylacteries."

That God is able to tie the knot indicates that God has fingers and other physical gifts. Furthermore, God is portrayed as wearing phylacteries. It follows that God has an arm and a forehead. There is no element of a figurative reading of the indicated traits. In the Talmud of Babylonia's stories God not only looks like a human being but also does the acts that human beings do. For example, God spends the day much as does a mortal ruler of Israel, at least as sages imagine such a figure. That is, he studies the Torah, makes practical decisions, and sustains the world (i.e., administers public funds for public needs)—just as sages do. What gives us a deeply human God is that for the final part of the day, God plays with his pet, Leviathan, who was like Hydra, the great sea serpent with multiple heads. Some alter that view and hold that God spends the rest of the day teaching youngsters. In passages such as these we therefore see the concrete expression of the personality of God:

Talmud of Babylonia tractate *'Abodah Zarah* 3b
Said R. Judah that Rab said, "The day is twelve hours long. During the first three, the Holy One, blessed be he, is engaged in the study of the Torah.

"During the next three God sits in judgment on the world, and when he sees the world sufficiently guilty to deserve destruction, he moves from the seat of justice to the seat of mercy.

"During the third he feeds the whole world, from the horned buffalo to vermin.

"During the fourth he plays with the leviathan, as it is said, 'There is Leviathan, whom you have made to play with' (Ps. 104:26)."

[Another authority denies this final point and says,] What then does God do in the fourth quarter of the day?

"He sits and teaches schoolchildren, as it is said, 'Whom shall one teach knowledge, and whom shall one make to understand the message? Those who are weaned from milk' (Isa. 28:9)."

And what does God do by night?

If you like, I shall propose that he does what he does in daytime.

Or if you prefer: he rides a translucent cherub and floats in eighteen thousand worlds. . . .

> Or if you prefer: he sits and listens to the song of the heavenly creatures, as it is said, "By the day the Lord will command his loving kindness and in the night his song shall be with me" (Ps. 42:9).

The personality of God encompassed not only physical but also emotional traits. In the final stage of the Judaism of the dual Torah God emerged as a fully exposed personality. The character of divinity, therefore, encompassed God's virtue, the specific traits of character and personality that God exhibited above and here below. God wanted people to be humble and therefore showed humility.

Talmud of Babylonia tractate *Shabbat* 89a
Said R. Joshua b. Levi, "When Moses came down from before the Holy One, blessed be he, Satan came and asked [God], 'Lord of the world, Where is the Torah? [What have you done with it? Do you really intend to give it to mortals?]'

"He said to him, 'I have given it to the earth. . . .' [Satan was ultimately told by God to look for the Torah by finding the son of Amram.]

"He went to Moses and asked him, 'Where is the Torah that the Holy One, blessed be he, gave you?'

"He said to him, 'Who am I that the Holy One, blessed be he, should give me the Torah?'

"Said the Holy One, blessed be he, to Moses, 'Moses, you are a liar!'

"He said to him, 'Lord of the world, you have a treasure in store that you have enjoyed every day. Shall I keep it to myself?'

"He said to him, 'Moses, since you have acted with humility, it will bear your name: "Remember the Torah of Moses, my servant" (Mal. 3:22).'"

God here is represented as favoring humility and rewarding the humble with honor. What is important is that God does not here cite Scripture or merely paraphrase it; the conversation is an exchange between two vivid personalities. True enough, Moses, not God, is the hero. But the personality of God emerges in vivid ways.

The Talmud of Babylonia: The Humanity of God

In stories found in the Talmud of Babylonia God negotiates, persuades, teaches, argues, exchanges reasons. The personality of God therefore comes to expression in a variety of portraits of how God will engage in arguments with men and angels, and so enters into the existence of ordinary people. These disputes, negotiations, and transactions yield a portrait of God who is reasonable and capable of give and take, as in the following:

Talmud of Babylonia tractate *'Arakin* 15a-b
Rabbah bar Mari said, "What is the meaning of this verse: 'But they were rebellious at the sea, even at the Red Sea; nonetheless he saved them for his name's sake' (Ps. 106:7)?

"This teaches that the Israelites were rebellious at that time, saying, 'Just as we will go up on this side, so the Egyptians will go up on the other side.' Said the Holy One, blessed be he, to the angelic prince who reigns over the sea, 'Cast them [the Israelites] out on dry land.'

"He said before him, 'Lord of the world, is there any case of a slave [namely, myself] to whom his master [you] gives a gift [the Israelites], and then the master goes and takes [the gift] away again? [You gave me the Israelites, now you want to take them away and place them on dry land.]'

He said to him, 'I'll give you one-and-a-half times their number.'

"He said before him, 'Lord of the world, is there a possibility that a slave can claim anything against his master? [How do I know that you will really do it?]'

"He said to him, 'The Kishon brook will be my pledge [that I shall carry out my word].

"Forthwith [the angelic prince of the sea] spit them out onto dry land, for it is written, 'And the Israelites saw the Egyptians dead on the seashore' (Exod. 14:30)."

God is willing to give a pledge to guarantee his word. He furthermore sees the right claim of the counterpart actor in the story. Hence we see how God obeys precisely the same social laws of exchange and reason that govern other incarnate beings.

Still more interesting is the picture of God's argument with Abraham. God is represented as accepting accountability, by the standards of humanity, for what God does.

Talmud of Babylonia tractate *Menahot* 53b
Said R. Isaac, "When the Temple was destroyed, the Holy One, blessed be he, found Abraham standing in the Temple. He said to him, 'What is my beloved doing in my house?'

"He said to him, 'I have come because of what is going on with my children.'

"He said to him, 'Your children sinned and have been sent into exile.'

"He said to him, 'But wasn't it by mistake that they sinned?'

"He said to him, 'She has wrought lewdness' (Jer. 11:15).

"He said to him, 'But wasn't it just a minority of them that did it?'

"He said to him, 'It was a majority' (Jer. 11:15).

"He said to him, 'You should at least have taken account of the covenant of circumcision [which should have secured forgiveness despite their sin]!'

"He said to him, 'The holy flesh is passed from you' (Jer. 11:15).

"And if you had waited for them, they might have repented!"

"He said to him, 'When you do evil, then you are happy' (Jer. 11:15).

"He said to him, 'He put his hands on his head, crying out and weeping, saying to them, "God forbid! Perhaps they have no remedy at all!"'

"A heavenly voice came forth and said, 'The Lord called you "a leafy olive tree, fair with excellent fruit" (Jer. 11:16).

"'Just as in the case of an olive tree, its future comes only at the end [that is, it is only after a long while that it produces its best fruit], so in the case of Israel, their future comes at the end of their time.'"

God relates to Abraham as to an equal. That is shown by God's implicit agreement that he is answerable to Abraham for what has taken place with the destruction of the Temple. God does not impose silence on Abraham, saying that that is a decree not to be contested but only accepted. God as a social being accepts that he must provide sound reasons for his actions, as must any other reasonable person in a world governed by rules applicable to everyone. God above all binds himself to the rule of justice.

Abraham is a fine choice for the protagonist, since he engaged in the argument concerning Sodom. His complaint is expressed: God is now called to explain himself. At each point then Abraham offers arguments in behalf of sinning Israel, and God responds, item by item. The climax has God promising Israel a future worth having. God emerges as both just and merciful, reasonable but sympathetic. The transaction attests to God's conformity to rules of reasoned transactions in a coherent society.

The Talmud of Babylonia: Divinity of God: God as Wholly Other

Though in the image of the sage, God towers over other sages, disposing of their lives and determining their destinies. Portraying God as sage allowed the storytellers to state in vivid way convictions on the disparity between the rabbinic sages' great intellectual achievements and their this-worldly standing and fate. But God remains within the model of other sages, takes up the rulings, follows the arguments, participates in the sessions that distinguish sages and mark them off from all other people:

Talmud of Babylonia tractate *Menahot* 29b

Said R. Judah said Rab, "When Moses went up to the height, he found the Holy One, blessed be he, sitting and tying crowns to the letters [of the Torah]."

"He said to him, 'Lord of the universe, why is this necessary?'

"He said to him, 'There is a certain man who is going to come into being at the end of some generations, by the name of Aqiba b. Joseph. He is going to find expositions to attach mounds and mounds of laws to each point [of a crown].'

"He said to him, 'Lord of the universe, show him to me.'

"He said to him, 'Turn around.'

"[Moses] went and took his seat at the end of eight rows, but he could not understand what the people were saying. He felt weak. When discourse came to a certain matter, one of [Aqiba's] disciples said to him, 'My lord, how do you know this?'

"He said to him, 'It is a law revealed by God to Moses at Mount Sinai.'

"Moses' spirits were restored.

"He turned back and returned to the Holy One, blessed be he. He said to him, 'Lord of the universe, now if you have such a man available, how can you give the Torah through me?'

"He said to him, 'Be silent. That is how I have decided matters.'

"He said to him, 'Lord of the universe, you have now shown me his mastery of the Torah. Now show me his reward.'

"He said to him, 'Turn around.'

"He turned around and saw people weighing out his flesh in the butcher shop.

"He said to him, 'Lord of the universe, such is his mastery of Torah, and such is his reward?'

"He said to him, 'Be silent. That is how I have decided matters.'"

When we notice that humanity is like God, but not to be confused with God, this story comes to mind. This is the single most important narrative about the personality of God. Here is the point at which humanity cannot imitate God but must relate to God in an attitude of profound humility and obedience.

Humanity may be in God's image, but God is always God. God makes all the decisions and guides the unfolding of the story. Moses then appears as the straight man. He asks the questions that permit God to make the stunning replies. Moses does not understand. God then tells him to shut up and accept his decree. God does what he likes, with whom he likes.

But that is not the last word. God above all is merciful. So when God prays, it is to elicit from himself forgiveness for Israel:

Talmud of Babylonia tractate *Berakot* 7a
Said R. Yohanan in the name of R. Yose, "How do we know that the Holy One, blessed be he, says prayers?

"Since it is said, 'Even them will I bring to my holy mountain and make them joyful in my house of prayer' (Isa. 56:7).

"'Their house of prayer' is not stated, but rather, 'my house of prayer.'

"On the basis of that usage we see that the Holy One, blessed be he, says prayers."

What prayers does he say?

Said R. Zutra bar Tobiah that Rab said, "'May it be my will that my mercy overcome my anger, and that my mercy prevail over my attributes, so that I may treat my children in accord with the trait of mercy and in their regard go beyond the strict measure of the law.'"

The sages' vision of God encompassed God's yearning for Israel, God's eagerness to forgive Israel its sins, and God's power to overcome anger in favor of mercy and love:

Talmud of Babylonia tractate *Berakot* 7a

Said R. Ishmael b. Elisha [who is supposed to have been a priest in Second Temple times], "One time I went in to offer up incense on the innermost altar, and I saw the crown of the Lord, enthroned on the highest throne, and he said to me, 'Ishmael, my son, bless me.'

"I said to him, 'May it be your will that your mercy overcome your anger, and that your mercy prevail over your attributes, so that you treat your children in accord with the trait of mercy and in their regard go beyond the strict measure of the law.'

"And he nodded his head to me."

And from that story we learn that the blessing of a common person should not be negligible in your view.

Here is another way in which God and humanity compare. Just as humanity feels joy, so does God. Just as humanity celebrates God, so does God celebrate Israel. Just as Israel declares God to be unique, so God declares Israel to be unique.

What, exactly, are we expected to be and to do because we wish to be "like God"? The answer is given at Leviticus 19:2, "You shall be holy, for I the Lord your God am holy." The rabbinic sages spell out the meaning of holiness: to be merciful and compassionate:

Talmud of Babylonia tractate *Shabbat* 133b

"This is my God and I will adorn him" (Exod. 15:2)—adorn yourself before him by truly elegant fulfillment of the religious duties, for example: a beautiful tabernacle, a beautiful palm branch, a beautiful ram's horn, beautiful show fringes, a beautiful scroll of the Torah, written in fine ink, with a fine reed, by a skilled penman, wrapped with beautiful silks.

Abba Saul says, "'I will adorn him'—be like him: just as he is gracious and compassionate, so you be gracious and compassionate."

Abba Saul's statement says in a few words the entire knowledge of God that in the end the Torah provides. For all of the truly pious conduct in doing religious duties, the real imitation of God comes about in our capacity to love one another.

God's mercy and love are expressed by the gift of the Torah. Wherein lies the gift? Humanity is not only in God's image—something they cannot have known on their own—but God has told them so. Israel are not only God's children—it would have been arrogance to have supposed so on their own—but God has stated this in so many words. Israel possesses the greatest gift of all. They know it, for God has said so:

Tractate 'Abot 3:13–14
R. Aqiba says, "Precious is the human being, who was created in the image [of God].

"It was an act of still greater love that it was made known to him that he was created in the image [of God], as it is said, 'For in the image of God he made man' (Gen. 9:6).

"Precious are Israelites, who are called children to the Omnipresent.

"It was an act of still greater love that they were called children to the Omnipresent, as it is said, 'You are the children of the Lord your God' (Deut. 14:1).

"Precious are Israelites, to whom was given the precious thing [the Torah].

"It was an act of still greater love that it was made known to them that to them was given that precious thing with which the world was made, as it is said, 'For I give you a good doctrine. Do not forsake my Torah' (Prov. 4:2)."

These statements of Aqiba speak not of truth alone, but of truth enhanced because of the Torah's validation. That is what it means to say that Israel knows God through the Torah. God is known because God makes himself known—by giving the Torah to Israel. The system is complete and self-sustaining.

PART III

Why Did, and Does, Judaism Thrive?

Chapter 6

Why Judaism Succeeded in Centuries of Competition with Christianity and Islam

The Success of Judaism

*B*y "success" I mean the capacity of a religious system to persuade those to whom it addresses its message that what it is has to say is self-evidently so. Why do I think Judaism succeeded in the competition with Christianity and Islam for the adherence of the Jewish people?

From the seventh century C.E. to the present day Judaism has competed with Christianity and Islam. The three religions shared much. All three spoke of one unique God (monotheism) made manifest to humanity. They concurred on many matters of theology and ethics. Both new monotheisms carried forward the narrative begun by Judaism in the Torah. Christianity acknowledged Moses and the Prophets and accepted the Torah as the Old Testament, and Islam recognized both Jews and Christians as people of the Book (the Bible), possessing in part the revelation that was completed by the prophet Muhammad. No wonder that Judaism met competition among religions claiming to perfect its revelation of God.

Some Jews adopted Christianity. Islam won Jewish converts as well. But in the main, among the Jews, Judaism triumphed. It retained the loyalty of the Jewish people. Over time, the Jews, who had been diverse in Temple times, became a people of one religion. Not only so, but Judaism attracted converts from various ethnic groups. So Judaism never would accept the standing of an ethnic religion, that is, a religion of one people only. It could hold its own with Christianity and Islam.

Given the worldly power of Christianity and Islam, we must regard the persistence of Judaism as a mark of its success. A religion may be said to succeed when it defines the worldview and way of life of the very group to whom it wishes to speak. By that criterion Judaism succeeded. That was because its ideas matched the everyday reality of its faithful—and made the believers accept and affirm their situation.

Judaism won the loyalty of the Jewish people, who did not go over to Christianity or to Islam during the long centuries of their hegemony. That is because Judaism successfully explained the Jews' condition and status. Specifically, it persuaded those it called "Israel," the people of the Torah, that forming a subordinated minority among the nations, accepting inferior status in the social order, served God's purpose. Israel's day would come when Israel fully realized that purpose. Everything fit together.

How do we know the Judaic system persuaded those to whom it spoke? The reason is simple. The success of Christianity in converting the Roman Empire did not obliterate Judaism. So too, when Islam conquered much of the Christian world, Judaism held its own.

In chapter 1 we reviewed the competition between Judaism and Christianity in the fourth century, covering the issues to which the Talmud of the Land of Israel responded. What about Islam?

Islam, born in the mid-seventh century, found in Judaism a tenacious adversary. After the death of Muhammad the Muslim armies swept over the Middle East and North Africa, subduing the great empire of Iran to the east, much of Byzantine Rome to the west, cutting across Egypt, Cyrenaica, what we know as Tunisia and North Africa, and reaching into Spain, with forays into France. Ancient Christian bishoprics fell. Vast Christian populations accepted the new monotheism, though they were not compelled to do so. But we have little evidence of similar mass conversions in the Jewish community, and that strongly suggests that Judaism stood firm. The reason is clear. Power based on arms proved nothing. Judaism's power lay in its weakness. Having dealt with the political triumph of Christianity, Judaism found itself entirely capable of coping with the military and therefore political victory of Islam as well.

Indeed, the stability of the Jewish communities in the newly conquered Islamic countries is noteworthy. It contrasts with the decline of Christianity in those same, long-Christian territories, for example, Syria, Palestine, Egypt, Cyrenaica, and the western provinces of North Africa, not to mention Spain. So we observe a simple fact. Judaism satisfactorily explained for Israel the events of the day. But Christianity, triumphant through the sword of Constantine, only with difficulty withstood the yet-sharper sword of Muhammad. On that account the great Christian establishments of the Middle East and North Africa fell away. Both Judaism and Christianity enjoyed precisely the same political status. Therefore the evident success of the one to hold its believers and the failure of the other to do so attests to what the fourth-century rabbinic sages had accomplished.

A word on the situation of Judaism and Christianity within Islamic countries is in order. In them only free male Muslims enjoyed the rank of a full member of society. Jews and Christians could accept Islam or submit, paying a tribute and accepting Muslim supremacy but continuing to practice their received religions. Bernard Lewis, the great scholar of Islam, characterizes the Islamic policy toward the conquered people of the Book, Christians and Jews, in these terms:

> This pattern was not one of equality but rather of dominance by one group and, usually, a hierarchic sequence of the others. Though this order did not concede equality, it permitted peaceful coexistence. While one group might dominate, it did not as a rule insist on suppressing or absorbing the others. . . . Communities professing recognized religions were allowed the tolerance of the Islamic state. They were allowed to practice their religions . . . . and to enjoy a measure of communal autonomy. . . . The Jews fell into the category of dhimmis; communities accorded a certain status, provided that they unequivocally recognized the primacy of Islam and the supremacy of the Muslims. This recognition was expressed in the payment of the poll tax and obedience to a series of restrictions defined in detail by the holy law.[1]

The Jews, like the Christians, were a subject group and had to accommodate themselves to that condition. But they had learned to make their peace with the remarkable success of Christianity in fourth-century Rome. So from the fourth century in Christendom, and from the seventh in Islam, Judaism remained stable and vital. Both Islam and Christendom presented a single challenge: the situation of subordination along with toleration.

Explaining the Condition of the Jews among the Nations

What traits of Judaism made its success possible? The power of Judaism lay in its capacity to do two things.

First, Judaism presented doctrines to explain the condition of subordination and toleration. Therefore the facts of everyday life served to reinforce the claims of the system. Judaism explained for Israel its subordinated but tolerated condition, indeed made that condition into God's will, and the acceptance of that condition in the heart as much as in the mind into the definition of virtue.

Second, that same Judaism so shaped the inner life of Israel as to define virtue in the very terms imposed by politics. Virtue meant to conciliate, to compromise, to make the best. This was expressed in many teachings concerning right attitudes. Loving the neighbor, forgiving the other, helping the weak—these were greatly prized. "Make your wishes into God's wishes, so God will make his wishes into your wishes"—so stated tractate *'Abot* 2:4. Israel recreated in its doctrine of virtue that exact condition of humility and accommodation that the people's political circumstance imposed from without. In simple language Judaism made a virtue of necessity.

So Judaism was able to meet the challenges of Christendom and Islam because of its power to match the inner life and outer circumstance. It joined together emotions and politics. Judaism created the condition of acceptance of a subordinated but tolerated position. That made possible the group's waiting for the Messiah in the end of days.

Because of its emphasis on Israel's forming God's community in humanity, Judaism had persuasively to explain the condition of the Jews. They formed a minority; as we just saw, they were ordinarily tolerated by the majority culture. Christianity blamed the Jews for the death of Christ, and Islam treated the Jews with contempt. They nowhere commanded their own destiny in a secular sense. That raised a challenge. If God gave the Torah and Israel lived by it, how come Christianity enjoyed its triumph in the fourth century at the time of Constantine, and commanded the loyalty of most of Europe? Islam, later on, in the seventh century C.E., the first century of Islam, conquered the Middle East to the gates of Constantinople, Egypt and North Africa, and most of Spain—fully half of the formerly Christian world. What purpose could God have had in such great events? Judaism had to explain the advent of the two competing religions. It had to figure out God's purpose in the success of Christianity and Islam.

Judaism found a powerful explanation for the condition of the Jews as a minority. It made Israel's very weakness into a source of strength for the faith. It did so by reworking the narrative of exile and return. It updated the story. It offered the condition of Israel as proof of the truth of that tale. The rabbinic system set forth in the Pentateuch, Mishnah, Talmud, and related documents deemed part of the Torah answered the pressing question. Its message of sanctification through a holy way of life of humility now, leading to salvation at the end of days, registered. That message held that God's people were in exile for their sins. When they repented, God would respond. People could take narrative personally because it corresponded to the world they experienced every day.

What—within the system of Judaism—of Christianity and Islam? Judaism maintained that God wanted the holy people to hold a subordinated but tolerated position within the world framed by the sibling rivals. Judaism found for Christianity and Islam a part in the scriptural story.

Abraham had two sons, Isaac and Ishmael. Isaac carried the blessing. But Ishmael was Abraham's descendant too. And in the narrative of Islam, Ishmael was the continuator of Islam.

Isaac had two sons, Jacob and Esau. Jacob carried the blessing, producing the children of Jacob, the children of Israel. But Esau was Jacob's descendant too. And Esau stood for Rome, and, in context, that meant Christian Rome.

Thus the Torah in the book of Genesis found a place for Islam and Christianity. Ishmael, the rival of Isaac, Esau, the rival of Jacob, were part of the story told by Israel in Judaism.

Exile and Return

What was the story that accounted for Israel's situation of subordination to Christianity and to Islam? In chapter 1 we met the basic pattern that emerging Judaism put forth, the pattern of exile and return. Now Israel was far from Eden, exiled from the land. Viewing Israel in exile accounted for the contrast between Israel's unimportance and its promised future greatness: "today if only you will . . . ," as the Messiah stories insisted. The road back was fully mapped out. People had now to remember who they were, where they were going, and what they had to do—or not to do—in order to get from here to there.

In telling its story, Judaism indeed made Israel's condition into God's will. Acceptance of that subordination to the nations as punishment for sin was turned into the definition of virtue. So the Prayer Book of Judaism would say, "Because of our sins we have been exiled from our land." The message of Judaism thus addressed precisely the situation envisaged by the original system. That is, the people are special, their life is contingent, their relationship to the land is subject to conditions, their collective life is lived at a level of heightened reality. The world beyond works out its affairs to accommodate God's will for Israel. But Israel was in control, though in a paradoxical way. For what Israel must do—as we saw in connection with the Messiah—is accept, submit, accommodate. Israel had to receive with humility the will and word of God in the Torah.

Explaining World History from Israel's Perspective

But there is more. Judaism explained more than Israel's fate. It accounted for the very course of world history in such a way that Judaism stood at the center of things. In Judaism's view the world beyond Israel—Christendom and Islam—works out its affairs to accommodate God's will for Israel. What followed from that fact?

The power to govern the fate of the nation rested with the nation. But that was true only so far as the nation accorded that power to God alone. God answered all questions through the Torah. Were people perplexed on who is Israel? The Torah answered the question: God's people, living out, here and now, the holy life prescribed by God. Did people wonder how long that people had to endure the government of gentiles? The Torah addressed that issue: so long as God willed.

The very God who had created the heavens and the earth dictated the fate of Israel—but also cared what each Jew ate for breakfast. God responded to the conduct of every Israelite and of all Israel. So the Torah laid emphasis upon the everyday life. That was where holiness was to be attained. And when it was, Israel would be saved. The subordinated status of Israel therefore served to attest to the true standing of Israel. It was small and inconsequential now. But it also was holy even now and destined for great reward at the end of time.

How Long and Why?

How long did the success of Judaism last? It endured so long as Christianity defined for the West, and Islam for the Near and Middle East, the paramount issues of culture and the social order. And that was until the eighteenth century for the Christian West, and to the twentieth century for the Islamic Near and Middle East.

Christianity in its many forms defined culture and politics for most of its history. It continues to do so in many parts of the world. But from the eighteenth century forward, in the West, Christianity met competition from secular ideas. It lost its standing as self-evident truth to important sectors of the West. Then in those same countries Judaism in its classical statement also found itself facing competition from other systems of behavior and belief. It too lost its monopoly as self-evident truth within the Jewish people. Other Judaic systems took shape to answer other questions, not addressed by the classical statement.

So the success of the Judaism that took shape in ancient times depended on the strength of its competition. Judaism had responded to the questions raised by Christianity. When other questions took priority, Judaism lost its standing as well.

The questions Christianity addressed to Jews were the very questions that Judaism answered. Specifically, Christianity had asked the Jews, Why are you not Christians? And Judaism told the Jews to respond, Because we are Israel, the people of the Torah, living a holy way of life. But Christianity's competition in nationalism asked the Jews, Why are you not like us? And that was a secular question of culture and politics.

Jews in the West proposed to reply: In some ways we are like you, in some ways, we are different. In matters of national identity and culture, we are like you. In religion, we are not like you. But the received system of Judaism had not provided a space for more than the single identity, "Israel," and for another way of life alongside the holy way of life that separated Israel from the nations. Then new Judaic systems would come to compete with the normative Judaism of the rabbinic sages, the Judaism of the Torah in writing and the Torah in memory.

So, faced with the political changes brought about by the American Constitution of 1787 and the French Revolution of 1789, Jews in Britain and central and western Europe and the United States aspired to a position equivalent to that of the majority population: citizenship, equality before the law. Then the urgent question emerged: How and why be *both* Jewish and German or Jewish and French or Jewish and British? The received system had no answer.

From the earliest decades of the nineteenth century new Judaisms took shape, dealing with other agenda of urgent questions and answering those questions in ways self-evidently right for those who believed. They offered explanations of how a Jew could be not solely "Israel" but something—anything—in addition to Israelite.

For that purpose people had to uncover a neutral realm in the life of individuals and consequently of the community alike, a realm left untouched by the processes of sanctification leading to salvation, that had for so long made Jews into "Israel," the community of Judaism. Each of these Judaisms claimed to continue in linear succession the Judaism that had flourished for so long, to develop in an incremental succession and so to connect, through the long past, to Sinai. But in fact each one responded to contemporary issues deemed urgent among one or another group of Jews. Between 1800 and 1850 the main systems had taken shape.

First in time is Reform Judaism, coming to expression in the early part of the nineteenth century and making changes in liturgy, then in doctrine and in way of life of the received Judaism of the dual Torah. Reform Judaism recognized the legitimacy of making changes and regarded change as reform, hence the name. Born in Germany, the Reform theologians thus invoked the language of the Protestant Reformation—another mark of the influence of Christianity upon Judaism.

Second was the reaction to Reform Judaism, called Orthodox Judaism, which in many ways was continuous with the received Judaism, but in some ways as selective as was Reform Judaism. Orthodox Judaism reached its first systematic expression in the middle of the nineteenth century. Orthodox Judaism addressed the issue of change, and held that Judaism lies beyond history. It is the work of God. It constitutes a set of facts of the same order as the facts of nature. But, at the same time, in principle no different from Reform Judaism, Orthodox Judaism affirmed that one could devote time to science, not only Torah study; that affirmation stood for an accommodation with contemporary politics and culture.

Third in line and somewhat after Orthodox Judaism came Positive Historical Judaism, the European name for Conservative Judaism in America. Conservative Judaism occupied the center between the two other Judaisms of continuation of the dual Torah. This Judaism maintained that change *could* become reform, but only in accord with the principles by which legitimate change may be separated from illegitimate change. Conservative Judaism would discover those principles through historical study. In an age in which historical facts were taken to represent theological truths, the emphasis on history meant much. All three successor Judaisms of Europe and the United States explained how one could be both an Israelite and something else, an American or a German. So they answered a question that modern nationalism asked, but that Christianity did not ask.

What about Judaism in the Islamic world? Through all its history the basic religiosity of the Islamic world reinforced the Judaic construction of the Jews' community as a holy community. Judaism had successfully answered the question, Why do you persist and not accept Islam? That question having been answered, Judaism in the received statement of the fourth century C.E. concerning the way of life and worldview of the holy people thrived in Islam from the beginning to the creation of the state of Israel in 1948. That political event brought to an end the life of the Jews and hence also of Judaism in most, though not all, Islamic nations (Morocco and Turkey representing the exceptions).

So Judaism answered for its "Israel" exactly those questions that the success of Christianity and Islam made urgent. All three religions, Judaism, Christianity, and Islam, dealt with the same issues, which concerned humanity's relationship to God, and God's self-revelation to humanity.

That is why Christianity and Islam account for the success of Judaism. So long as Christianity defined the civilization of the West, and Islam of North Africa, the Near and Middle East, and Central Asia, Judaism in its fourth-century, classical statement triumphed in Israel, the Jewish people. That is why, by most Jews in the world, Judaism's questions were deemed urgent, its answers found self-evidently true. And when not, not: when other questions pressed, other Judaic systems took shape.[2] And each of them would tell its own story within the pattern of exile and return.

NOTES TO CHAPTER 6

1. Bernard Lewis, *The Jews of Islam* (Princeton, N.J.: Princeton University Press, 1984), 8.
2. See my *Death and Birth of Judaism: The Impact of Christianity, Secularism, and the Holocaust on Jewish Faith* (1987; reprint, Lanham, Md.: University Press of America, 2000).

PART IV

Exemplary Figures in the Emergence of Judaism

Introduction

*J*udaism values persons not for their individuality but for their power to exemplify virtue held in common. Therefore the stories that we have tell us not about heroic individuals but about how individuals embody the values of the community formed by the Torah. Links in the chain of tradition, individuals make a difference at that point at which they lose all individuality. They embody virtue required of all.

Anecdotes about men and women deepen our grasp of what the Torah requires. These stories are not random and they are not aimed at providing a secular biography of a particular purpose. Rather they show the particularization of virtue. Of special interest to the rabbinic storytellers are how the individual sage mastered the Torah and taught it and how the individual dies. Learning, virtue, and a dignified death form the points of interest.

Accordingly, we do not have resources for a biography of any rabbinic sage. The stories that the rabbinic sources tell about sages yield the model of the life framed by the Torah. Anecdotes of individual conduct show how someone fulfilled the ideal that the Torah sets forth for every Israelite. What marked the person as special was how he or she did in an exemplary manner what all were supposed to do anyhow. No continuous "life" emerges, and no individual stands out for his or her unique qualities.

That preference for the exemplary over the personal marks the culture of Judaism in ancient times. The official writings of Judaism present a collective consensus. Not one authoritative writing comes to us from a single, named author. That is why they also do not narrate biographies. There is no counterpart in Judaism to the Gospels, centered on the life and teachings of one person in particular.

Chapter 7

God

*T*he most heroic of the exemplary figures about whom stories are told is God. We already know that God is presented in human form. But there were things that the rabbinic sages wished to say about God that could be said best, and perhaps only, through stories. That is why God's response to the destruction of the Temple in 586 B.C.E. and thus also in 70 C.E. takes the form of a narrative. It is the only way for the rabbinic sages to express the picture of how God wept at the loss of the sanctuary.

> *Lamentations Rabbah* XXIV.II.1
> "My Lord God of hosts summoned on that day to weeping and lamenting, to tonsuring and girding with sackcloth" (Isa. 22:14):
> When the Holy One, blessed be he, considered destroying the house of the sanctuary, he said, "So long as I am within it, the nations of the world cannot lay a hand on it.
> "I shall close my eyes to it and take an oath that I shall not become engaged with it until the time of the end."
> Then the enemies came and destroyed it.
> Forthwith the Holy One, blessed be he, took an oath by his right hand and put it behind him: "He has drawn back his right hand from before the enemy" (Lam. 2:3).
> At that moment the enemies entered the sanctuary and burned it up.
> When it had burned, the Holy One, blessed be he, said, "I do not have any dwelling on earth any more. I shall take up my presence from there and go up to my earlier dwelling."
> That is in line with this verse: "I will go and return to my place, until they acknowledge their guilt and seek my face" (Hos. 5:15).
> At that moment the Holy One, blessed be he, wept, saying, "Woe is me! What have I done! I have brought my Presence to dwell below on account of the Israelites, and now that they have sinned, I have gone back to my ear-

lier dwelling. Heaven forfend that I now become a joke to the nations and a source of ridicule among people."

At that moment Metatron came, prostrated himself, and said before him, "Lord of the world, let me weep, but don't you weep!"

He said to him, "If you do not let me weep now, I shall retreat to a place in which you have no right to enter, and there I shall weep."

That is in line with this verse: "But if you will not hear it, my soul shall weep in secret for pride" (Jer. 13:17).

Said the Holy One, blessed be he, to the ministering angels, "Let's go and see what the enemies have done to my house."

Forthwith the Holy One, blessed be he, and the ministering angels went forth, with Jeremiah before them.

When the Holy One, blessed be he, saw the house of the sanctuary, he said, "This is certainly my house, and this is my resting place, and the enemies have come and done whatever they pleased with it!"

At that moment the Holy One, blessed be he, wept, saying, "Woe is me for my house! O children of mine—where are you? O priests of mine—where are you? O you who love me—where are you? What shall I do for you? I warned you, but you did not repent."

Said the Holy One, blessed be he, to Jeremiah, "Today I am like a man who had an only son, who made a marriage canopy for him, and the son died under his marriage canopy. Should you not feel pain for me and for my son?

"Go and call Abraham, Isaac, Jacob, and Moses from their graves, for they know how to weep."

He said before him, "Lord of the world, I don't know where Moses is buried."

The Holy One, blessed be he, said to him, "Go and stand at the bank of the Jordan and raise your voice and call him, 'Son of Amram, son of Amram, rise up and see your flock, which the enemy has swallowed up!'"

Jeremiah immediately went to the cave of Machpelah and said to the founders of the world, "Arise, for the time has come for you to be called before the Holy One, blessed be he."

They said to him, "Why?"

He said to them, "I don't know," because he was afraid that they would say to him, "In your time this has come upon our children!"

Jeremiah left them and went to the bank of the Jordan and cried out, "Son of Amram, son of Amram, rise up, for the time has come for you to be called before the Holy One, blessed be he."

He said to him, "What makes this day so special, that I am called before the Holy One, blessed be he?"

He said to him, "I don't know."

Moses left him and went to the ministering angels, for he had known them from the time of the giving of the Torah. He said to them, "You who serve on high! Do you know on what account I am summoned before the Holy One, blessed be he?"

They said to him, "Son of Amram! Don't you know that the house of the sanctuary has been destroyed, and the Israelites taken away into exile?"

So he cried and wept until he came to the fathers of the world. They too forthwith tore their garments and put their hands on their heads, crying and weeping, up to the gates of the house of the sanctuary.

When the Holy One, blessed be he, saw them, forthwith: "My Lord God of hosts summoned on that day to weeping and lamenting, to tonsuring and girding with sackcloth."

Were it not stated explicitly in a verse of Scripture, it would not be possible to make this statement.

And they went weeping from this gate to that, like a man whose deceased lies before him,

and the Holy One, blessed be he, wept, lamenting, "Woe for a king who prospers in his youth and not in his old age."

Chapter 8

Abraham

Abraham is the first human being to know and obey God, and the rabbinic sages provide a picture of how he came to the conclusion that idolatry is false.

Genesis Rabbah XXXVIII:XIII.1

"Haran died in the presence of his father Terah in the land of his birth, in Ur of the Chaldeans" (Gen. 11:28):

Said R. Hiyya [in explanation of how Haran died in his father's presence], "Terah was an idol manufacturer. Once he went off on a trip and put Abraham in charge of the store. Someone would come in and want to buy an idol. He would say to him, 'How old are you?'

"He said, 'Fifty years old.'

"He said, 'Woe to that man, who is fifty years old and is going to bow down to something a day old.' So the man would be ashamed and go his way.

"One time a woman came in with a bowl of flour, and said to him, 'Take this and offer it before them.'

"He went and took a stick, broke the idols, and put the stick in the hand of the biggest idol.

"When his father came back, he said to him, 'Why in the world have you been doing these things?'

"He said to him, 'How can I hide it from you? One time a woman came in with a bowl of flour, and said to me, "Take this and offer it before them." Then this idol said, "I'll eat first," and that idol said, "I'll eat first." One of them, the largest, got up and grabbed the stick and broke the others.'

"[Terah] said to him, 'Why are you making fun of me! Do those idols know anything [that such a thing could possibly happen]? [Obviously not!]'

"He said to him, 'And should your ears not hear what your mouth is saying?' He took him and handed him over to Nimrod.

"He [Nimrod] said to him [Abraham], 'Bow down to the fire.'

"He said to him, 'We really should bow down to water, which puts out fire.'

"He said to him, 'Bow down to water.'

109

"He said to him, 'We really should bow down to the clouds, which bear the water.'

"He said to him, 'Then let's bow down to the clouds.'

"He said to him, 'We really should bow down to the wind, which disperses the clouds.'

"He said to him, 'Then let's bow down to the wind.'

"He said to him, 'We really should bow down to human beings, who can stand up to the wind.'

"He said to him, 'You're just playing word games with me. Let's bow down to the fire. So now, look, I am going to throw you into the fire, and let your God whom you worship come and save you from the fire.'

"Now Haran was standing there undecided. He said, 'What's the choice? If Abram wins, I'll say I'm on Abram's side, and if Nimrod wins, I'll say I'm on Nimrod's side. [So how can I lose?]'

"When Abram went down into the burning furnace and was saved, Nimrod said to him, 'On whose side are you?'

"He said to him, 'Abram's.'

"They took him and threw him into the fire, and his guts burned up and came out, and he died in the presence of his father.

"That is in line with the verse of Scripture: 'And Haran died in the presence of his father, Terah' (Gen. 11:28)."

Chapter 9

Isaac

*I*saac's heroism consisted in his willingness to be sacrificed, even in the face of temptation to rebel. He attained merit by accepting God's commandment even unto death.

Genesis Rabbah LVI:III.1 to Genesis 22:6
  "And Abraham took the wood of the burnt offering and laid it on Isaac, his son; [and he took in his hand the fire and the knife]" (Gen. 22:6):
  It is like one who carries his own cross on his shoulder.

Genesis Rabbah LVI:IV.1 to Genesis 22:7
  "And Isaac said to his father Abraham, 'My father'" (Gen. 22:7):
  Samael [the tempter] came to our father, Abraham. He said to him, "What sort of nonsense is troubling your heart? The son that was given to you at the age of a hundred are you going to slaughter?"
  He said to him, "Indeed so."
  He said to him, "And if he tests you still further than this, can you stand the test? 'If a thing be put to you as a trial, will you be wearied' (Job 4:2)?"
  He said to him, "And still more."
  He said to him, "Tomorrow he will [reverse himself and] tell you that you are a murderer, and you are liable."
  He said to him, "Indeed so."
  When Samael saw that he could accomplish nothing with him, he came to Isaac. He said to him, "Oh son of a miserable mother. He is going to slaughter you."
  He said to him, "Indeed so!"
  He said to him, "If so, all those lovely cloaks that your mother made will be the inheritance of Ishmael, the hated one of her house."
  If a word does not make its way entirely, it makes its way in part. That is in line with this verse: "And Isaac said to his father Abraham, 'My father'" (Gen. 22:7). [That is, Isaac began to waver in his faith.]

And he said, "Behold the fire and the wood, but where is the lamb for a burnt offering?"

Abraham said, "May that man who incited you drown."

In any event: "'God will provide himself the lamb for a burnt offering,' and if not, then: 'the lamb for the burnt offering will be my son'" (Gen. 21:8).

"So they went both of them together" (Gen. 22:6):

This one went to tie up and the other to be tied up, this one went to slaughter and the other to be slaughtered.

Chapter 10

Rachel

Among the rabbinic sages' heroic figures is Rachel, Jacob's wife, who can accomplish in relationship with God what no patriarch or prophet and not even the ministering angels could achieve. When God dismissed the reproach of Abraham, Isaac, Jacob, Moses, and Jeremiah, he finally met Rachel, and because of her supplications, had mercy on the Israelites in their hour of suffering.

Lamentations Rabbah XXIV.II.3

Said R. Samuel bar Nahman, "When the Temple was destroyed, Abraham came before the Holy One, blessed be he, weeping, pulling at his beard and tearing his hair, striking his face, tearing his clothes, with ashes on his head, walking about the Temple, weeping and crying, saying before the Holy One, blessed be he,

"'How does it happen that I am treated differently from every other nation and language, that I should be brought to such humiliation and shame!'

"When the ministering angels saw him, they too composed lamentations, arranging themselves in rows, saying . . .

"'You have broken the covenant':

"Said the ministering angels before the Holy One, blessed be he, 'Lord of the world, the covenant that was made with their father, Abraham, has been broken, the one through which the world was settled and through which you were made known in the world, that you are the most high God, the one who possesses heaven and earth.'

"At that moment the Holy One, blessed be he, responded to the ministering angels, saying to them, 'How does it happen that you are composing lamentations, arranging yourselves in rows, on this account?'

"They said to him, 'Lord of the world! It is on account of Abraham, who loved you, who came to your house and lamented and wept. How does it happen that you didn't pay any attention to him?'

"He said to them, 'From the day on which my beloved died, going off to his eternal house, he has not come to my house, and now "what is my beloved doing in my house" (Jer. 11:15)?'

"Said Abraham before the Holy One, blessed be he, 'Lord of the world! How does it happen that you have sent my children into exile and handed them over to the nations? And they have killed them with all manner of disgusting forms of death! And you have destroyed the house of the sanctuary, the place on which I offered up my son Isaac as a burnt offering before you!?'

"Said to Abraham the Holy One, blessed be he, 'Your children sinned and violated the whole Torah, transgressing the twenty-two letters that are used to write it: "Yes, all Israel have transgressed your Torah" (Dan. 9:11).'

"Said Abraham before the Holy One, blessed be he, 'Lord of the world, who will give testimony against the Israelites, that they have violated your Torah?'

"He said to him, 'Let the Torah come and give testimony against the Israelites.'

"Forthwith the Torah came to give testimony against them.

"Said Abraham to her, 'My daughter, have you come to give testimony against the Israelites that they have violated your religious duties? And are you not ashamed on my account? Remember the day on which the Holy One, blessed be he, tried to sell you to all the nations and languages of the world, and no one wanted to accept you, until my children came to Mount Sinai and they accepted you and honored you! And now are you coming to give testimony against them on their day of disaster?'

"When the Torah heard this, she went off to one side and did not testify against them.

"Said the Holy One, blessed be he, to Abraham, 'Then let the twenty-two letters of the alphabet come and give testimony against the Israelites.'

"Forthwith the twenty-two letters of the alphabet came to give testimony against them.

"The aleph came to give testimony against the Israelites, that they had violated the Torah.

"Said Abraham to her, 'Aleph, you are the head of all of the letters of the alphabet, and have you now come to give testimony against the Israelites on the day of their disaster?

"'Remember the day on which the Holy One, blessed be he, revealed himself on Mount Sinai and began his discourse with you: "I ['anoki, beginning with aleph] am the Lord your God who brought you out of the Land of Egypt, out of the house of bondage" (Exod. 20:2).

"'But not a single nation or language was willing to take you on, except for my children! And are you now going to give testimony against my children?'

"Forthwith the aleph went off to one side and did not testify against them.

"The beth came to give testimony against the Israelites.

"Said Abraham to her, 'My daughter, have you come to give testimony against my children, who are meticulous about the five books of the Torah, at the head of which you stand, as it is said, "In the beginning [*bereshit*] God created . . ." (Gen. 1:1)?'

"Forthwith the beth went off to one side and did not testify against them.

"The gimel came to give testimony against the Israelites.

"Said Abraham to her, 'Gimel, have you come to give testimony against my children, that they have violated the Torah? Is there any nation, besides my children, that carries out the religious duty of wearing show-fringes, at the head of which you stand, as it is said, "Twisted cords [*gedelim*] you shall make for yourself" (Deut. 22:12)?'

"Forthwith the gimel went off to one said and did not testify against them.

"Now when all of the letters of the alphabet in succession then realized that Abraham had silenced them, they were ashamed and stood off and would not testify against Israel.

"Abraham forthwith commenced speaking before the Holy One, blessed be he, saying to him, 'Lord of the world, when I was a hundred years old, you gave me a son. And when he had already reached the age of volition, a boy thirty-seven years of age, you told me, "offer him up as a burnt offering before me"!

"'And I became harsh to him and had no mercy for him, but I myself tied him up. Are you not going to remember this and have mercy on my children?'

"Isaac forthwith commenced speaking before the Holy One, blessed be he, saying to him, 'Lord of the world, when father said to me, "God will see to the lamb for the offering for himself, my son" (Gen. 22:8), I did not object to what you had said, but I was bound willingly, with all my heart, on the altar, and spread forth my neck under the knife. Are you not going to remember this and have mercy on my children!'

"Jacob forthwith commenced speaking before the Holy One, blessed be he, saying to him, 'Lord of the world, did I not remain in the house of Laban for twenty years? And when I went forth from his house, the wicked Esau met me and wanted to kill my children, and I gave myself over to death in their behalf. Now my children are handed over to their enemies like sheep for slaughter, after I raised them like fledglings of chickens. I bore on their account the anguish of raising children, for through most of my life I was pained greatly on their account. And now are you not going to remember this and have mercy on my children!'

"Moses forthwith commenced speaking before the Holy One, blessed be he, saying to him, 'Lord of the world, was I not a faithful shepherd for the Israelites for forty years? I ran before them in the desert like a horse. And when the time came for them to enter the land, you issued a decree against me in the wilderness that there my bones would fall. And now that they have gone into exile, you have sent to me to mourn and weep for them.'

"This is in line with the proverb people say: "When it's good for my master, it's not good for me, but when it's bad for him, it's bad for me!""

"Then Moses said to Jeremiah, 'Go before me, so I may go and bring them in and see who will lay a hand on them.'

"Jeremiah said to him, 'It isn't even possible to go along the road, because of the corpses.'

"He said to him, 'Nonetheless.'

"Forthwith Moses went along, with Jeremiah leading the way, until they came to the waters of Babylon.

"They saw Moses and said to one another, 'Here comes the son of Amram from his grave to redeem us from the hand of our oppressors.'

"An echo went forth and said, 'It is a decree from before me.'

"Then said Moses to them, 'My children, to bring you back is not possible, for the decree has already been issued. But the Omnipresent will bring you back quickly.' Then he left them.

"Then they raised up their voices in weeping until the sound rose on high: 'By the rivers of Babylon there we sat down, yes, we wept' (Ps. 137:1).

"When Moses came back to the founders of the world [the patriarchs and matriarchs], they said to him, 'What have the enemies done to our children?'

"He said to them, 'Some of them he killed, the hands of some of them he bound behind their back, some of them he put in iron chains, some of them he stripped naked, some of them died on the way, and their corpses were left for the vultures of heaven and the hyenas of the earth, some of them were left for the sun, starving and thirsting.'

"Then they began to weep and sing dirges: 'Woe for what has happened to our children! How have you become orphans without a father! How have you had to sleep in the hot sun during the summer without clothes and covers! How have you had to walk over rocks and stones without shoes and sandals! How were you burdened with a heavy bundle of sand! How were your hands bound behind your backs! How were you left unable even to swallow the spit in your mouths!'

"Moses then said, 'Cursed are you, O sun! Why did you not grow dark when the enemy went into the house of the sanctuary?'

"The sun answered him, 'By your life, Moses, faithful shepherd! They would not let me nor did they leave me alone, but beat me with sixty whips of fire, saying, "Go, pour out your light."'

"Moses then said, 'Woe for your brilliance, O Temple, how has it become darkened? Woe that its time has come to be destroyed, for the building to be reduced to ruins, for the school children to be killed, for their parents to go into captivity and exile and the sword!'

"Moses then said, 'O you who have taken the captives! I impose an oath on you by your lives! If you kill, do not kill with a cruel form of death, do not exterminate them utterly, do not kill a son before his father, a daughter before her mother, for the time will come for the Lord of heaven to exact a full reckoning from you!'

"The wicked Chaldeans did not do things this way, but they brought a son before his mother and said to the father, 'Go, kill him!' The mother wept, her tears flowing over him, and the father hung his head.

"And further Moses said before him, 'Lord of the world! You have written in your Torah, "Whether it is a cow or a ewe, you shall not kill it and its young both in one day" (Lev. 22:28).

"'But have they not killed any number of children along with their mothers, and yet you remain silent!'

"Then Rachel, our mother, leapt to the fray and said to the Holy One, blessed be he, 'Lord of the world! It is perfectly self-evident to you that your servant, Jacob, loved me with a mighty love, and worked for me for my father for seven years, but when those seven years were fulfilled, and the time came for my wedding to my husband, my father planned to substitute my sister for me in the marriage to my husband. Now that matter was very hard for me, for I knew the deceit, and I told my husband and gave him a sign by which he would know the difference between me and my sister, so that my father would not be able to trade me off. But then I regretted it and I bore my passion, and I had mercy for my sister, that she should not be shamed. So in the evening for my husband they substituted my sister for me, and I gave my sister all the signs that I had given to my husband, so that he would think that she was Rachel.

"'And not only so, but I crawled under the bed on which he was lying with my sister, while she remained silent, and I made all the replies so that he would not discern the voice of my sister.

"'I paid my sister only kindness, and I was not jealous of her, and I did not allow her to be shamed, and I am a mere mortal, dust and ashes. Now I had no envy of my rival, and I did not place her at risk for shame and humiliation. But you are the King, living and enduring and merciful. How does it happen that you are jealous of idolatry, which is nothing, and so have sent my children into exile, allowed them to be killed by the sword, permitted the enemy to do whatever they wanted to them?!'

"Forthwith the mercy of the Holy One, blessed be he, welled up, and he said, 'For Rachel I am going to bring the Israelites back to their land.'

"That is in line with this verse of Scripture: 'Thus said the Lord: A cry is heard in Ramah, wailing, bitter weeping, Rachel weeping for her children. She refuses to be comforted for her children, who are gone. Thus said the Lord, Restrain your voice from weeping, your eyes from shedding tears; for there is a reward for your labor, declares the Lord; they shall return from the enemy's land, and there is hope for your future, declares the Lord: your children shall return to their country' (Jer. 31:15–17)."

Chapter 11

Moses

*T*he story in which Rachel emerges as the principal illustrates a quality of the mode of thought of Judaism. Specifically, in Judaism there is no conception of history. The rabbinic sages say, "There is neither 'earlier' nor 'later' in the Torah," but narratives unfold in accord with their own logic. Thus Abraham and Moses are represented in conversation with God at the destruction of the Temple.

That same conception extends to the portrait of the study of Torah. All begins with Moses. But that is not a temporal statement. It is rather a judgment of the inner logic, the potential reason, that inheres in the Torah Moses received from God. That is what "originates" with Moses: a timeless truth. Only later sages uncover that ever-present truth.

There is a story that shows how Moses witnessed the Torah teaching, in his name, of the great master, Aqiba. The point is that God is always God—not just the model for humanity but fundamentally different. In the end people must accept God's decree, even though it contradicts their expectations of justice, as we saw earlier at pp. 86–87.

Chapter 12

Hillel

*P*atience and forbearance, necessary traits of the sage, serve to win people to the Torah and so to give them their share in eternal life. Here Hillel patiently teaches the entire Torah while standing on one foot. What emerges is a reworking of Leviticus 19:18: "You will love your neighbor as yourself."

Babylonian Talmud tractate *Shabbat* 2:5 I.12/31a
There was a case of a gentile who came before Shammai. He said to him, "Convert me on the stipulation that you teach me the entire Torah while I am standing on one foot." He drove him off with the building cubit that he had in his hand.
He came before Hillel: "Convert me."
He said to him, "'What is hateful to you, to your fellow don't do.
"That's the entirety of the Torah; everything else is elaboration. So go, study."

Chapter 13

Honi the Circle Drawer

*T*he rabbinic sages recognized that outside the Torah camp there were other holy men who enjoyed God's special grace. Here is the story of the most famous of them, Honi the Circle Drawer, and of why he drew circles. It was to bring rain in the right volume and of the right type. Later on we shall meet others who enjoyed Heaven's favor, both women and men who by reason of their special virtue could pray for rain but who were not masters of the Torah.

> Mishnah tractate *Ta'anit* 3:9–10
> They said to Honi the Circle Drawer, "Pray for rain."
> He said to them, "Go and take in the clay ovens used for [baking unleavened bread for] Passover, so that they do not soften in the rain which is coming."
> He prayed, but it did not rain.
> What did he do?
> He drew a circle and stood in the middle of it and said before him, "Lord of the world! Your children have turned to me, for before you, I am like a member of the family. I swear by your great name—I'm simply not moving from here until you take pity on your children!"
> It began to rain drop by drop.
> He said, "This is not what I wanted, but rain for filling up cisterns, pits, and caverns."
> It began to rain violently.
> He said, "This is not what I wanted, but rain of goodwill, blessing, and graciousness."
> Now it rained the right way, until the Israelites had to flee from Jerusalem up to the Temple Mount because of the rain.
> Now they came and said to him, "Just as you prayed for it to rain, now pray for it to go away."
> He said to them, "Go, see whether the stone of those who stray has disappeared [under water]."

Simeon b. Shatah said to him, "If you were not Honi, I should decree a ban of excommunication against you. But what am I going to do to you? For you importune before the Omnipresent, so he does what you want, like a son who importunes his father, so he does what he wants.

"Concerning you Scripture says, 'Let your father and your mother be glad, and let her that bore you rejoice'" (Prov. 23:25).

Chapter 14

Yohanan ben Zakkai

*B*efore the Temple was destroyed in the siege of Jerusalem that began in 68 C.E. and ended on the 9th of the lunar month of Ab (corresponding to August) in 70, the greatest sage of the Torah of the day reconciled with the Romans in exchange for the right to continue to teach the Torah. The Israelites would accept Roman rule so long as they could continue to be ruled by God. Here is the story of how he escaped from the besieged city and made his peace with the Romans.

The Fathers According to Rabbi Nathan IV:VI.1
   Now when Vespasian came to destroy Jerusalem, he said [to the inhabitants of the city], "Idiots! why do you want to destroy this city and burn the house of the sanctuary? For what do I want of you, except that you send me a bow or an arrow [as marks of submission to my rule], and I shall go on my way."
   They said to him, "Just as we sallied out against the first two who came before you and killed them, so shall we sally out and kill you."
   When Rabban Yohanan ben Zakkai heard, he proclaimed to the men of Jerusalem, saying to them, "My sons, why do you want to destroy this city and burn the house of the sanctuary? For what does he want of you, except that you send him a bow or an arrow, and he will go on his way."
   They said to him, "Just as we sallied out against the first two who came before him and killed them, so shall we sally out and kill him."
   Vespasian had stationed men near the walls of the city, and whatever they heard, they would write on an arrow and shoot out over the wall. [They reported] that Rabban Yohanan ben Zakkai was a loyalist of Caesar's.
   After Rabban Yohanan ben Zakkai had spoken to them one day, a second, and a third, and the people did not accept his counsel, he sent and called his disciples, R. Eliezer and R. Joshua, saying to them, "My sons, go and get me out of here. Make me an ark and I shall go to sleep in it."

R. Eliezer took the head and R. Joshua the feet, and toward sunset they carried him until they came to the gates of Jerusalem.

The gatekeepers said to them, "Who is this?"

They said to him, "It is a corpse. Do you not know that a corpse is not kept overnight in Jerusalem?"

They said to them, "If it is a corpse, take him out," so they took him and brought him out at sunset, until they came to Vespasian.

They opened the ark and he stood before him.

He said to him, "Are you Rabban Yohanan ben Zakkai? Indicate what I should give you."

He said to him, "I ask from you only Yavneh, to which I shall go, and where I shall teach my disciples, establish prayer, and carry out all of the religious duties."

He said to him, "Go and do whatever you want."

He said to him, "Would you mind if I said something to you?"

He said to him, "Go ahead."

He said to him, "Lo, you are going to be made sovereign."

He said to him, "How do you know?"

He said to him, "It is a tradition of ours that the house of the sanctuary will be given over not into the power of a commoner but of a king, for it is said, 'And he shall cut down the thickets of the forest with iron, and Lebanon [which refers to the Temple] shall fall by a mighty one' (Isa. 10:34)."

People say that not a day, two, or three passed before a delegation came to him from his city indicating that the [former] Caesar had died and they had voted for him to ascend the throne.

They brought him a catapult and drew it up against the wall of Jerusalem.

They brought him cedar beams and put them into the catapult, and he struck them against the wall until a breach had been made in it. They brought the head of a pig and put it into the catapult and tossed it toward the limbs that were on the Temple altar.

At that moment Jerusalem was captured.

Rabban Yohanan ben Zakkai was in session and with trembling was looking outward, in the way that Eli had sat and waited: "Lo, Eli sat upon his seat by the wayside watching, for his heart trembled for the ark of God" (1 Sam. 4:13).

When Rabban Yohanan ben Zakkai heard that Jerusalem had been destroyed and the house of the sanctuary burned in flames, he tore his garments, and his disciples tore their garments, and they wept and cried and mourned.

Chapter 15

Joshua ben Hananiah
and Gamaliel II

*Y*ohanan ben Zakkai formed the critical link in the chain of tradition to Sinai. The center for Torah study that he founded at Yavneh formed the basis for the Roman-sponsored Jewish government of the Jewish people of the Land of Israel. The rabbinic sages served in the Roman-sponsored government headed by the patriarch, who derived from the family of Hillel. The Jewish government set up at Yavneh did not acknowledge Rome as the source of its authority. The presiding figure after 70, Gamaliel, descended from Hillel, who for his part descended from King David, from whom the Messiah would come forth in due course. That was one basis for ruling Israel. The other, in Judaism, was knowledge of the Torah. The claim of the sage to rule by the authority of the Torah competed with the claim of the patriarch to rule by the authority of the house of David.

Here is how the two sources of authority—the Messiah, the Torah, genealogy versus learning—resolved their conflict. Joshua stands for the rabbinic sages, qualified by the recognition of Yohanan ben Zakkai, the founding master of the school after 70, and Gamaliel stands for the patriarchate.

Mishnah tractate *Rosh Hashanah* 2:8–9
A picture of the shapes of the moon did Rabban Gamaliel have on a tablet and on the wall of his upper room, which he would show ordinary folk, saying, "Did you see it like this or like that?"

Two witnesses came and said, "We saw it at dawn on the morning [of the twenty-ninth] in the east and at eve in the west."

Said R. Yohanan b. Nuri, "They are false witnesses."

Now when they came to Yavneh, Rabban Gamaliel accepted their testimony [assuming they erred at dawn].

And furthermore two came along and said, "We saw it at its proper time, but on the night of the added day it did not appear [to the court]."

Then Rabban Gamaliel accepted their testimony.

Said R. Dosa b. Harkinas, "They are false witnesses.

"How can they testify that a woman has given birth, when, on the very next day, her stomach is still up there between her teeth [for there was no new moon!]?"

Said to him [Dosa] R. Joshua, "I can see your position [and affirm it over Gamaliel's]."

Said to him [to Joshua] Rabban Gamaliel, "I decree that you come to me with your staff and purse on the Day of Atonement that is determined in accord with your reckoning [so publicly renouncing his ruling in favor of Gamaliel's]."

R. Aqiba went and found him troubled.

He said to him, "I can provide grounds for showing that everything that Rabban Gamaliel has done is validly done, since it says, 'These are the set feasts of the Lord, even holy convocations, which you shall proclaim' (Lev. 23:4). Whether they are in their proper time or not in their proper time, I have no set feasts but these ['which you shall proclaim']."

He came along to R. Dosa b. Harkinas.

He [Dosa] said to him, "Now if we're going to take issue with the court of Rabban Gamaliel, we have to take issue with every single court that has come into being from the time of Moses to the present day, since it says, 'Then went up Moses and Aaron, Nadab and Abihu, and seventy of the elders of Israel' (Exod. 24:9). Now why have the names of the elders not been given? To teach that every group of three [elders] who came into being as a court of Israel—lo, they are equivalent to the court of Moses himself."

[Joshua] took his staff with his purse in his hand and went along to Yavneh, to Rabban Gamaliel, on the Day of Atonement that is determined in accord with his [Gamaliel's] reckoning.

Rabban Gamaliel stood up and kissed him on his head and said to him, "Come in peace, my master and my disciple—my master in wisdom, and my disciple in accepting my rulings."

Chapter 16

Eliezer ben Hyrcanus

Yohanan ben Zakkai's other principal disciple was Eliezer ben Hyrcanus. Here is the story of the origins, in the Torah, of Eliezer, with special reference to how he commenced Torah study in his mature years and pursued learning in poverty but eventually enjoyed great success, a common motif in rabbinic lives.

The Fathers According to Rabbi Nathan VI:VI.1, 4

How did R. Eliezer ben Hyrcanus begin [his Torah study]?

He had reached the age of twenty-two years and had not yet studied the Torah. One time he said, "I shall go and study the Torah before Rabban Yohanan ben Zakkai."

His father Hyrcanus said to him, "You are not going to taste a bit of food until you have ploughed the entire furrow."

He got up in the morning and ploughed the entire furrow.

They say that that day was Friday. He went and took a meal with his father-in-law.

And some say that he tasted nothing from the sixth hour on Friday until the sixth hour on Sunday.

Hyrcanus, his father, heard that he was studying the Torah with Rabban Yohanan ben Zakkai. He decided, "I shall go and impose on Eliezer my son a vow not to derive benefit from my property."

They say that that day Rabban Yohanan ben Zakkai was in session and expounding [the Torah] in Jerusalem, and all the great men of Israel were in session before him. He heard that he was coming. He set up guards, saying to them, "If he comes to take a seat, do not let him."

He came to take a seat and they did not let him [sit in the back of the gathering].

He kept stepping over people and moving forward until he came to Ben Sisit Hakkesset and Naqdimon b. Gurion and Ben Kalba Sabua. He sat among them, trembling.

They say that on that day Rabban Yohanan ben Zakkai looked at R. Eliezer, indicating to him, "Cite an appropriate passage and give an exposition."

He said to him, "I cannot cite an appropriate passage."

He urged him, and the other disciples urged him.

He went and cited an opening passage and expounded matters the like of which no ear had ever heard.

And at every word that he said, Rabban Yohanan ben Zakkai arose and kissed him on his head and said, "My lord, Eliezer, my lord, you have taught us truth."

As the time came to break up, Hyrcanus his father stood up and said, "My lords, I came here only to impose a vow on my son, Eliezer, not to derive benefit from my possession. Now all of my possessions are given over to Eliezer my son, and all my other sons are disinherited and will have no share in them."

Chapter 17

Eliezer ben Hyrcanus
and Joshua ben Hananiah

*E*liezer and Joshua received their knowledge of the Torah from the same master, Yohanan ben Zakkai, yet they differed on one point after another. The differences concerned not only the definition of facts of tradition, but the right reasoning concerning those facts. The most striking quality of the writings of Judaism is respect for disputes resolved through reasoned argument. Difference of opinion is honored. Contention is a mark of devotion to the Torah. Reason overrides authority and tradition in deciding the law. Here is a statement of how rabbinic sages carried on an argument on a point of law. We begin in the middle; what was at issue is not important to us. The players are Eliezer ben Hyrcanus and Joshua ben Hananiah.

Babylonian Talmud tractate *Baba Mesia* 4:10 I.15/59a-b
On that day [on which Eliezer and Joshua argued about a point of law] R. Eliezer produced all of the arguments in the world, but they did not accept them from him. So he said to them, "If the law accords with my position, this carob tree will prove it."
The carob was uprooted from its place by a hundred cubits—and some say, four hundred cubits.
They said to him, "There is no proof from a carob tree."
So he went and said to them, "If the law accords with my position, let the stream of water prove it."
The stream of water reversed flow.
They said to him, "There is no proof from a stream of water."
So he went and said to them, "If the law accords with my position, let the walls of the schoolhouse prove it."
The walls of the schoolhouse tilted toward falling.
R. Joshua rebuked them, saying to them, "If disciples of sages are contending with one another in matters of law, what business do you have?"

They did not fall on account of the honor owing to R. Joshua, but they also did not straighten up on account of the honor owing to R. Eliezer, and to this day they are still tilted.

So he went and said to them, "If the law accords with my position, let the Heaven prove it!"

An echo from Heaven came forth, saying, "What business have you with R. Eliezer, for the law accords with his position under all circumstances!"

R. Joshua stood up on his feet and said, "'It is not in heaven' (Deut. 30:12)."

What is the sense of, "'It is not in heaven' (Deut. 30:12)"?

Said R. Jeremiah, "[The sense of Joshua's statement is this:] For the Torah has already been given from Mount Sinai, so we do not pay attention to echoes, since you have already written in the Torah at Mount Sinai, 'After the majority you are to incline' (Exod. 23:2)."

R. Nathan came upon Elijah and said to him, "What did the Holy One, blessed be he, do at that moment?"

He said to him, "He laughed and said, 'My children have overcome me, my children have overcome me!'"

Chapter 18

Eliezer ben Hyrcanus
and Yohanan ben Zakkai

*T*he rabbinic sages stressed that the Torah governed how a disciple conducts intimate aspects of everyday life. Here we see how the disciple, Eliezer ben Hyrcanus, and his master, Yohanan ben Zakkai, conducted the ritual of dying. The humility is noteworthy. After a life of Torah study, Yohanan still is concerned with the final judgment for his life.

Babylonian Talmud tractate *Berakot* 4:2 I.2/28a
When R. Eliezer fell ill, his disciples came in to pay a call on him. They said to him, "Our master, teach us the ways of life, so that through them we may merit the world to come."

He said to them, "Be attentive to the honor owing to your fellows, keep your children from excessive reflection, and set them among the knees of disciples of sages, and when you pray, know before whom you stand, and on that account you will merit the life of the world to come."

And when R. Yohanan b. Zakkai fell ill, his disciples came in to pay a call on him. When he saw them, he began to cry. His disciples said to him, "Light of Israel! Pillar at the right hand! Mighty hammer! On what account are you crying?"

He said to them, "If I were going to be brought before a mortal king, who is here today and tomorrow gone to the grave, who, should he be angry with me, will not be angry forever, and, if he should imprison me, will not imprison me forever, and if he should put me to death, whose sentence of death is not for eternity, and whom I can appease with the right words or bribe with money, even so, I should weep.

"But now that I am being brought before the King of kings of kings, the Holy One, blessed be he, who endures forever and ever, who, should he be angry with me, will be angry forever, and if he should imprison me, will imprison me forever, and if he should put me to death, whose sentence of death is for eternity, and whom I cannot appease with the right words or bribe with money, "and not only so, but before me are two paths, one to the garden of Eden and the other to Gehenna, and I do not know by which path I shall be brought,

"and should I not weep?"

They said to him, "Our master, bless us."

He said to them, "May it be God's will that the fear of Heaven be upon you as much as the fear of mortals."

His disciples said, "Just so much?"

He said to them, "Would that it were that much. You should know that, when a person commits a transgression, he says, 'I hope no one sees me.'"

Chapter 19

Elisha ben Abbuya

*N*ot all rabbinic masters set a good example. Here is the story of one who did not, the apostate Elisha ben Abbuya. He tells the reason he gave up his faith in God made known in the Torah. He saw a tragic event that contradicted the promises of the Torah. But he turned out to have a flawed understanding of the matter.

Talmud of the Land of Israel tractate *Hagigah* 2:1.III:7–8

Why did [Elisha abandon the Torah and become a heretic]?

Once Elisha was sitting and studying in the plain of Gennesaret, and he saw a man climb to the top of a palm tree, take a mother bird with her young, and descend safely. The following day he saw another man climbing to the top of the palm tree; he took the young birds but released the mother. When he descended a snake bit him and he died.

Elisha thought, "It is written, '[If you chance to come upon a bird's nest, in any tree or on the ground, with young ones or eggs, you shall not take the mother with the young;] you shall let the mother go, but the young shall you take to yourself; that it may go well with you, and that you may live long' (Deut. 22:6–7). Where is the welfare of this man, and where his length of days?"

He did not know that R. Jacob had explained it before him: "That it may go well with you" in the world to come that is wholly good, "And that you may live long," in the time that is wholly long.

Some say [he defected] because he saw the tongue of Rabbi Judah the Baker, dripping blood, in the mouth of a dog. He said, "This is the Torah, and this its reward! This is the tongue that was bringing forth the words of the Torah as befits them. This is the tongue that labored in the Torah all its days. This is the Torah, and this its reward! It seems as though there is no reward [for righteousness] and no resurrection of the dead."

But some say that when his mother was pregnant with him, she passed by some heathen temples and smelled their particular kind of incense. And that odor pierced her body like the poison of a snake.

Sometime later Elisha fell sick. They came and told R. Meir, "Behold, your master is ill." He went, intending to visit him, and he found him ill. He said to him, "Will you not repent?"

He said, "If sinners repent, are they accepted?"

[Meir] replied, "Is it not written thus: 'You cause a man to repent up to the point when he becomes dust' (Ps. 90:3)? Up to the time when life is crushed are repentant sinners received."

At that moment, Elisha wept, then he departed [this life] and died. And R. Meir rejoiced in his heart, thinking, "My master died in repentance."

Chapter 20

Aqiba

A qiba, disciple of Joshua and Eliezer, had the power to see the true meaning of events. In this narrative, he finds in the fulfillment of prophecies of disaster the promise of coming redemption. He reasoned, if the predictions of suffering for sin come true, then the predictions of consolation on account of repentance also will be realized.

> *Sifre Deuteronomy* XLIII:III.7–8
>
> "for Mount Zion which lies desolate; jackals prowl over it" (Lam. 5:18):
>
> Rabban Gamaliel, R. Joshua, R. Eleazar b. Azariah, and R. Aqiba went to Rome. They heard the din of the city of Rome from a distance of a hundred and twenty miles.
>
> They all begin to cry, but R. Aqiba began to laugh.
>
> They said to him, "Aqiba, we are crying and you laugh?"
>
> He said to them, "Why are you crying?"
>
> They said to him, "Should we not cry, that idolators and those who sacrifice to idols and bow down to images live securely and prosperously, while the footstool of our God has been burned down by fire and become a dwelling place for the beasts of the field? So shouldn't we cry?"
>
> He said to them, "That is precisely the reason that I was laughing. For if those who outrage him he treats in such a way, those who do his will all the more so!"
>
> There was the further case of when they were going up to Jerusalem. When they came to the Mount of Olives they tore their clothing. When they came to the Temple Mount and a fox came out of the house of the Holy of Holies, they began to cry. But R. Aqiba began to laugh.
>
> "Aqiba, you are always surprising us. Now we are crying and you laugh?"
>
> He said to them, "Why are you crying?"
>
> They said to him, "Should we not cry, that from the place of which it is written, 'And the ordinary person that comes near shall be put to death'

(Num. 1:51) a fox comes out? So the verse of Scripture is carried out: 'for Mount Zion which lies desolate; jackals prowl over it.'"

He said to them, "That is precisely the reason that I was laughing. For Scripture says, 'And I will take for myself faithful witnesses to record, Uriah the priest and Zechariah the son of Jeberechiah' (Isa. 8:2).

"Now what is the relationship between Uriah and Zechariah? Uriah lived in the time of the first temple, Zechariah in the time of the second!

"But Uriah said, 'Thus says the Lord of hosts: Zion shall be plowed as a field, and Jerusalem shall become heaps' (Jer. 26:18).

"And Zechariah said, 'There shall yet be old men and old women sitting in the squares of Jerusalem, every man with his staff in his hand for old age' (Zech. 8:4).

"And further: 'And the squares of the city shall be full of boys and girls playing in the squares thereof' (Zech. 8:5).

"Said the Holy One, blessed be he, 'Now lo, I have these two witnesses. So if the words of Uriah are carried out, the words of Zechariah will be carried out, while if the words of Uriah prove false, then the words of Zechariah will not be true either.'

"I was laughing with pleasure because the words of Uriah have been carried out, and that means that the words of Zechariah in the future will be carried out."

They said to him, "Aqiba, you have given us consolation. May you be comforted among those who are comforted."

Chapter 21

Bar Kokhba

*T*he rabbinic sages represent in their own way Bar Kokhba, the leader of the second revolt against Rome under the Emperor Hadrian, in 132–135. They favor humility, and Bar Kokhba is shown arrogant. They want Israel to obey God's will in the Torah, and Bar Kokhba rejects God's will. His arrogance, they hold, resulted in the loss of Jerusalem and the permanent closure of the Temple there, and that accords with their theology.

Consistent with his optimism about the outcome of suffering and repentance, which would be consolation and restoration, Aqiba is represented as recognizing Bar Kokhba as a messiah, come to save Israel. The point of the story is to refute his view.

Lamentations Rabbah LVIII:II.7–10 to Lamentations 2:2

When R. Aqiba saw Bar Koziba [Kokhba], he said, "This is the royal messiah."

R. Yohanan b. Torta said to him, "Aqiba, grass will grow from your cheeks and he will still not have come."

Eighty thousand trumpeters besieged Betar. There Bar Koziba was encamped, with two hundred thousand men with an amputated finger.

Sages sent word to him, saying, "How long are you going to produce blemished men in Israel?"

He said to them, "And what shall I do to examine them [to see whether they are brave]?"

They said to him, "Whoever cannot uproot a cedar of Lebanon do not enroll in your army."

He had two hundred thousand men of each sort [half with an amputated finger, half proved by uprooting a cedar].

When they went out to battle, he would say, "Lord of all ages, don't help us and don't hinder us!"

That is in line with this verse: "Have you not, O God, cast us off? And do not go forth, O God, with our hosts" (Ps. 60:12).

What did Bar Koziba do?

He could catch a missile from the enemy's catapult on one of his knees and throw it back, killing many of the enemy.

That is why R. Aqiba said what he said [about Bar Koziba's being the royal messiah].

For three and a half years [the roman emperor] Hadrian besieged Betar.

R. Eleazar the Modiite was sitting in sackcloth and ashes, praying and saying, "Lord of all the ages, do not sit in judgment today, do not sit in judgment today."

Since [Hadrian] could not conquer the place, he considered going home.

There was with him a Samaritan, who said to him, "My lord, as long as that old cock [Eleazar] wallows in ashes, you will not conquer the city.

"But be patient, and I shall do something so you can conquer it today."

He went into the gate of the city and found R. Eleazar standing in prayer.

He pretended to whisper something into his ear, but the other paid no attention to him.

People went and told Bar Koziba, "Your friend wants to betray the city."

He sent and summoned the Samaritan and said to him, "What did you say to him?"

He said to him, "If I say, Caesar will kill me, and if not, you will kill me. Best that I kill myself and not betray state secrets."

Nonetheless, Bar Koziba reached the conclusion that he wanted to betray the city.

When R. Eleazar had finished his prayer, he sent and summoned him, saying to him, "What did this one say to you?"

He said to him, "I never saw that man."

He kicked him and killed him.

At that moment an echo proclaimed: "Woe to the worthless shepherd who leaves the flock, the sword shall be upon his arm and upon his right eye" (Zech. 11:17).

Said the Holy One, blessed be he, "You have broken the right arm of Israel and blinded their right eye. Therefore your arm will wither and your eye grow dark."

Forthwith Betar was conquered and Ben Koziba was killed.

They went, carrying his head to Hadrian. He said, "Who killed this one?"

They said, "One of the Goths [troops in Roman service] killed him," but he did not believe them.

He said to them, "Go and bring me his body."

They went to bring his body and found a snake around the neck.

He said, "If the God of this one had not killed him, who could have vanquished him?"

That illustrates the following verse of Scripture: "If their Rock had not given them over . . ." (Deut. 32:30).

Chapter 22

Simeon ben Gamaliel

*I*n the aftermath of the war, the Romans for a time sought to repress the practice of Judaism—for example, observing the Sabbath, the wearing of ritual objects, and Torah study—which they deemed the source of sedition and rebellion. After the country was pacified, they would reconstitute the Judaic government under Judah the Patriarch, who sponsored the Mishnah.

In the interim important sages would die, including Judah's father, Simeon ben Gamaliel. Here is how the sages found a theological explanation for their fate, which they attributed to God's will, not to the Romans' persecution.

The Fathers According to Rabbi Nathan XXXVIII:V.2
When they seized Rabban Simeon b. Gamaliel and R. Ishmael on the count of death, Rabban Simeon b. Gamaliel was in session and was perplexed, saying, "Woe is us! For we are put to death like those who profane the Sabbath and worship idols and practice fornication and kill."

Said to him R. Ishmael b. Elisha, "Would it please you if I said something before you?"

He said to him, "Go ahead."

He said to him, "Is it possible that when you were sitting at a banquet, poor folk came and stood at your door, and you did not let them come in and eat?"

He said to him, "By heaven [may I be cursed] if I ever did such a thing! Rather, I set up guards at the gate. When poor folk came along, they would bring them in to me and eat and drink with me and say a blessing for the sake of Heaven."

He said to him, "Is it possible that when you were in session and expounding [the Torah] on the Temple Mount and the vast populations of Israelites were in session before you, you took pride in yourself?"

He said to him, "Ishmael my brother, one has to be ready to accept his failing. [That is why I am being put to death, the pride that I felt on such an occasion.]"

They went on appealing to the executioner for grace. This one [Ishmael] said to him, "I am a priest, son of a high priest, kill me first, so that I do not have to witness the death of my companion."

And the other [Simeon] said, "I am the patriarch, son of the patriarch, kill me first, so that I do not have to witness the death of my companion."

He said to him, "Cast lots." They cast lots, and the lot fell on Rabban Simeon b. Gamaliel.

The executioner took the sword and cut off his head.

R. Ishmael b. Elisha took it and held it in his breast and wept and cried out: "Oh holy mouth, oh faithful mouth, oh mouth that brought forth beautiful gems, precious stones, and pearls! Who has laid you in the dust, who has filled your mouth with dirt and dust?

"Concerning you Scripture says, 'Awake, O sword, against my shepherd and against the man who is near to me' (Zech. 13:7)."

He had not finished speaking before the executioner took the sword and cut off his head.

Concerning them Scripture says, "My wrath shall wax hot, and I will kill you with the sword, and your wives shall be widows, and your children fatherless" (Exod. 22:23).

Chapter 23

A Pious Man
from Kefar Imi

*N*ot all heroic figures in Judaism qualify through Torah study, and not all saints are sages. Some of the most vivid heroic figures are nameless. And they are not sages. Here is an example of morality that wins admiration: humility and punctilious observance of the law.

Talmud of the Land of Israel tractate *Ta'anit* 1:4.I.3
A pious man from Kefar Imi appeared [in a dream] to the rabbis. He prayed for rain and it rained. The rabbis went up to him. His householders told them that he was sitting on a hill. They went out to him, saying to him, "Greetings," but he did not answer them.

He was sitting and eating, and he did not say to them, "You break bread too."

When he went back home, he made a bundle of faggots and put his cloak on top of the bundle [instead of on his shoulder].

When he came home, he said to his household [i.e., his wife], "These rabbis are here [because] they want me to pray for rain. If I pray and it rains, it is a disgrace for them, and if not, it is a profanation of the Name of Heaven. But come, you and I will go up [to the roof] and pray. If it rains, we shall tell them, 'We are not worthy to pray and have our prayers answered.'"

They went up and prayed and it rained.

They came down to them [and asked], "Why have the rabbis troubled themselves to come here today?"

They said to him, "We wanted you to pray so that it would rain."

He said to them, "Now do you really need my prayers? Heaven already has done its miracle."

They said to him, "Why, when you were on the hill, did we say hello to you, and you did not reply?"

He said to them, "I was then doing my job. Should I then interrupt my concentration [on my work]?"

They said to him, "And why, when you sat down to eat, did you not say to us, 'You break bread too'?"

He said to them, "Because I had only my small ration of bread. Why would I have invited you to eat by way of mere flattery [when I knew I could not give you anything at all]?"

They said to him, "And why when you came to go down, did you put your cloak on top of the bundle?"

He said to them, "Because the cloak was not mine. It was borrowed for use at prayer. I did not want to tear it."

They said to him, "And why, when you were on the hill, did your wife wear dirty clothes, but when you came down from the mountain, did she put on clean clothes?"

He said to them, "When I was on the hill, she put on dirty clothes, so that no one would gaze at her. But when I came home from the hill, she put on clean clothes, so that I would not gaze on any other woman."

They said to him, "It is well that you pray and have your prayers answered."

Chapter 24

Two Virtuous Wives

Not all heroic figures were men or truly famous women in the model of Rachel, matriarch of Israel, or Esther and Ruth, whom we shall meet later. Here are stories about two women prepared to sell themselves to save their husbands. The stories center on unlettered and humble men. They are able to bring rain through their prayers, and the rabbinic sages want to know why. But a second look shows who is the center of the story, and it is the heroines, the wives who are ready to give up their virtue to save their husbands. So far as Heaven's favor is concerned, self-sacrifice for the other outweighs even Torah study in the scale of Judaic virtues. Woman do not participate in the chain of tradition from Sinai through mastery of the Torah. But they turn out to win God's favor through self-sacrifice, a virtue that outweighs Torah study.

Talmud of the Land of Israel tractate *Ta'anit* 1:4.I.3
A certain ass driver appeared before the rabbis [in a dream] and prayed, and rain came. The rabbis sent and brought him and said to him, "What is your trade?"

He said to them, "I am an ass driver."

They said to him, "And how do you conduct your business?"

He said to them, "One time I rented my ass to a certain woman, and she was weeping on the way, and I said to her, 'What's with you?' and she said to me, 'The husband of that woman [me] is in prison [for debt], and I wanted to see what I can do to free him.' So I sold my ass and I gave her the proceeds, and I said to her, 'Here is your money, free your husband, but do not sin [by becoming a prostitute to raise the necessary funds].'"

They said to him, "You are worthy of praying and having your prayers answered."

In a dream of R. Abbahu, Mr. Pentakaka ["five sins"] appeared, who prayed that rain would come, and it rained. R. Abbahu sent and summoned him. He said to him, "What is your trade?"

143

He said to him, "Five sins does that man [I] do every day, [for I am a pimp:] hiring whores, cleaning up the theater, bringing home their garments for washing, dancing, and performing before them."

He said to him, "And what sort of decent thing have you ever done?"

He said to him, "One day that man [I] was cleaning the theater, and a woman came and stood behind a pillar and cried. I said to her, 'What's with you?' And she said to me, 'That woman's [my] husband is in prison, and I wanted to see what I can do to free him,' so I sold my bed and cover, and I gave the proceeds to her. I said to her, 'Here is your money, free your husband, but do not sin.'"

He said to him, "You are worthy of praying and having your prayers answered."

Chapter 25

Judah the Patriarch

*H*umility characterized not only unlettered ass drivers and housewives but even Judah the Patriarch himself. The story of his dying commandments to his family and staff stresses how he did not want to be treated with an excess of honor upon death.

Babylonian Talmud tractate *Ketubot* 12:3 II:3–20/103a–104a

At the time that Rabbi [Judah the Patriarch] was dying, he said, "I need my children."

His children came in to him. He said to them, "Take good care of the honor owing to your mother. Let a light be kindled in its proper place, a table set in its proper place, a bed laid in its proper place.

"Joseph Hofni, Simeon Efrati—they are the ones who served me when I was alive, and they will take care of me when I have died.

"Let a light be kindled in its proper place, a table set in its proper place, a bed laid in its proper place:"

He further said to them, "I need the sages of Israel."

The sages of Israel came to him. He said to them, "Call the session back after thirty days [beyond my death].

"I'm not better than our lord, Moses, of whom it is written, 'And the children of Israel mourned for Moses in the plains of Moab thirty days' (Deut. 34:8)."

Thirty days they mourned him day and night; from that point on, they mourned by day and studied by night or mourned by night and studied by day, until twelve months of mourning had gone by.

As Rabbi lay dying, R. Hiyya came in to him, and found him weeping. He said to him, "My lord, how come you're weeping? And has it not been taught on Tannaite authority, 'If someone died smiling, it is a good sign for him; if he died weeping, it is a bad sign for him; if he is facing upward, it is a good sign for him; if he is facing downward, it is a bad sign for him; if his face is toward people, it is a good sign for him; if his face is toward the wall, it is a bad sign for him; if his face is green, it is a bad sign for him; if his face is bright and red, it is a good sign for him; if it is on the Sabbath eve, it is a good sign for him; if it is at the end of the Sabbath, it is a bad sign for him; if it is on the eve of the Day of Atonement, it is a bad sign for him; if it is at the end of the Day of Atonement, it is a good sign for him; if it is on account of dysentery, it is a good sign for him, since most righteous men die of dysentery'?"

And he said to him, "I am weeping because of the Torah and the commandments [from which I now take my leave]."

On the day on which Rabbi died, rabbis decreed a fast and prayed for mercy, saying, "Whoever says that Rabbi is dead will be stabbed with a sword."

The servant girl of Rabbi went up to the roof. She said, "Those in the upper world want Rabbi, and those in the lower world down here want Rabbi. May it be God's will that those of the lower world will overcome those in the upper world."

But when she saw how many times he went to the privy, removing his prayer boxes containing verses of Scripture and putting them back on, and how pained he was, she said, "May it be God's will that those of the upper world will overcome those in the lower world."

Now since the rabbis did not fall silent but kept praying for mercy for him, she took a cruse and threw it from the roof to earth. They shut up for a moment from asking for mercy, and Rabbi's soul found its rest.

The rabbis said to Bar Qappara, "Go, see how he is." He went and found that his soul had found its rest. He tore his cloak and turned the tear of the garment backward. When he got back, he opened with these words: "The angels and the mortals have seized the holy ark. The angels have overcome the mortals and the holy ark has been captured."

They said to him, "Has he died?"

He said to them, "You said it, I didn't."

When Rabbi died, he raised his ten fingers heavenward and said, "Lord of the world, you know full well that with these ten fingers of mine, I have labored in the Torah, and I didn't take any selfish benefit from even my littlest finger. May it please you that there be peace where I am laid to rest."

An echo came forth and said, "'He shall enter into peace, they shall rest on their biers' (Isa. 57:2)."

Chapter 26

Yohanan and Simeon ben Laqish

*T*he heroes among the rabbinic sages valued argument, not for the sake of contention but in quest of truth. They accorded a cool welcome to yes-men, deeming them mere politicians. Friendship meant debate. We recall how Joshua b. Hananiah rebuked Heaven for intervening in a dispute between sages. Here is the other half of the story: the high value placed on unrelenting pursuit of truth. The participants are Yohanan bar Nappaha and Simeon ben Laqish, important authorities of the Talmud.

Babylonian Talmud tractate *Baba Mesia* 7:1 I:12/84a
One day there was a dispute in the schoolhouse [on the following matter]: As to a sword, knife, dagger, spear, handsaw, and scythe—at what point in making them do they become susceptible to become unclean? It is when the process of manufacturing them has been completed [at which point they are deemed useful and therefore susceptible]. And when is the process of manufacturing them completed?

R. Yohanan said, "When one has tempered them in the crucible."

R. Simeon b. Laqish said, "When one has furbished them in water."

[Simeon b. Laqish had originally been a robber and was converted to study of the Torah by Yohanan.] [Referring to his origins as a thug,] R. Yohanan said to him, "Never con a con man."

He said to him, "So what good did you ever do for me? When I was a robber, people called me, 'my lord' [rabbi], and now people call me 'my lord.'"

He said to him, "I'll tell you what good I've done for you, I brought you under the wings of the Presence of God."

R. Yohanan was offended, and R. Simeon b. Laqish fell ill. His [Yohanan's] sister [Simeon b. Laqish's wife] came to him weeping, saying to him, "[Heal my husband,] do it for my children's sake!"

He said to her, "'Leave your fatherless children. I will preserve them alive' (Jer. 49:11)."

"Then do it on account of my widowhood!"

He said to her, "'and let your widows trust in me' (Jer. 49:11)."

R. Simeon b. Laqish died, and R. Yohanan was much distressed afterward. The rabbis said, "Who will go and restore his spirits? Let R. Eleazar b. Pedat go, because his traditions are well honed."

He went and took a seat before him. At every statement that R. Yohanan made, he comments, "There is a Tannaite teaching [of the authority of the Mishnah or the Tosefta] that sustains your view."

He said to him, "Are you like the son of Laqish? When I would state something, the son of Laqish would raise questions against my position on twenty-four grounds, and I would find twenty-four solutions, and it naturally followed that the tradition was broadened, but you say to me merely, 'There is a Tannaite teaching that sustains your view.' Don't I know that what I say is sound?"

So he went on tearing his clothes and weeping, "Where are you, the son of Laqish, where are you, the son of Laqish," and he cried until his mind turned from him. The rabbis asked mercy for him, and he died.

Chapter 27

Simeon ben Eleazar

A further story conveys the importance of patience and humility as the marks of the personality nurtured by the Torah.

Fathers According to Rabbi Nathan XLI:III.1
There is the case of R. Simeon b. Eleazar, who was coming from the house of his master in Migdal Eder, riding on an ass and making his way along the seashore. He saw an unusually ugly man. He said to him, "Empty head! What a beast you are! Is it possible that everyone in your town is as ugly as you are?"

He said to him, "And what can I do about it? Go to the craftsman who made me and tell him, 'How ugly is that utensil that you have made!'"

When R. Simeon b. Eleazar realized that he had sinned, he got off his ass and prostrated himself before the man, saying to him, "I beg you to forgive me."

The ugly man said to him, "I shall not forgive you until you go to the craftsman who made me and tell him, 'How ugly is that utensil that you have made!'"

Simeon ran after the man for three miles. The people of the town came out to meet him. They said to him, "Peace be to you, my lord."

The ugly man said to them, "Whom do you call, 'my lord'?"

They said to him, "To the one [Simeon] who is going along after you."

The ugly man said to them, "If this is a 'my lord,' may there not be many more like him in Israel."

They said to him, "God forbid! And what has he done to you?"

He said to them, "Thus and so did he do to me."

They said to him, "Nonetheless, forgive him."

He said to them, "Lo, I forgive him, on the condition that he not make a habit of acting in that way."

On that same day R. Simeon entered the great study house that was his and gave an exposition: "One should always be as soft as a reed and not as tough as a cedar.

"In the case of a reed, all the winds in the world can go on blowing against it but it sways with them, so that when the winds grow silent, it reverts and stands in its place. And what is the destiny of a reed? In the end a pen is cut from it with which to write a scroll of the Torah.

"But in the case of a cedar it will not stand in place, but when the south wind blows against it, it uproots the cedar and turns it over. And what is the destiny of a cedar? Foresters come and cut it down and use it to roof houses, and the rest they toss into the fire.

"On the basis of this fact they have said, 'One should always be as soft as a reed and not as tough as a cedar.'"

Chapter 28

Esther

The book of Esther tells the story of how the Persian prime minister, Haman, sought from the emperor Ahasuerus the right to kill all the Jews. He was thwarted in his plan by Mordecai, a Jewish sage, who placed his niece, Esther, in the emperor's court. At the crucial moment, Esther revealed to Ahasuerus that as a Jew she was subject to Haman's plot. She won his support for the Jews, who therefore overcame their enemies.

Esther took her position in a long line of heroic figures. She learned from the Torah how to behave. Specifically, she realized how to conduct herself. In keeping her true identity hidden from the emperor until events required her to act, she took as her model Rachel and Benjamin, as well as King Saul, all of whom were her ancestors and all of whom kept silent until required to reveal themselves.

> *Esther Rabbah* I to Esther 2:20/LI:I
> "Now Esther had not made known her kindred or her people, as Mordecai had charged her; for Esther obeyed Mordecai just as when she was brought up by him" (Esth. 2:20):
> This teaches that she kept silent like Rachel, her ancestor, who kept silent.
> All of her great ancestors had kept silent.
> Rachel kept silent when she saw her wedding band on the hand of her sister but shut up about it.
> Benjamin, her son, kept silent.
> You may know that that is so, for the stone that stood for him on the high priest's breastplate was a jasper, indicating that he knew of the sale of Joseph, but he kept silent.
> [The word for jasper contains letters that stand for] "there is a mouth" [i.e., he could have told], but he kept silent.

Saul, from whom she descended: "Concerning the matter of the kingdom he did not tell him" (1 Sam. 10:16).

Esther: "Now Esther had not made known her kindred or her people, as Mordecai had charged her" (Esth. 2:20).

Chapter 29

Ruth

*T*he book of Ruth tells the story of the loyalty of Ruth, who came from Moab, not from the land of Israel, to her Israelite mother-in-law after the death of Ruth's husband. She followed her mother-in-law, rather than returning to her homeland, Moab. There, in Bethlehem, Ruth married Boaz and with him produced an heir who was King David. Since the Messiah would at the end of time emerge from the house of David, the point of the book is clear. The Messiah will derive from a Moabite woman, by reason of her loyalty.

Ruth's personal loyalty to Naomi is shown not to be the principal motivation. Rather, it is a religious conversion.

Ruth Rabbah to Ruth 1:16 XX:I

But Ruth said, "Entreat me not to leave you or to return from following you; for where you go I will go, and where you lodge I will lodge; your people shall be my people, and your God my God . . ." (Ruth 1:16):

. . . "to leave you or to return from following you; for where you go I will go, and where you lodge I will lodge; your people shall be my people, and your God my God":

"Under all circumstances I intend to convert, but it is better that it be through your action and not through that of another."

When Naomi heard her say this, she began laying out for her the laws that govern proselytes.

She said to her, "My daughter, it is not the way of Israelite women to go to theaters and circuses put on by idolators."

She said to her, "Where you go I will go."

She said to her, "My daughter, it is not the way of Israelite women to live in a house that lacks a mezuzah."

She said to her, "Where you lodge I will lodge."

. . . "your people shall be my people":

This refers to the penalties and admonitions against sinning.

. . . "and your God my God":

This refers to the other religious duties.

Another interpretation of the statement, "for where you go I will go":

[This refers to the places where Israel offered sacrifices to God:] to the tent of meeting, Gilgal, Shiloh, Nob, Gibeon, and the eternal house.

. . . "and where you lodge I will lodge":

"I shall spend the night concerned about the offerings."

. . . "your people shall be my people":

"so nullifying my idol."

. . . "and your God my God":

"to pay a full recompense for my action."

PART V   Primary Documents

Introduction

Beyond the written Torah, the Hebrew Scriptures of ancient Israel, the primary documents of Judaism are the writings produced by the rabbinic sages of the first six centuries C.E. They divide into two groups, each responding to half of the Torah, the oral and the written. One set of writings comments on the oral part of the Torah and sets forth the law (Hebrew: *halakah*), the other deals with the written part of the Torah and sets forth lore (Hebrew: *haggadah*, narrative).

The documents that present the law, chapters 30 through 33 below, begin with the Mishnah—the record of the oral tradition of Sinai—and continue in commentaries organized around the Mishnah. These are the Tosefta (supplements to the Mishnah) and the two Talmuds (systematic analysis of the Mishnah and the law).

The documents of lore, chapters 34 through 44 below, comment on the books of the written Torah that are read in the synagogue in public worship. These are as follows: the five books of Moses (Genesis, Exodus, Leviticus, Numbers, and Deuteronomy), and books read on special occasions in synagogue worship. These are Ruth (read on Pentecost, marking the revelation of the Torah at Sinai), Lamentations (read on the ninth of Ab, commemorating the destruction of the First Temple of Jerusalem in 586 B.C.E. and the Second Temple in 70 C.E., and other calamities), Song of Songs (read on Passover), and Esther (read on Purim).

In addition, at chapter 44 we find a collection of wise sayings, *'Abot,* and a systematic commentary on tractate *'Abot* (the Fathers), in the *Fathers According to Rabbi Nathan.*

In each chapter an introduction is followed by an excerpt. In my translations of the rabbinic writings I have provided a reference system, corresponding to chapter and verse references in the Bible: a letter for a sentence, an Arabic numeral for a paragraph, and a Roman numeral for a chapter.

Chapter 30

The Mishnah

*T*he Mishnah is a philosophical law code. That is, it presents laws systematically, as part of a logical, coherent statement. That statement sets forth the principles for the perfection of Israel's social order. It was produced ca. 200 C.E. under the sponsorship of Judah the Patriarch, whom we met in chapter 1. The Mishnah is comprised by six divisions, which cover sixty-two topics, in expositions called tractates.

Some of the laws were practical. They concerned everyday realities in the here and now. Others covered rules for situations not then in existence or transactions not subject to the authority of the rabbinic sages. In the former category are civil laws concerning torts and damages. In the latter are laws about the Temple, then in ruins. Laws not pertinent to everyday life are included to guide the restoration of Israel's sacred society in the end of days.

The Mishnah's principal interest is in the sanctification of Israelite society. In volume, the laws on purity in the Temple, the sixth division, cover approximately a quarter of the entire document. Topics of interest to the priesthood and the Temple, such as priestly fees, conduct of the cult on holy and on ordinary days and management and upkeep of the Temple, and the rules of cultic cleanness, predominate in the first, second, fifth, and sixth divisions. So approximately two-thirds of the law code had no bearing on practical affairs at the time of the completion of that code. Viewed whole, the Mishnah was meant as a design for the restoration, which the Israelites expected at the end of days. But it also legislated for the world of the day. Practical rules governing the social order form the bulk of the third and fourth divisions.

I give the Hebrew name for each of the six divisions and of the tractate and in parentheses the topic, in English, as well.

1. *Zera'im* ("seeds" = Agriculture): *Berakot* (Blessings); *Pe'ah* (the corner of the field); *Demai* (doubtfully tithed produce); *Kil'ayim* (mixed seeds); *Shebi'it* (the prohibition of produce in the seventh year); *Terumot* (heave

offering or priestly rations); *Ma'aserot* (tithes); *Ma'aser Sheni* (second tithe); *Hallah* (dough offering); *'Orlah* (produce of trees in the first three years after planting, which is prohibited); and *Bikkurim* (firstfruits).

2. *Mo'ed* (Appointed Times): *Shabbat* (the Sabbath); *'Erubin* (the fictive fusion meal or boundary); *Pesahim* (Passover); *Sheqalim* (the Temple tax); *Yoma* (the Day of Atonement); *Sukkah* (the Festival of Tabernacles); *Besah* (the preparation of food on the festivals and Sabbath); *Rosh Hashanah* (the New Year); *Ta'anit* (fast days); *Megillah* (Purim); *Mo'ed Qatan* (the intermediate days of the Festivals of Passover and Tabernacles); *Hagigah* (the festal offering).

3. *Nashim* (Women = marriage, family): *Yebamot* (the levirate widow); *Ketubbot* (the marriage contract); *Nedarim* (vows); *Nazir* (the special vow of the Nazirite); *Sotah* (the wife accused of adultery); *Gittin* (writs of divorce); *Qiddushin* (betrothal).

4. *Neziqin* (Damages = civil law): *Baba Qamma, Baba Mesi'a, Baba Batra* (civil law, covering damages and torts, then correct conduct of business, labor, and real estate transactions); *Sanhedrin* (institutions of government; criminal penalties); *Makkot* (civil penalties, flogging); *Shebu'ot* (oaths); *'Eduyyot* (a collection arranged on other than topical lines); *Horayot* (rules governing improper conduct of civil authorities).

5. *Qodashim* (Holy Things): *Zebahim* (everyday animal offerings); *Menahot* (meal offerings); *Hullin* (animals slaughtered for secular purposes, not as Temple offerings); *Bekorot* (firstlings); *'Arakin* (vows of valuation); *Temurah* (vows of exchange of a beast for an already consecrated beast); *Keritot* (penalty of extirpation or premature death); *Me'ilah* (sacrilege); *Tamid* (the daily whole offering); *Middot* (the layout of the Temple building); *Qinnim* (how to deal with bird offerings designated for a given purpose and then mixed up).

6. *Tohorot* (Purity = uncleanness, its sources and means of purification): *Kelim* (susceptibility of utensils to uncleanness); *'Ohalot* (transmission of corpse uncleanness in the tent of a corpse); *Nega'im* (the uncleanness described at Leviticus 13–14); *Parah* (the preparation of purification water); *Tohorot* (problems of doubt in connection with matters of cleanness); *Miqwa'ot* (immersion pools); *Niddah* (menstrual uncleanness); *Makshirin* (rendering susceptible to uncleanness produce that is dry and so not susceptible); *Zabim* (the uncleanness covered at Leviticus 15); *Tebul Yom* (the uncleanness of one who has immersed on that same day and awaits sunset for completion of the purification rites); *Yadayim* (the uncleanness of hands); *'Uqsin* (the uncleanness transmitted through what is connected to unclean produce).

Our sample passage is Mishnah tractate *Sanhedrin* 2:1–5. It concerns the theoretical institutions of Israelite government, the king and the high priest. The author wishes to say that Israel has two heads, one the head of state, king, the other the head of the religion, the high priest, respectively. The exercise classifies and orders the two. They form a common genus, and each is a species of that genus. The genus is "head of holy Israel." The species are king and high priest. The purpose of the presentation is to indicate which of the species takes priority. To underscore the elements of comparison and contrast, I have added heads in boldface type.

Mishnah tractate *Sanhedrin* Chapter 2

1. The rules of the high priest: subject to the law, marital rites, conduct in bereavement

    2:1 A. A high priest judges, and [others] judge him;

        B. gives testimony, and [others] give testimony about him;

        C. performs the rite of removing the shoe [Deut. 25:7–9], and [others] perform the rite of removing the shoe with his wife.

        D. [Others] enter levirate marriage with his wife, but he does not enter into levirate marriage,

        E. because he is prohibited to marry a widow.

        F. [If] he suffers a death [in his family], he does not follow the bier. . . .

        K. And when he gives comfort to others

        L. the accepted practice is for all the people to pass one after another, and the appointed [prefect of the priests] stands between him and the people.

        M. And when he receives consolation from others,

        N. all the people say to him, "Let us be your atonement."

        O. And he says to them, "May you be blessed by Heaven."

        P. And when they provide him with the funeral meal,

        Q. all the people sit on the ground, while he sits on a stool.

2. The rules of the king: not subject to the law, marital rites, conduct in bereavement

    2:2 A. The king does not judge, and [others] do not judge him;

        B. does not give testimony, and [others] do not give testimony about him;

        C. does not perform the rite of removing the shoe, and others do not perform the rite of removing the shoe with his wife;

        D. does not enter into levirate marriage, nor [do his brothers] enter levirate marriage with his wife.

        E. R. Judah says, "If he wanted to perform the rite of removing the shoe or to enter into levirate marriage, his memory is a blessing."

        F. They said to him, "They pay no attention to him [if he expressed the wish to do so]."

        G. [Others] do not marry his widow.

        H. R. Judah says, "A king may marry the widow of a king.

    I. "For so we find in the case of David, that he married the widow of Saul,

    J. "For it is said, 'And I gave you your master's house and your master's wives into your embrace' (2 Sam. 12:8)."

2:3 A. [If the king] suffers a death in his family, he does not leave the gate of his palace.

    B. R. Judah says, "If he wants to go out after the bier, he goes out,

    C. "for thus we find in the case of David, that he went out after the bier of Abner,

    D. "since it is said, 'And King David followed the bier' (2 Sam. 3:31)."

    E. They said to him, "This action was only to appease the people."

    F. And when they provide him with the funeral meal, all the people sit on the ground, while he sits on a couch.

3. Special rules pertinent to the king because of his calling

2:4 A. [The king] calls out [the army to wage] a war fought by choice on the instructions of a court of seventy-one.

    B. He [may exercise the right to] open a road for himself, and [others] may not stop him.

    C. The royal road has no required measure.

    D. All the people plunder and lay before him [what they have seized], and he takes the first portion.

    E. "He should not multiply wives to himself" (Deut. 17:17)—only eighteen.

    F. R. Judah says, "He may have as many as he wants, so long as they do not entice him [to abandon the Lord (Deut. 7:4)]."

    G. R. Simeon says, "Even if there is only one who entices him [to abandon the Lord]—lo, this one should not marry her."

    H. If so, why is it said, "He should not multiply wives to himself"?

    I. Even though they should be like Abigail [1 Sam. 25:3].

    J. "He should not multiply horses to himself" (Deut. 17:16)—only enough for his chariot.

    K. "Neither shall he greatly multiply to himself silver and gold" (Deut. 17:16)—only enough to pay his army.

    L. "And he writes out a scroll of the Torah for himself" (Deut. 17:17).

    M. When he goes to war, he takes it out with him; when he comes back, he brings it back with him; when he is in session in court, it is with him; when he is reclining, it is before him,

    N. as it is said, "And it shall be with him, and he shall read in it all the days of his life" (Deut. 17:19).

2:5 A. [Others may] not ride on his horse, sit on his throne, handle his scepter.

B. And [others may] not watch him while he is getting a haircut, or while he is nude, or in the bathhouse,

C. since it is said, "You shall surely set him as king over you" (Deut. 17:15)—that reverence for him will be upon you.

The details of the rules form a pattern that is not arbitrary. The pattern allows us to see how the two heads of Israel are alike, how are they not alike, and what accounts for the differences. By matching the details and then comparing and contrasting two things that are like and not alike, we see that the king emerges at the higher position of the two. He is not subject to judgment, the high priest is. That marks the king as higher in the hierarchy. That is how the Mishnah sets forth the rules of Israel's social order, showing how reason prevails.

Chapter 31

The Tosefta

*T*he Tosefta (Supplements), ca. 300 C.E., forms a huge collection of laws that complement the Mishnah. It is four times larger than the document that it amplifies.

Read on its own, the Tosefta is unintelligible. Read side by side with the Mishnah, it makes sense. That is because it completely depends on the Mishnah's model. It follows the Mishnah's topical program and it formulates laws as does the Mishnah. The Tosefta is a vine on the Mishnah's trellis. Moreover, its sentences by themselves do not hold together at all. Their order consistently refers to that of the Mishnah's statements. For most of the Tosefta we simply cannot understand a line without first consulting the Mishnah's counterpart statement.

The document contains three kinds of writings. The first consists of verbatim citations and glosses of sentences of the Mishnah. The second is made up of freestanding statements that complement the sense of the Mishnah but do not cite a Mishnah paragraph verbatim. These statements can be fully understood only in dialogue with the Mishnah's counterpart. The third comprises freestanding, autonomous statements, formulated in the manner of the Mishnah but fully comprehensible on their own.

The editors or compilers of the Tosefta arranged their materials in accord with a simple plan. First come statements that cite and expand upon what the Mishnah's sentences say. Second, the compilers present sentences that do not cite the Mishnah's corresponding ones, but that cannot be understood without reference to the Mishnah's rule or sense. Third in sequence are the small number of freestanding statements, which can be wholly understood on their own and without appeal to the sense or principle of the corresponding Mishnah passage; and in some few cases, these compositions and even composites will have no parallel in the Mishnah at all.

Here is how the Tosefta confronts the same themes and also cites some of the passages verbatim. I have abbreviated the passage to highlight its relationship to the Mishnah excerpt (included in the previous chapter), which I give in boldface type.

Tosefta *Sanhedrin* 4:1–2

4:1 A. A high priest who committed homicide—

B. [if he did so] deliberately, he is executed; [if he did so] inadvertently, he goes into exile to the cities of refuge [as at Num. 35:9ff.].

C. [If] he transgressed a positive or negative commandment or indeed any of the commandments, lo, he is treated like an ordinary person in every respect.

D. He does not perform the rite of removing the shoe [Deut. 25:7–9], and others do not perform the rite of removing the shoe with his wife [vs. Mishnah *Sanhedrin* 2:1C].

E. He does not enter into levirate marriage, and [others] do not enter into levirate marriage with his wife [cf. Mishnah *Sanhedrin* 2:1C-E].

F. [When] he stands in the line [to receive comfort as a mourner], the prefect of the priests is at his right hand, and the head of the father's houses [the priestly courses] at his left hand.

G. And all the people say to him, "Let us be your atonement."

H. And he says to them, "May you be blessed by Heaven" [Mishnah *Sanhedrin* 2:1N-O].

I. [And when] he stands in the line to give comfort to others, the prefect of the priests and the [high] priest who has now passed out of his position of grandeur are at his right hand, and the mourner is at his left.

J. [People may] not watch him while he is getting a haircut, [while he is nude] or in the bathhouse [Mishnah *Sanhedrin* 2:5B],

K. since it is said, "And he who is high priest among his brothers" (Lev. 21:10)—that his brethren should treat him with grandeur. . . .

L. But if he wanted to permit others to wash with him, the right is his.

4:2 A. An Israelite king does not stand in line to receive comfort [in the time of bereavement],

B. nor does he stand in line to give comfort to others.

C. And he does not go to provide a funeral meal for others.

D. But others come to him to give him a funeral meal [Mishnah *Sanhedrin* 2:3F],

E. as it is said, "And the people went to provide a funeral meal for David" (2 Sam. 3:35).

F. And if he transgressed a positive or a negative commandment or indeed any of the commandments, lo, he is treated like an ordinary person in every respect.

G. **He does not perform the rite of removing the shoe, and others do not perform the rite of removing the shoe with his wife,**

H. **he does not enter into levirate marriage, nor do his brothers enter into levirate marriage with his wife [Mishnah *Sanhedrin* 2:2C-D].**

I. **R. Judah says, "If he wanted to perform the rite of removing the shoe [Mishnah *Sanhedrin* 2:2E], he has the right to do so."**

J. They said to him, "You turn out to diminish the glory owing to a king."

K. **And [others] do not marry his widow [Mishnah *Sanhedrin* 2:2G],** as it is said, "So they were shut up to the day of their death, living in widowhood" (2 Sam. 20:3).

L. And he has the right to choose wives for himself from any source he wants, whether daughters of priests, Levites, or Israelites.

M. **And they do not ride on his horse, sit on his throne, handle his crown or scepter or any of his regalia [Mishnah *Sanhedrin* 2:5].**

N. [When] he dies, all of them are burned along with him, as it is said, "You shall die in peace and with the burnings of your fathers, the former kings" (Jer. 34:5).

We see how the Mishnah is given a commentary. The commentary cites the Mishnah's text and adds information to make the Mishnah's rule clearer or to place it in context. It adds texts of Scripture to validate laws of the Mishnah.

Clearly, the Tosefta has a variety of materials. Some of the materials are freestanding, but some simply cite and gloss the Mishnah. Tosefta *Sanhedrin* 4:1 starts with a topic not treated in the Mishnah, at A-C. This statement cannot be understood fully unless we recall that the high priest is judged, the king is not subject to judgment. Hence, in the present instance, we have a case in which the high priest is judged. Then at Tosefta *Sanhedrin* 4:1D-L, we go over the law of the Mishnah. We find the Mishnah's language cited and glossed. One kind of gloss is a proof text, as at Tosefta *Sanhedrin* 4:1K, for a statement of the Mishnah, which is cited at Tosefta *Sanhedrin* 4:1J. Tosefta *Sanhedrin* 4:2A-C reprise the Mishnah's rule on the king, but only in detail. The main principle is taken for granted and illustrated.

Chapter 32

The Talmud
of the Land of Israel

A talmud is a sustained, systematic amplification and analysis of passages of the Mishnah and the Tosefta and other legal teachings of the same standing. There are two of them, the Talmud of the Land of Israel, ca. 400 C.E., and the Talmud of Babylonia, ca. 600 C.E.

Both Talmuds invariably do to the Mishnah one of these four things: (1) text criticism, establishing the wording of the legal statement under discussion; (2) explanation of the meaning of the Mishnah, including glosses and amplifications; (3) addition of scriptural proof texts of the Mishnah's central propositions; and (4) harmonization of one Mishnah passage with another passage on the same problem, deriving from the Mishnah or the Tosefta or another legal teaching of the same standing.

The first two of these four procedures remain wholly within the narrow frame of the Mishnah passage subject to discussion. The second pair take an essentially independent stance vis-à-vis the Mishnah passage at hand. Ordinarily, the order for both Talmuds is the same as given above: text criticism, explanation, scriptural proof texts, harmonization or analysis of the law.

Once more I cite the Mishnah's language in boldface type. Both Talmuds are bilingual, part in Hebrew, part in Aramaic. They cite the law texts and Scripture in Hebrew, but they conduct their analysis and discussion in Aramaic, a language akin to Hebrew that was spoken in the land of Israel in the early centuries C.E. I signal the Aramaic passages in italics, the Hebrew in plain type. By my marking them off, the Talmud's program of broadening and deepening the presentation of the law emerges clearly.

Our excerpt is the Talmud of the Land of Israel's treatment of the same passage of the Mishnah already familiar.

Mishnah tractate *Sanhedrin* 2:1
> **A. A high priest judges, and [others] judge him;**
> **B. gives testimony, and [others] give testimony about him;**

C. performs the rite of removing the shoe [Deut. 25:7–9], and [others] perform the rite of removing the shoe with his wife.

D. [Others] enter levirate marriage with his wife, but he does not enter into levirate marriage,

E. because he is prohibited to marry a widow.

F. [If] he suffers a death [in his family], he does not follow the bier.

G. "But when [the bearers of the bier] are not visible, he is visible; when they are visible, he is not.

H. "And he goes with them to the city gate," the words of R. Meir.

I. R. Judah says, "He never leaves the sanctuary,

J. "since it says, 'Nor shall he go out of the sanctuary' (Lev. 21:12)."

Talmud of the Land of Israel tractate *Sanhedrin* 2:1 units I:1–4

I:1 A. *It is understandable that* he judges others.

B. But as to others judging him, [is it appropriate to his station?]

C. Let him appoint a mandatory.

D. Now take note: What if he has to take an oath?

E. Can the mandatory take an oath for his client?

I:2 A. Property cases involving [a high priest]—in how large a court is the trial conducted?

B. With a court of twenty-three judges.

C. *Let us demonstrate that fact from the following:*

D. **A king does not sit in the Sanhedrin, nor do a king and a high priest join in the court session for intercalation [Tosefta *Sanhedrin* 2:15].**

E. *[In this regard,] R. Haninah and R. Mana—one of them said,* "The king does not take a seat on the Sanhedrin, on account of suspicion [of influencing the other judges].

F. "Nor does he take a seat in a session for intercalation, because of suspicion [that it is in the government's interest to intercalate the year].

G. "And a king and a high priest do not take a seat for intercalation, for it is not appropriate to the station of the king [or the high priest] to take a seat with seven judges."

H. *Now look here*: If it is not appropriate to his station to take a seat with seven judges, is it not an argument a fortiori that he should not [be judged] by three? *That is why one must say*, Property cases involving him are tried in a court of twenty-three.

I:3 A. Said R. Eleazar, "A high priest who sinned—they administer lashes to him, but they do not remove him from his high office."

B. Said R. Mana, "It is written, 'For the consecration of the anointing oil of his God is upon him: I am the Lord' (Lev. 21:12).

C. "That is as if to say, 'Just as I [stand firm] in my consecration, so Aaron [stands firm] in his consecration.'"

D. R. Haninah Ketobah [said that], R. Aha in the name of R. Simeon b. Laqish [said]: "An anointed priest who sinned—they administer lashes to him [by the judgment of a court of three judges].

E. *"If you rule that* it is by the decision of a court of twenty-three judges [that the lashes are administered], it turns out that his ascension [to high office] is descent [to public humiliation, since if he sins he is publicly humiliated by a sizable court]."

I:4 A. R. Simeon b. Laqish said, "A ruler who sinned—they administer lashes to him by the decision of a court of three judges."

B. What is the law as to restoring him to office?

C. Said R. Haggai, "By Moses! *If we put him back into office, he will kill us!"*

D. *R. Judah the Patriarch heard this ruling [of R. Simeon b. Laqish's] and was outraged. He sent a troop of Goths [Roman soldiers, placed at his disposal by the imperial government] to arrest R. Simeon b. Laqish. [R. Simeon b. Laqish] fled to the tower, and, some say, it was to Kefar Hittayya.*

E. *The next day R. Yohanan went up to the meetinghouse, and R. Judah the Patriarch went up to the meetinghouse. He said to him, "Why does my master not state a teaching of Torah?"*

F. *[Yohanan] began to clap with one hand [only].*

G. *[Judah the Patriarch] said to him, "Now do people clap with only one hand?"*

H. *He said to him, "No, nor is ben Laqish here [and just as one cannot clap with one hand only, so I cannot teach Torah if my colleague, Simeon b. Laqish, is absent]."*

I. *[Judah] said to him, "Then where is he hidden?"*

J. *He said to him, "In a certain tower."*

K. *He said to him, "You and I shall go out to greet him tomorrow."*

L. *R. Yohanan sent word to R. Simeon b. Laqish, "Get a teaching of Torah ready, because the patriarch is coming over to see you."*

M. *[Simeon b. Laqish] came forth to receive them and said, "The example that you [Judah] set is to be compared to the paradigm of your Creator.* For when the All-Merciful came forth to redeem Israel [from Egypt], he did not send a messenger or an angel, but the Holy One, blessed be he, himself came forth, as it is said, 'For I will pass through the land of Egypt that night' (Exod. 12:12)— *and not only so, but he and his entire retinue.*

N. *[Judah the Patriarch] said to him, "Now why in the world did you see fit to teach this particular statement [that a ruler who sinned is subject to lashes]?"*

O. *He said to him, "Now did you really think that because I was afraid of you, I would hold back the teaching of the All-Merciful?*

P. "[And lo, citing 1 Sam. 2:23–24,] R. Samuel b. R. Isaac said, '[Why do you do such things? For I hear of your evil dealings from all the people.] No, my sons, it is no good report [that I hear the people of the Lord spreading abroad]. If a man sins against a man, God will mediate for him but if a man sins against the Lord, who can intercede for him? But they would not listen to the voice of their father, for it was the will of the Lord to slay them' (1 Sam. 2:23–25).]

Q. "When the people of the Lord spread about [an evil report about a man], they remove him [even though he is the patriarch]."

The Talmud of the Land of Israel to the Mishnah passage under study begins with an explanation of the rule of the Mishnah that the high priest is subject to judgment. This is not fitting for his high status. But there is no other way, because he cannot appoint someone to take his place in court. Paragraph I:2 raises an interesting question. Property cases are ordinarily judged in a court of three judges. But how many are required for the high priest? The answer is, it is judged by an enlarged court, a fact proved by reference to a parallel case, paragraph I:2C-H. The facts are supplied at C-G, and then interpreted at H.

Paragraph I:3 raises a new but very relevant question. What happens if the high priest sins? Is he flogged and is he removed from office? He is flogged, but not removed from office.

Paragraph I:4 then pursues the same issue, now asking about a ruler: is he restored to office? The patriarch intervened in the matter and sent troops to deal with the rabbinic sage, Simeon b. Laqish.

The Talmud of the Land of Israel has therefore both clarified the rule of the Mishnah and also extended it to apply to cases not treated in the Mishnah.

Chapter 33

The Talmud
of Babylonia

*T*he second of the two Talmuds, produced ca. 600 C.E., the Talmud of Babylonia (present-day Iraq), is by far the more important. It has served as the constitution and bylaws of Judaism to this day. It comments on thirty-seven tractates of the Mishnah.

The Talmud of Babylonia speaks about the Mishnah in essentially a single voice, about a limited number of problems. Wherever you turn, the same sorts of questions are phrased in the same rhetoric. It favors an argument made up of questions and answers that lead to more questions and more answers. The questions and answers pertain equally well to every subject and problem. So essentially the Talmud of Babylonia says the same thing about everything. Over and over again it makes the point that many cases embody one principle, a governing law of reason and consistency.

The two Talmuds routinely treat the same passage of the Mishnah or the Tosefta. But they differ in how to do so in the following ways: (1) the first Talmud analyzes evidence, the second investigates premises; (2) the first remains wholly within the limits of its case, the second treats the case as an example of a rule; (3) the first wants to know the rule, the second asks about the implications of the rule for other cases altogether.

Now let us see how the Talmud of Babylonia reads the same paragraphs that we met in the Mishnah, Tosefta, and Talmud of the Land of Israel. Italics indicate Aramaic; plain type, Hebrew; boldface type signals a passage of the Mishnah or the Tosefta.

Mishnah tractate *Sanhedrin* 2:1 = Talmud of Babylonia tractate *Sanhedrin* 18a
  A. A high priest judges, and [others] judge him;
  B. gives testimony, and [others] give testimony about him;
  C. performs the rite of removing the shoe [Deut. 25:7–9], and [others] perform the rite of removing the shoe with his wife.

D. [Others] enter levirate marriage with his wife, but he does not enter into levirate marriage,

E. because he is prohibited to marry a widow.

F. [If] he suffers a death [in his family], he does not follow the bier.

G. "But when [the bearers of the bier] are not visible, he is visible; when they are visible, he is not.

H. "And he goes with them to the city gate," the words of R. Meir.

I. R. Judah says, "He never leaves the sanctuary,

J. "since it says, 'Nor shall he go out of the sanctuary' (Lev. 21:12)."

Talmud of Babylonia tractate *Sanhedrin* 18a/2:1 I:1

I.1 A. **A high priest judges [Misnah *Sanhedrin* 2:1A]:**

B. *That is self-evident. [Why should anyone have thought otherwise?]*

C. *It was necessary to make that point in the context of the statement that* **others judge him.**

D. *That too is self-evident.* If others do not judge him, how can he serve as a judge? *For has it not been written,* "Gather yourselves together, yes, gather together" (Zeph. 2:1), on which R. Simeon b. Laqish said, "[The word for 'gather together' bears the meaning of adorn, in consequence of which:] Adorn yourself and afterward adorn others." [Why, again, should anyone have thought otherwise?]

E. *Rather, since the framer of the passage wished to make reference to* **the king, who does not judge others and is not judged by others,** *he made reference in his clause on the high priest to the fact that* **he does judge and is judged by others.**

The exposition of the Mishnah paragraph begins with the question, Why was it necessary for the Mishnah's author to state the law before us? That is because the law is self-evident, and did not require articulation. The detail subject to that question is included only for formal reasons, to balance the detail that is required concerning the king.

Now the Talmud proceeds to read the Mishnah in the light of the Tosefta's presentation, making reference to the opening clause of the passage that we cited earlier. Note that once more the text raises questions of a critical nature, for example, why it was necessary to state something so self-evident. I indent the secondary developments of the discussion.

F. *And if you wish, I shall propose that what the framer of the passage teaches is in line with that which has been taught on Tannaite authority:* **A high priest who committed homicide [if he did so]**

deliberately, he is executed; [if he did so] inadvertently, he goes
into exile to the cities of refuge [Num. 35:9ff.]. [If] he transgressed a positive or negative commandment, [Tosefta: or,
indeed, any of the commandments,] lo, he is treated like an ordinary person in every respect [Tosefta *Sanhedrin* 4:1A-C].

G. [Proceeding to the exegesis of the passage of Tosefta just now cited:]
If he did so deliberately, he is executed:

H. *That is self-evident.*

I. *It was included because of the other part of the statement,* **If he did
so inadvertently, he goes into exile to the cities of refuge.**

J. *But that fact also is self-evident.*

Here the Talmud finds a case that is not self-evident, one involving a high
priest who has committed manslaughter. Ordinarily, such a one goes into exile
in a city of refuge. At the death of the next high priest, his term in exile is over.
But if it is a high priest himself, perhaps the rule is otherwise. So we are told
that the rule is the same.

K. *It was necessary to make it explicit. It might have entered your mind
to claim that since it is written, "And he shall dwell therein until the
death of the high priest" (Num. 35:25), only one who is subject to
the remedy of return [at the death of the high priest] is subject to the
rule [of taking refuge in the city to begin with]. But someone who is
not subject to the remedy of return [at the death of the high priest]
should not go into exile at all. For we have learned in the Mishnah:*
**[18B] He who kills a high priest and a high priest who commit-
ted involuntary manslaughter never leaves [the city of refuge]**
[Mishnah *Sanhedrin* 2:7B-D].

L. *I might then have concluded that such a one should not go into exile
at all.*

M. *[The framer of the passage] tells us that that is not the case.*

N. *But might I say that it is indeed the case?*

O. Scripture has said, "Every man slayer may flee there" (Deut. 19:3)—
including even a high priest.

P. **If he transgressed a positive or negative commandment, or
indeed any of the commandments, lo, he is treated like an ordinary person in every respect** [Tosefta *Sanhedrin* 4:1C].

Q. *Is it not possible that he will not transgress?*

R. *This is the sense of the passage:* If he transgressed a positive or negative commandment, lo, he is treated like an ordinary person in every
respect.

S. *That is self-evident.*

T. *It might have entered our mind to say that, since we have learned in the Mishnah,* **A tribe, a false prophet, and a high priest are judged only by a court of seventy-one judges [Mishnah *Sanhedrin* 1:6],** in which connection R. Ada bar Ahbah said, "'Every great matter they shall bring to you' (Exod. 18:22), meaning matters involving a great [important] man [such as the high priest], one should reach the conclusion that any and every matter affecting a great man [must come to such a court].

U. *So we are informed [that that is not the case].*

V. *But perhaps that indeed is the case?*

W. *Is it written,* "Matters affecting a great man"? *What is written is,* "A great matter," meaning, something that is quite literally a matter of importance.

The comments on the Mishnah and the received law follow a clear-cut pattern, which is exemplified here. We see that the comment takes the form of a series of arguments, each connected to the one before and leading to the one following. Notice the contentious spirit of the analysis: "that is self-evident!" "perhaps that is indeed the case!" and the like. The Talmud systematically takes up the sentences of the Mishnah and the Tosefta and explains them. The secondary expansions do not change the picture of a carefully crafted document.

Chapter 34

Genesis and *Genesis Rabbah*

*T*he book of Genesis tells the story of creation and the fall of Adam and Eve from Eden, then the call to Abraham and Sarah and the beginnings of their extended family, Israel. *Genesis Rabbah* comments on the book of Genesis. It transforms the book of Genesis from a genealogy and family history of Abraham, Isaac, Jacob, then Joseph, into a book of the laws of history and rules of the salvation of Israel. In the reading of Genesis by *Genesis Rabbah* the deeds of the founders become omens and signs for the final generations.

Genesis Rabbah in its final form emerges ca. 400 C.E., the end of that momentous century in which the Roman Empire passed from pagan to Christian rule. In *Genesis Rabbah* the entire narrative of Genesis is so formed as to point toward the sacred history of Israel, the Jewish people: its slavery and redemption; its coming Temple in Jerusalem; its exile and salvation at the end of time. The deeds of the founders supply signals for the children about what is going to come in the future. So the biography of Abraham, Isaac, and Jacob also provides a protracted account of the history of Israel later on.

Genesis Rabbah Parashah LXX to Genesis 28:20–29:30
LXX:VI.1 A. ["Then Jacob made a vow, saying, 'If God will be with me and will keep me in this way that I go and will give me bread to eat and clothing to wear, so that I come again to my father's house in peace, then the Lord shall be my God. And this stone, which I have set up for a pillar, shall be God's house; and of all that you give me, I will give the tenth to you'" (Gen. 28:20–22)] . . . "so that I come again to my father's house in peace, then the Lord shall be my God" (Gen. 28:20–22):
B. R. Joshua of Sikhnin in the name of R. Levi: "The Holy One, blessed be he, took the language used by the patriarchs and turned it into a key to the redemption of their descendants."

Now we see how the deeds of the matriarchs and patriarchs and of God's love for them prefigure the story of Israel long after the time of the matriarchs and patriarchs.

C. "Said the Holy One, blessed be he, to Jacob, 'You have said, "Then the Lord shall be my God." By your life, all of the acts of goodness, blessing, and consolation that I am going to carry out for your descendants I shall bestow only by using the same language:

D. ""'Then, in that day, living waters shall go out from Jerusalem" (Zech. 14:8). "Then, in that day a man shall rear a young cow and two sheep" (Isa. 7:21). "Then, in that day, the Lord will set his hand again the second time to recover the remnant of his people" (Isa. 11:11). "Then, in that day, the mountains shall drop down sweet wine" (Joel 4:18). "Then, in that day, a great horn shall be blown and they shall come who were lost in the land of Assyria" (Isa. 27:13).""'

The union of Jacob's biography and Israel's history yields the passage at hand. The trigger is the word "then" and the passages that use that same word. They are held to flow together to make the same point, beginning with Jacob.

LXX:X.1. A. "Jacob said to them, 'My brothers, where do you come from?' They said, 'We are from Haran'" (Gen. 29:40):

B. R. Yose bar Haninah interpreted the verse at hand with reference to the exile.

C. "'Jacob said to them, "My brothers, where do you come from?"' They said, "We are from Haran": that is, 'We are flying from the wrath of the Holy One, blessed be he.' [Here there is a play on the words for "Haran" and "wrath," which share the same consonants.]

D. "'He said to them, "Do you know Laban the son of Nahor?"' The sense is this, 'Do you know him who is destined to bleach your sins as white as snow?' [Here there is a play on the words for "Laban" and "bleach," which share the same consonants.]

E. "'They said, "We know him." He said to them, "Is it well with him?" They said, "It is well."'" On account of what sort of merit?

F. [Yose continues his interpretation:] "'[The brothers go on,] . . . "and see, Rachel his daughter is coming with the sheep"'" (Gen. 29:6–7).

G. "That is in line with this verse: 'Thus says the Lord, "A voice is heard in Ramah, lamentation and bitter weeping, Rachel weeping for her children. She refuses to be comforted." Thus says the Lord, "Refrain your voice from weeping . . . and there is hope for your future," says the Lord, and your children shall return to their own border'" (Jer. 31:15–16)."

Now the history of the redemption of Israel is located in the conversation between Jacob and Laban's sons. We have already met in chapter 10 the story of how, when Abraham and Moses and Jeremiah could make no headway with God, Rachel's weeping made God forgive her children when they went into exile.

Chapter 35

Exodus and *Mekilta Attributed to R. Ishmael*

*T*he book of Exodus tells how God freed the Israelites when they were enslaved in Egypt and sets forth a variety of rules for Israelite life, including instructions on building the tabernacle in the wilderness. *Mekilta Attributed to R. Ishmael,* an interpretation of the book of Exodus, is to be dated some time after 300 C.E. It presents a composite of three kinds of materials concerning the book of Exodus. The first is a set of explanations of some passages of Exodus. The second is a group of propositional and argumentative essays in the form of commentaries, in which theological principles are set forth and demonstrated. The third consists of topical articles, some of them sustained, many of them well crafted, about important subjects of Judaism. Here is the way in which the commandment concerning the Sabbath, Exodus 20:8–11, is expounded.

> *Mekilta Attributed to R. Ishmael* LIII
>   II.1.A. "Remember the Sabbath day to keep it holy":
>   B. [In the two versions of the Ten Commandments, at Exodus 20 and Deuteronomy 5] "Remember" and "Keep" [at Deut. 5:12: "Keep the Sabbath day to keep it holy"] were both part of a single act of speech.

The Torah thus contains two versions of the commandment concerning the Sabbath, one using the language "Remember," the other, "Keep." The comment is that both formulations were set forth in a single act of speech. How is that possible? We are now given other examples in which two different ways of wording were spoken in a single act of speech.

> II.2.A. "Everyone who profanes it shall surely be put to death" (Exod. 31:14),

   B. and "And on the Sabbath day two he-lambs" (Num. 28:9) were both part of a single act of speech.
II.3.A. "You shall not uncover the nakedness of your brother's wife" (Lev. 18:16),
   B. and "Her husband's brother shall go in to her" (Deut. 25:5) were both part of a single act of speech.
II.4.A. "You shall not wear a mingled stuff" (Deut. 22:11) and "You shall make yourself twisted cords" (Deut. 22:12) were both part of a single act of speech.
II.5.A. For it is said, "God has spoken once, but we have heard two things" (Ps. 62:12).
   B. And, "Is not my word like fire, says the Lord, and like a hammer that breaks the rock into pieces?" (Jer. 23:29).
II.6.A. "Remember" and "Keep":
   B. "Remember" in advance, and "keep" afterward.
   C. In this connection sages have said, "They add time from an ordinary day to a holy day."
   D. It is like a wolf who moves backward and forward.

Now attention shifts to the wording in front of us, "Remember the Sabbath day. . . ." What act of remembering is involved?

II.7.A. Eleazar b. Hananiah b. Hezekiah b. Garon says, "'Remember the Sabbath day to keep it holy':
   B. "you should remember it from Sunday, so that if something nice comes to hand, you should set it aside for the sake of the Sabbath."
   C. R. Isaac says, "You should not count the days of the week the way others do, but rather, you should count for the sake of the Sabbath [the first day, the second day, upward to the seventh, which is the Sabbath]."

The next clause, "to keep it holy," is spelled out, and in the next paragraphs, further statements are amplified along the same lines.

II.8.A. "[Remember the Sabbath day] to keep it holy":
   B. to keep it holy by reciting a blessing.
   C. In this connection sages have said, "They recite a prayer of sanctification over wine when the Sabbath enters."
   D. I know only that there is a prayer of sanctification recited by day. How do I know that there is a prayer of sanctification recited by night?
   E. Scripture says, "You shall keep the Sabbath" (Exod. 31:14).

    F. I know only that there is a prayer of sanctification for the Sabbath. How about festival days?

    G. Scripture says, "These are the appointed seasons of the Lord" (Lev. 23:4).

II.9.A. "Six days you shall labor and do all your work":

    B. But can a mortal carry out all of one's work in only six days?

    C. But the nature of Sabbath rest is such that it should be as though all of your labor has been carried out.

II.10.A. Another teaching [as to "Six days you shall labor and do all your work"]:

    B. "Take a Sabbath rest from the very thought of work."

    C. And so Scripture says, "If you turn away your foot because of the Sabbath" (Isa. 58:13), and then, "Then you shall delight yourself in the Lord" (Isa. 58:14).

Numbers 1–5 construct a set of examples of the same fact, that where we have duplications or contradictions, these are harmonized; God made statements that seem to contradict one another at one and the same time, indicating that there is a harmony to be discovered. The rest of the exposition spells out the meaning of Scripture for everyday life.

Chapter 36

Leviticus and
Leviticus Rabbah

*T*he book of Leviticus sets forth the rules governing the animal sacrifices that God commands Israel to offer, the priests that are to prepare them, and the rules of uncleanness and cleanness that pertain to the place where the offerings are presented, the Temple. So the issues concern sanctification, how Israel is to be holy: "You shall be holy, for I the Lord your God am holy" (Lev. 19:2).

Leviticus Rabbah, completed in ca. 450 C.E., asks how Israel is to be saved from its present situation; that is, it concerns salvation. So the work links sanctification to salvation: Israel is to become holy, and when it forms a holy community, it will look forward to being saved. Specifically, Leviticus tells the story of how Israel, purified from social sin and sanctified, would be saved.

The message of *Leviticus Rabbah*—like that of *Genesis Rabbah*—is that the laws of history may be known. The Torah, properly understood, reveals them. These laws, so far as Israel is concerned, focus upon the holy life of the community. If Israel then obeys the laws of society aimed at Israel's sanctification, then the history, resting on the merit of the ancestors, will unfold in the pattern shown by the patriarchs and matriarchs. The point is, then, that salvation at the end of history depends upon sanctification in the here and now. To prove it the authors make lists of facts contained in the Torah that bear the same traits and show the working of rules of history. These lists then through the power of repetition make a single enormous point or prove a social law of history.

Here is an example of how Scripture produces facts that prove a point. The point derives from Qohelet (Ecclesiastes) 3:15: "God seeks what has been driven away," thus, God prefers the pursued over the pursuer, thus Israel over the nations.

Leviticus Rabbah XXVII:V
    1.A. "God seeks what has been driven away" (Qoh. 3:15).

B. R. Huna in the name of R. Joseph said, "It is always the case that 'God seeks what has been driven away' [favoring the victim].

C. "You find when a righteous man pursues a righteous man, 'God seeks what has been driven away.'

D. "When a wicked man pursues a wicked man, 'God seeks what has been driven away.'

E. "All the more so when a wicked man pursues a righteous man, 'God seeks what has been driven away.'

F. "[The same principle applies] even when you come around to a case in which a righteous man pursues a wicked man, 'God seeks what has been driven away.'"

2.A. R. Yose b. R. Yudan in the name of R. Yose b. R. Nehorai says, "It is always the case that the Holy One, blessed be he, demands an accounting for the blood of those who have been pursued from the hand of the pursuer.

B. "Abel was pursued by Cain, and God sought [an accounting for] the pursued: 'And the Lord looked [favorably] upon Abel and his meal offering' (Gen. 4:4).

C. "Noah was pursued by his generation, and God sought [an accounting for] the pursued: 'You and all your household shall come into the ark' (Gen. 7:1). And it says, 'For this is like the days of Noah to me, as I swore [that the waters of Noah should no more go over the earth]' (Isa. 54:9).

D. "Abraham was pursued by Nimrod, 'and God seeks what has been driven away': 'You are the Lord, the God who chose Abram and brought him out of Ur' (Neh. 9:7).

E. "Isaac was pursued by Ishmael, 'and God seeks what has been driven away': 'For through Isaac will seed be called for you' (Gen. 21:12).

F. "Jacob was pursued by Esau, 'and God seeks what has been driven away': 'For the Lord has chosen Jacob, Israel for his prized possession' (Ps. 135:4).

G. "Moses was pursued by Pharaoh, 'and God seeks what has been driven away': 'Had not Moses his chosen stood in the breach before him' (Ps. 106:23).

H. "David was pursued by Saul, 'and God seeks what has been driven away': 'And he chose David, his servant' (Ps. 78:70).

I. "Israel was pursued by the nations, 'and God seeks what has been driven away': 'And you has the Lord chosen to be a people to him' (Deut. 14:2).

J. "And the rule applies also to the matter of offerings. A bull is pursued by a lion, a sheep is pursued by a wolf, a goat is pursued by a leopard.

K. "Therefore the Holy One, blessed be he, has said, 'Do not make offerings before me from those animals that pursue, but from those that are pursued: "When a bull, a sheep, or a goat is born"' (Lev. 22:27)."

God selects for the animals to be offered as sacrifices those that are pursued, not those that are pursuers; herbivores, not carnivores. And that fact of the holy Temple is consistent with facts of history. Abel, Noah, Abraham, Isaac, Jacob, Moses, David, Israel—all conform to the same pattern. We see how the proposition that God favors the pursued over the pursuer is proved. History recorded in the Torah contains examples of that fact. When we collect the cases, we discover the rule.

Chapter 37

Numbers and *Sifre to Numbers*

*T*he book of Numbers recounts incidents in the wandering of the people of Israel in the wilderness for forty years. *Sifre to Numbers,* ca. 300 C.E., provides a reading of most of the book of Numbers. It follows no topical program distinct from that of Scripture, which is systematically clarified, as we shall see in our sample of the document. The purpose of the clarification of Scripture is to highlight the reasonable character of the law.

In the present case, a story is told to illustrate the explicit explanation that Scripture assigns to a commandment. Israelites are commanded to wear show-fringes on their garments, "to look upon and to remember all the commandments." Exactly how the show-fringes (ordinarily worn beneath other garments, so the story takes for granted) remind the wearer of "all the commandments" is then the issue that is clarified.

Sifre to Numbers CXV:I.1
- A. "The Lord said to Moses, 'Speak to the people of Israel and say to them to make tassels [fringes] [on the corners of their garments throughout their generations, and put upon the tassel of each corner a cord of blue; and it shall be to you a tassel to look upon and remember all the commandments of the Lord to do them, not to follow after your own heart and your own eyes, which you are inclined to go after wantonly. So you shall remember and do all my commandments and be holy to your God. I am the Lord your God who brought you out of the land of Egypt to be your God. I am the Lord your God]'" (Num. 15:37–41):
- B. [Since the phrasing is "say to them,"] even women are included in the requirement.
- C. R. Simeon declares women exempt from the religious duty of wearing fringes, because it is a religious duty involving an act of

commission dependent on a particular time, and from a religious
duty in that classification women are exempt.

D. This is the encompassing rule that R. Simeon stated, "As to all religious duties involving an act of commission dependent on a particular time, men are liable and women are exempt, and such duties do
not apply to women, for those duties apply to those fit for doing them
and not to those unfit."

E. R. Judah b. Baba says, "In particular sages have exempted the
woman's veil from the requirement of fringes, while they did not
require her to wear a prayer cloak only because there are times that
her husband wraps himself in it."

The issue of women's place within Israel's covenanted relationship with
God is addressed head-on. Are they part of that "Israel" that accepted the
Torah? Yes, they are, but they have particular duties that differentiate them
from male Israelites. How that principle applies to the show-fringes is then
articulated at E.

Sifre to Numbers CXV:I.2

A. . . . "to look upon and remember all the commandments of the Lord
to do them":

B. Scripture indicates that whoever carries out the religious duty of
wearing fringes is credited as if he had carried out all of the religious
duties.

C. And lo, this produces an argument a fortiori: if someone who carries
out the religious duty of wearing fringes is given credit as if he had
carried out all of the religious duties, all the more so is that the case
for any of the other religious duties enjoined by the Torah.

Sifre to Numbers CXV:IV

1. A. . . . "not to follow after your own heart and your own eyes":

B. This refers to heresy, along the lines of the following verse: "The
wiles of a woman I find more bitter than death, her heart is a trap to
catch you and her arms are fetters" (Qoh. 7:28).

C. And Scripture says, "The king will rejoice in God" (Ps. 63:12).

2. A. . . . "and your own eyes":

B. This refers to prostitution, as it is said, "And Samson said, 'Take that
one for me, for she is right in my eyes'" (Judg. 14:3).

The show-fringes take their position in the holy way of life that defines
Israel. They stand for the entire body of religious duties that Israel undertakes
in its service to God. The same point is made again in the next discussion.

Sifre to Numbers CXV:IV.6–7

6. A. R. Nathan says, "You have not got a single religious duty that is listed in the Torah, the reward of the doing of which is not made explicit right alongside.

   B. "Go and learn the lesson from the religious duty of the fringes."

7. A. There is the case of a man who was meticulous about carrying out the religious duty of the fringes. He heard that there was a certain whore in one of the coastal towns, who would collect a fee of four hundred gold coins. He sent her four hundred gold coins and made a date with her.

   B. When his time came, he came along and took a seat at the door of her house. Her maid came and told her, "That man with whom you made a date, lo, he is sitting at the door of the house."

   C. She said to her, "Let him come in."

   D. When he came in, she spread out for him seven silver mattresses and one gold one, and she was on the top, and between each one were silver stools, and on the top, gold ones. When he came to do the deed, the four fringes fell out [of his garment] and appeared to him like four witnesses. The man slapped himself in the face and immediately withdrew and took a seat on the ground.

   E. The whore too withdrew and took a seat on the ground.

   F. She said to him, "By the winged god of Rome! I shall not let you go until you tell me what blemish you have found in me."

   G. He said to her, "By the Temple service! I did not find any blemish at all in you, for in the whole world there is none so beautiful as you. But the Lord, our God, has imposed upon me a rather small duty, but concerning [even that minor matter] he wrote, 'I am the Lord your God who brought you out of the land of Egypt to be your God. I am the Lord your God'—two times.

   H. "'I am the Lord your God,' I am destined to pay a good reward.

   I. "'I am the Lord your God,' I am destined to exact punishment.'"

   J. She said to him, "By the Temple service! I shall not let you go until you write me your name, the name of your town, and the name of your school in which you study Torah."

   K. So he wrote for her his name, the name of his town, and the name of his master, and the name of the school in which he had studied Torah.

   L. She went and split up her entire wealth, a third to the government, a third to the poor, and a third she took with her and came and stood at the schoolhouse of R. Hiyya.

   M. She said to him, "My lord, accept me as a proselyte."

   N. He said to her, "Is it possible that you have laid eyes on one of the disciples [and are converting in order to marry him]?"

   O. She took out the slip that was in her hand.

P. He said to [the disciple who had paid the money but not gone through with the act], "Stand up and acquire possession of what you have purchased. Those spreads that she spread out for you in violation of a prohibition she will now spread out for you in full remission of the prohibition.

Q. "As to this one, the recompense is paid out in this world, and as to the world to come, I do not know how much [more he will receive]!"

The story illustrates the proposition that looking at the show-fringes reminds one of the duty of living a holy way of life. The Israelite who was meticulous about wearing the show-fringes had to look at them before he could accomplish his goal, and they reminded him of who he was and what his obligations to God were. The result was a magnificent act of sanctification of God's name: the woman herself accepted the Torah and became part of Israel.

Chapter 38

Deuteronomy and *Sifre to Deuteronomy*

*I*n the book of Deuteronomy, a protracted reprise of the law and narrative of the first four books of the Pentateuch, Moses explicitly sets forth a vision of Israel's future history. The rabbinic sages in *Sifre to Deuteronomy,* ca. 300 C.E., examined that vision to uncover the rules that explain what happens to Israel. That issue drew attention to the cases that yield generalizations. The sages turned incidents or statements into general rules. In their commentary upon the book of Deuteronomy they set forth a systematic account of Israel's future history. They found the key to Israel's recovery of command of its destiny. They located it in the details of cases and carefully reframed them into rules pertaining to all cases.

Our sample shows how the rabbinic sages try to find the rules of history— why do things happen as they do—and so to figure out the future.

Sifre to Deuteronomy Pisqa CCCVII:I

1. A. ["The Rock—his deeds are perfect. Yes, all his ways are just; a faithful God, never false, true and upright is he. Children unworthy of him—that crooked perverse generation—their baseness has played him false. Do you thus requite the Lord, O dull and witless people? Is not he the father who created you, fashioned you, and made you endure?" (Deut. 32:4–6).]
   B. "The Rock": [The letters for the word 'rock' may be read to mean "artist," "design," and "form or create," thus yielding this sense:] the artist, for he designed the world first, and formed man in it [and all of these deeds are perfect].
   C. For it is said, "The Lord God formed man" (Gen. 2:7).
2. A. . . . "his deeds are perfect":
   B. What he does is entirely perfect with all those who are in the world, and none may complain against his deeds, even the most minor nitpicking.

    C. Nor may anyone look askance and say, "Would that I had three eyes," "would that I had three hands," "would that I had three legs," "would that I walked on my head," "would that my face were turned around toward my back"—"how nice it would be for me!"

    D. Scripture states, . . . "his deeds are perfect."

3. A. . . . "his deeds are perfect":

    B. [Since the word translated "perfect" can also be read as "just," we interpret as follows:] He sits as judge for every single person and gives to each what is coming to him.

4. A. ". . . a faithful God":

    B. For he believed in the world and created it.

5. A. ". . . never false":

    B. For people were not created to be wicked but to be righteous, and so Scripture says, "Behold, this only have I found, that God made man upright, but they have sought out many inventions" (Qoh. 7:29).

6. A. ". . . true and upright is he":

    B. He conducts himself in uprightness with everyone in the world.

The proposition yielded by the base verse is made explicit throughout: creation is perfect and was meant to be perfect. God is unflawed, even though creation did not work out as planned. The proposition rests on the reading of the letters for "rock" to mean "creator," and the entire program unfolds with precision from that point.

CCCVII:II

1. A. Another comment concerning the verse, "The Rock—[his deeds are perfect. Yes, all his ways are just; a faithful God, never false, true and upright is he]":

    B. ["Rock" means] "the mighty."

2. A. ". . . his deeds are perfect":

    B. What he does is entirely perfect with all those who are in the world, and none may complain against his deeds, even the most minor nit-picking.

    C. Nor may anyone look askance and say, "Why did the generation of the flood drown in water?" "Why did the generation of the tower of Babylon get dispersed to the ends of the world?" "Why did the people of Sodom drown in fire and brimstone?" "Why did Aaron take the priesthood?" "Why did David take the monarchy?" "Why did Korah and his conspiracy get swallowed up by the earth?"

    D. Scripture says, ". . . his deeds are perfect."

    E. [Since the word translated "perfect" can also be read as "just," we interpret as follows:] He sits as judge for every single person and gives to each what is coming to him.

3. A. ". . . a faithful God":
   B. He is like a bailee [who keeps his trust].
4. A. ". . . never false":
   B. He collects what is coming to him only at the end, for the trait of the Holy One, blessed be he, is different from the trait of mortals.
   C. A mortal leaves a deposit with his fellow, a pouch of two hundred *zuz* and he owes the bailee a hundred, when he comes to get what is his, the bailee says to him, "I'll take the *maneh* [the hundred *zuz*] which you owe me, and you keep the rest."
   D. So too in the case of a worker who worked for a householder and who is owed a denar. When he comes to collect his wage, the other says, to him, "I'll take the denar you owe me, and here's the rest of what is coming to you."
   E. But the One who spoke and brought the world into being is not like that.
   F. Rather: ". . . a faithful God":
   G. He is like a bailee [Hammer: who keeps his trust].
   H. He collects what is coming to him only at the end.
5. A. ". . . true and upright is he":
   B. In line with this verse: "For the Lord is righteous, he loves righteousness" (Ps. 11:7).

The proposition of nos. 1 and 2 is given everyday meaning at nos. 3ff. That is, God is patient but in the end he imposes a very appropriate penalty upon sinners. Numbers 1–2 present that proposition. Numbers 3–6 illustrate it. God collects what is coming, but only at the end, and not in midtransaction.

CCCVII:III

1. A. Another comment concerning the verse, "The Rock—[his deeds are perfect. Yes, all his ways are just; a faithful God, never false, true and upright is he]":
   B. ["Rock" means] "the mighty."
2. A. ". . . his deeds are perfect":
   B. What he does is entirely perfect with all those who are in the world.
   C. The recompense of the righteous and the punishment of the wicked [are entirely correct, for] the former have gotten nothing of what is coming to them in this world, and the latter have never gotten what is coming to them in this world either.
   D. And how on the basis of Scripture do we know that the righteous have never gotten what is coming to them in this world?
   E. As it is said, "Oh, how abundant is your goodness, which you have laid up for them who fear you" (Ps. 31:20).
   F. And how on the basis of Scripture do we know that the wicked have never gotten what is coming to them in this world?

     G. As it is said, "Is not this laid up in store with me, sealed up in my treasuries" (Deut. 32:34).

     H. When does each get what is coming to him?

     I. ". . . all his deeds are perfect."

     J. [Since the word translated "perfect" can also be read as "just," we interpret as follows:] Tomorrow, when he takes his seat in the throne of justice, he sits as judge for every single person and gives to each what is coming to him.

3. A. ". . . a faithful God":

     B. Just in the world to come as he pays back a completely righteous person a reward for the religious duty that he did in this world,

     C. so in this world he pays the completely wicked person a reward for every minor religious duty that he did in this world.

     D. And in the world to come just as he exacts punishment from a completely wicked person for the transgression that he did in this world,

     E. so in this world he exacts from the completely righteous person a penalty for every minor transgression that he did in this world.

4. A. ". . . never false":

     B. When someone dies, all the person's deeds come and are spelled out before him, saying to him, "Thus and so did you do on such and such a day, and thus and so did you do on such and such a day.

     C. "Do you confess these things?":

     D. And he says, "Yes."

     E. They say to him, "Sign here,"

     F. as it is said, "The hand of every man shall seal it, so that all men may know his deeds" (Job 37:7).

5. A. ". . . true and upright is he":

     B. Then he justifies the decision saying, "I have been fairly judged,"

     C. as Scripture says, "That you may justify the judgment when you speak" (Ps. 51:6).

The proposition begun at the outset is repeated in yet a new mode. Just as the fate meted out to famous sinners and famous saints is just, so the fate meted out to each individual is equally accurate and well construed. So a single implicit proposition, concerning God's judgment, is restated out of the base verse, which makes exactly that point.

CCCVII:IV

1. A. Another comment concerning the verse, "The Rock—his deeds are perfect. [Yes, all his ways are just; a faithful God, never false, true and upright is he]":

     B. When they arrested R. Haninah b. Teradion, a decree against him was issued, that he be executed by burning, along with his scroll.

    C. They told him, "A decree against you has been issued, that you be executed by burning, along with your scroll."

    D. He recited this verse: "The Rock—his deeds are perfect."

    E. They informed his wife, "A decree against your husband has been issued, that he be executed by burning, along with his scroll, and against you that you be put to death," and she recited this verse: "'a faithful God, never false, true and upright is he.'"

    F. They told his daughter, "A decree against your father has been issued, that he be executed by burning, along with his scroll, and against your mother, that she be executed, and against you, that you 'do work,'" and she recited this verse: "'Great in counsel and mighty in work, whose eyes are open' (Jer. 32:19)."

    G. Said Rabbi, "What great righteous people are these, for in their hour of trouble they called forth three verses that justify God's decree in a way that none of the rest of the verses of Scripture do it.

    H. "All three of them formed the exact intention in such a way as to justify the judgment of God concerning them."

2. A. A philosopher went to the ruler and said to him, "My lord, [following Hammer:] do not boast that you have burned the Torah, for to the place [heaven] from which it has come forth, it now returns, namely, to the house of its father."

    B. He said to him, "Tomorrow you will be judged in the same way as these [and be put to death]."

    C. He said to him, "You give me very good news, that tomorrow my share will be with theirs in the world to come."

If God's ways are perfect, how to make sense of the martyrdom of the saints? The answer shows that the saints attained their sainthood by knowing how to accept and to justify God's decree concerning them. It then proceeds to draw evidence from an outsider, impressed by the saints' conduct and convictions.

Chapter 39

Pesiqta de Rab Kahana

*I*n the synagogue, the Torah, the five books of Moses, is read weekly, so that over a year (some places: three years), the entire Pentateuch is publicly declaimed. In addition there are particular readings on special Sabbaths, for example, the Sabbath that falls between the New Year and the Day of Atonement. *Pesiqta de Rab Kahana,* ca. 500 C.E., sets forth expositions of themes dictated by those special Sabbaths or festivals and their scriptural readings. The twenty-eight chapters of *Pesiqta de Rab Kahana* in order follow the synagogal lections from early spring through fall, from late February or early March through late September or early October, approximately half of the solar year, twenty-seven weeks.

Here we see how the author expounds the theme of the Sabbath of Return, which falls between the Day of Judgment—the New Year (Rosh Hashanah)—and the Day of Atonement (Yom Kippur). On the Sabbath that comes in the ten days between the New Year and the Day of Atonement, the theme of repentance is expounded. Here we see how that is done.

Pesiqta de Rab Kahana XXIV:XI.1–8
1. A. ["Return O Israel to the Lord your God, for you have stumbled because of your iniquity. Take with you words and return to the Lord and say to him, Take away all iniquity; accept that which is good, and we will render the fruit of our lips. Assyria shall not save us, we will not ride upon horses; and we will say no more, Our God to the work of our hands. In you the orphan finds mercy" (Hos. 14:1–3).] What is written prior to Hosea 14:2? It is the following: "Samaria shall bear her guilt [for she has rebelled against her God]" (Hos. 14:1).
   B. And thereafter: "Return O Israel [to the Lord your God, for you have stumbled because of your iniquity. Take with you words and return to the Lord and say to him, Take away all iniquity; accept that which is good, and we will render the fruit of our lips. Assyria shall

192

not save us, we will not ride upon horses; and we will say no more,
Our God to the work of our hands. In you the orphan finds mercy]"
(Hos. 14:1–3).

The point is, if Israel returns to God in repentance, God will forgive Israel
its sins. This proposition is now illustrated by a parable.

C. R. Eleazar in the name of R. Samuel bar Nahman: "The matter may
   be compared to the case of a town that rebelled against the king, who
   sent against it a general of the army to destroy it. The general was
   skilled and cool.
D. "He said to them, 'Take time for yourselves, so that the king not do
   to you what he did to such-and-such a town and its environs, and to
   such-and-such a district and its area.'
E. "So said Hosea to Israel, 'My children, repent, so that the Holy One,
   blessed be he, will not do to you what he did to Samaria and its environs.'
F. "Said Israel before the Holy One, blessed be he, 'Lord of the ages,
   if we repent, will you accept us?'
G. "He said to them, 'The repentance of Cain I accepted, will I not
   accept yours?'
H. "'For a harsh decree was issued against him.'"

The basic proposition has now been expounded: If I accepted the repentance of Cain, will I not accept your repentance too? That is the point of E-H.
We now are given an exposition of how Cain repented.

2. A. That is in line with this verse of Scripture: "When you till the ground,
      it will no more yield its strength to you; a fugitive and a wanderer
      shall you be" (Gen. 4:12).
   B. But since he repented, he was relieved of half of the harsh decree.
   C. How do we know that he repented? "And Cain said to the Lord, 'Too
      great is my sin for me to bear it'" (Gen. 4:13).
   D. And how do we know that he was relieved of half of the harsh
      decree? "And Cain went away from the presence of the Lord and
      dwelled in the land of the wanderer" (Gen. 4:17).
   E. What is written is not "in the land of the fugitive and the wanderer,"
      but only, "in the land of the wanderer, to the east of Eden."
3. A. What is the meaning of "And Cain went away [from the presence of
      the Lord]"?
   B. R. Yudan in the name of R. Aibu said, "He shouted over the shoul-
      der and went away, as if to deceive the ones above. [He rejected
      God's reproof, as though murder was a light matter.]"

C. R. Berekhiah in the name of R. Eleazar b. R. Simeon: "He went away like the [pig] that shows a cloven hoof [pretending to be a valid animal, when it is not,] like one who would deceive the Creator."

D. R. Hunah in the name of R. Hinena bar Isaac said, "He went out rejoicing, in line with this verse: 'He goes forth to meet you and when he sees you, he will be glad in his heart' (Exod. 4:14).

E. "Adam met him and said to him, 'What happened at your trial?'

F. "He said to him, I repented and am reconciled.'

G. "Then Adam began to beat on his face: 'So great is the power of repentance, and I never knew it!'

H. "He forthwith went and said: 'It is a good thing to confess to the Lord' (Ps. 92:1)."

I. Said R. Levi, "It was Adam who stated this psalm: 'A psalm for the Sabbath day' (Ps. 92:1).

J. "And shall I not accept your repentance?"

The exposition of the case of Cain is now complete, and the narrative proceeds to Ahab, a sinner who repented and was forgiven.

4. A. "I accepted the repentance of Ahab, and shall I not accept your repentance?"

B. For a harsh decree was issued against him, in line with this verse: You shall speak to him, saying, "Have you killed and also taken possession?" And you shall speak to him, saying, "Thus says the Lord: In the place where dogs licked the blood of Naboth shall dogs lick your blood, even yours" (1 Kgs. 21:19).

C. "And it came to pass when Ahab heard these words that he tore his clothes and put sackcloth on his flesh and fasted and lay in sackcloth" (1 Kgs. 21:27). . . .

G. What is written there? "The word of the Lord came to Elijah the Tishbite saying, Do you see that Ahab humbles himself before me? Because he humbles himself before me, I will not bring the evil in his days" (1 Kgs. 21:28–29).

H. Said the Holy One, blessed be he, to Elijah, "You have seen that Ahab repented: Do you see that Ahab humbles himself before me? [Because he humbles himself before me, I will not bring the evil in his days.]

I. "And shall I not accept your repentance?"

5. A. "I accepted the repentance of the men of Anathoth, and shall I not accept your repentance?"

B. For a harsh decree was issued against them: "Thus says the Lord concerning the men of Anathoth who seek your life, saying, 'You shall not prophesy in the name of the Lord that you die not by our hand,' therefore thus says the Lord, 'Behold I will punish them . . . there shall be no remnant of them'" (Jer. 11:21, 23).

   C. But when they repented, they had the merit of producing descendants: "The men of Anathoth a hundred and twenty-eight" (Ezra 2:23).

   D. "And shall I not accept your repentance?"

6. A. "I accepted the repentance of the men of Nineveh, and shall I not accept your repentance?"

   B. For a harsh decree was issued against them, in line with this verse of Scripture: "Jonah began to enter into the city a day's journey [and he proclaimed and said, 'Yet forty days and Nineveh shall be overthrown']" (Jonah 3:4).

   C. "And the tidings reached the king of Nineveh and he arose from his throne and laid his robe from him and covered himself with sackcloth and proclaimed through Nineveh by the decree of the king and his nobles, saying, ['Let neither man nor beast . . . taste anything; let them not feed nor drink water; but let them be covered with sackcloth both man and beast and let them cry mightily to God']" (Jonah 3:7–8). . . .

   M. "And rend your hearts and not your garments" (Joel 2:13):

   N. Said R. Joshua b. Levi, "If you rend your hearts in repentance, you will not have to render your garments on account of the death of your sons and daughters.

   O. "Why not?

   P. "'Because he is merciful and long-suffering' (Joel 2:13)."

   Q. R. Aha and R. Tanhum in the name of R. Hiyya in the name of R. Yohanan, "What is written is not long-suffering [in the singular] but longer-suffering [in the dual], indicating that he is patient with the righteous but also patient with the wicked.

   R. "He is patient with the righteous and collects from them the modicum on account of the bad deeds that they did in this world so as to give them their full and complete reward in the world to come.

   S. "And he accords prosperity to the wicked in this world so as to give them the modicum of the reward for the good deeds that they have done in this world in order to exact from them full and complete penalty in the world to come."

   T. R. Samuel bar Nahman in the name of R. Yohanan: "What is written is not long-suffering [in the singular] but longer-suffering [in the dual], indicating that he is patient before he comes to collect [exacting punishment], and what he comes to collect, he extends the time [same word as patience] for collecting payment."

7. A. "I accepted the repentance of Manasseh, and shall I not accept your repentance?"

   B. For a harsh decree was issued against him.

C. This is in line with this verse of Scripture: "The Lord spoke to Manasseh and to his people but they did not listen. Therefore the Lord brought upon them the captains of the host of the king of Assyria, who took Manasseh with hooks" (2 Chr. 33:10, 11). . . .

I. "But when nothing helped, he said, 'I remember that my father would recite for me this verse: "In your distress when all these things come upon you in the end of days return to the Lord your God and listen to his voice, for the Lord your God is a merciful God, he will not fail you nor destroy you" (Deut. 4:30, 31).

J. "'Lo, I shall call on him. If he answers me, well and good, and if not, then they're all alike.'

K. "Now the ministering angels were closing the windows of the firmament, so that the prayer of Manasseh would not come before the Holy One, blessed be he, 'Lord of the ages, a man who set up an idol in the temple—should such a man be able to repent?'

L. "Said to them the Holy One, blessed be he, 'If I do not accept him in repentance, lo, I shall lock the door before all those who come to repent.'

M. "What did the Holy One, blessed be he, do for him?

N. "He dug a little opening under the throne of glory that was his, and through it he listened to his supplication. That is in line with this verse of Scripture: 'And he prayed to the Lord and he was entreated of him' (2 Chr. 33:13).

O. "What is written in the verse for the word for entreat is dug for him."

P. "And he listened to his supplications" (2 Chr. 33:13):

Q. "And he brought him back to Jerusalem to his kingdom" (2 Chr. 33:13). . . :

U. "Manasseh knew that the Lord is God" (2 Chr. 33:13): At that time said Manasseh, "There is justice and a Judge."

V. "I accepted the repentance of Jeconiaiah, and shall I not accept your repentance?"

8. A. "I accepted the repentance of Jeconaiah, and shall I not accept your repentance?"

B. For a harsh decree was issued against him.

C. That is in line with the following verse of Scripture: "Is this man Coniah a despised, broken pot, a vessel no one cares for? Why are he and his children hurled and cast into a land which they do not know?" (Jer. 22:28). . . .

I. Said R. Meir, "The Holy One, blessed be he, took an oath that he would not bring from Jeconaiah son of Jehoiakim, another king of Judah, in line with this verse: As I live says the Lord, if Coniah the son of Jehoiakim were the signet on a hand, yet by my right hand I would pluck you hence (Jer. 22:24)."

J. R. Hinena bar Isaac said, "'From there [that is, from Jeconaiah] I
shall pull up the kingdom from the house of David.'"

The main point throughout is that if God could accept the repentance of the
most reprobate of sinners, God also can accept the repentance of Israel. This
point is stated clearly at no. 1, and then the theme is resumed at no. 3. The
opening statement of the proposition is somewhat complicated, but what follows is clear and accords with a simple pattern throughout. The case of Ahab
shows the pattern: proposition, case, conclusion.

Chapter 40

Ruth and *Ruth Rabbah*

*T*he book of Ruth celebrates the loyalty of the outsider, Ruth, to her Israelite mother-in-law, and Ruth's entry into Israel. The rabbinic sages who interpret the book of Ruth in *Ruth Rabbah* have only one message. It concerns the outsider who becomes the principal, the Messiah out of Moab, and this miracle is accomplished through mastery of the Torah. Anyone, without regard to genealogy or origin, can know God through God's self-revelation in the Torah.

The admission of the outsider depends upon the rules of the Torah. These differentiate among outsiders. Those who know the rules are able to apply them accurately and mercifully. The proselyte is accepted because the Torah makes it possible to do so, and the condition of acceptance is complete and total submission to the Torah. Boaz taught Ruth the rules of the Torah, and she obeyed them carefully. Those proselytes who are accepted are respected by God and are completely equal to all other Israelites. Those who marry them are masters of the Torah, and their descendants are masters of the Torah, typified by David. Boaz in his day and David in his day were the same in this regard. What the proselyte therefore accomplishes is to take shelter under the wings of God's Presence, and the proselyte who does so stands in the royal line of David, Solomon, and the Messiah.

Over and over again the point is made that Ruth the Moabitess, perceived by the ignorant as an outsider, enjoyed complete equality with all other Israelites, because she had accepted the yoke of the Torah, married a great sage, and through her descendants produced the Messiah-sage, David.

Ruth Rabbah XL:I

    1. A.   "And at mealtime Boaz said to her, 'Come here and eat some bread, and dip your morsel in the wine.' So she sat beside the reapers, and he passed to her parched grain; and she ate until she was satisfied, and she had some left over" (Ruth 2:14):

B. R. Yohanan interpreted the phrase "come here" in six ways:

C. "The first speaks of David.

D. "'Come here': means, to the throne: 'That you have brought me here' (2 Sam. 7:18).

E. "'. . . and eat some bread:' the bread of the throne.

F. "'. . . and dip your morsel in vinegar:' this speaks of his sufferings: 'O Lord, do not rebuke me in your anger' (Ps. 6:2).

G. "'So she sat beside the reapers': for the throne was taken from him for a time."

I. [Resuming from G:] "'and he passed to her parched grain': he was restored to the throne: 'Now I know that the Lord saves his anointed' (Ps. 20:7).

J. "'. . . and she ate and was satisfied and left some over': this indicates that he would eat in this world, in the days of the Messiah, and in the age to come.

2. A. "The second interpretation refers to Solomon: 'Come here': means, to the throne.

B. "'. . . and eat some bread': this is the bread of the throne: "And Solomon's provision for one day was thirty measures of fine flour and three score measures of meal' (1 Kgs. 5:2).

C. "'. . . and dip your morsel in vinegar': this refers to the dirty of the deeds [that he did].

D. "'So she sat beside the reapers': for the throne was taken from him for a time."

G. [Reverting to D:] "'and he passed to her parched grain': for he was restored to the throne.

H. "'. . . and she ate and was satisfied and left some over': this indicates that he would eat in this world, in the days of the Messiah, and in the age to come.

3. A. "The third interpretation speaks of Hezekiah: 'Come here': means, to the throne.

B. "'. . . and eat some bread': this is the bread of the throne.

C. "'. . . and dip your morsel in vinegar': this refers to sufferings [Isa. 5:1]: 'And Isaiah said, Let them take a cake of figs' (Isa. 38:21).

D. "'So she sat beside the reapers': for the throne was taken from him for a time: 'Thus says Hezekiah, This day is a day of trouble and rebuke' (Isa. 37:3).

E. "'. . . and he passed to her parched grain': for he was restored to the throne: 'So that he was exalted in the sight of all nations from then on' (2 Chr. 32:23).

F. "'. . . and she ate and was satisfied and left some over': this indicates that he would eat in this world, in the days of the Messiah, and in the age to come.

4. A. "The fourth interpretation refers to Manasseh: 'Come here': means, to the throne.

  B. "'. . . and eat some bread': this is the bread of the throne.

  C. "'. . . and dip your morsel in vinegar': for his dirty deeds were like vinegar, on account of wicked actions.

  D. "'So she sat beside the reapers': for the throne was taken from him for a time: 'And the Lord spoke to Manasseh and to his people, but they did not listen. So the Lord brought them the captains of the host of the king of Assyria, who took Manasseh with hooks' (2 Chr. 33:10–11)."

  K. [Reverting to D:] "'and he passed to her parched grain': for he was restored to the throne: 'And brought him back to Jerusalem to his kingdom' (2 Chr. 33:13).

5. A. "The fifth interpretation refers to the Messiah: 'Come here': means, to the throne.

  B. "'. . . and eat some bread': this is the bread of the throne.

  C. "'. . . and dip your morsel in vinegar': this refers to suffering: 'But he was wounded because of our transgressions' (Isa. 53:5).

  D. "'So she sat beside the reapers': for the throne is destined to be taken from him for a time: 'For I will gather all nations against Jerusalem to battle and the city shall be taken' (Zech. 14:2).

  E. "'. . . and he passed to her parched grain': for he will be restored to the throne: 'And he shall smite the land with the rod of his mouth' (Isa. 11:4)."

  F. R. Berekhiah in the name of R. Levi: "As was the first redeemer, so is the last redeemer:

  G. "Just as the first redeemer was revealed and then hidden from them—"

  H. And how long was he hidden? Three months: "And they met Moses and Aaron" (Exod. 5:20),

  I. [reverting to G:] "so the last redeemer will be revealed to them and then hidden from them."

6. A. "The sixth interpretation refers to Boaz: 'Come here': [supply:] means, to the throne.

  B. "'. . . and eat some bread': this refers to the bread of the reapers.

  C. "'. . . and dip your morsel in vinegar': it is the practice of reapers to dip their bread in vinegar."

  E. [Reverting to C:] "'So she sat beside the reapers': this is meant literally.

  F. "'. . . and he passed to her parched grain': a pinch between his two fingers."

Ruth's actions, like Abraham's, Isaac's, and Jacob's, prefigure the story of their descendants, Israel. When Boaz said to Ruth, "Come here and eat some bread," he spoke not only of that instant but of time to come: David, Solomon, Hezekiah, Manasseh, the Messiah, as well as to Ruth herself. Here we see how the whole of Scripture's narrative is brought to bear upon any one detail within that narrative.

Chapter 41

Lamentations and
Lamentations Rabbah

*T*he biblical book of Lamentations contains a sustained dirge for the destruction of Jerusalem by the Babylonians in ca. 586 B.C.E. The issue is, does God still care about Israel, even after the destruction of the Temple on account of Israel's sin? The theme of *Lamentations Rabbah,* a commentary on the book of Lamentations produced in the sixth century C.E., is Israel's relationship with God. The message concerning that theme is that the covenant still governs that relationship. Therefore everything that happens to Israel makes sense and bears meaning. Israel is not helpless before its fate but controls its own destiny. The destruction of the Temple in Jerusalem in 70 C.E.—as much as in 586 B.C.E.—proves the enduring validity of the covenant. Because the rules govern when Israel sinned, so they will govern when Israel repents. That certainty bears the promise of redemption.

Lamentations Rabbah L.I.9
There was the case of Miriam, daughter of Tanhum, who was taken captive with her seven sons with her.
The ruler took and imprisoned them within seven rooms.
Then he went and brought the eldest and said to him, "Bow down before the idol."
He said to him, "God forbid! I will not bow down before the idol."
"Why not?"
"Because it is written in the Torah, 'I am the Lord your God' (Exod. 20:2)."
He forthwith had him taken off and killed.
Then he went and brought the next and said to him, "Bow down before the idol."
He said to him, "God forbid! I will not bow down before the idol."
"Why not?"
"Because it is written in the Torah, 'You shall have no other gods before me' (Exod. 20:3)."
He forthwith had him taken off and killed.

202

Then he went and brought the next and said to him, "Bow down before the idol."

He said to him, "God forbid! I will not bow down before the idol."

"Why not?"

"Because it is written in the Torah, 'For you shall not bow down to any other god' (Exod. 34:14)."

He forthwith had him taken off and killed.

Then he went and brought the next and said to him, "Bow down before the idol."

He said to him, "God forbid! I will not bow down before the idol."

"Why not?"

"Because it is written in the Torah, 'He who sacrifices unto the gods, except for the Lord only, shall be utterly destroyed' (Exod. 22:19)."

He forthwith had him taken off and killed.

Then he went and brought the next and said to him, "Bow down before the idol."

He said to him, "God forbid! I will not bow down before the idol."

"Why not?"

"Because it is written in the Torah, 'Hear O Israel, the Lord our God, the Lord is one' (Deut. 6:4)."

He forthwith had him taken off and killed.

Then he went and brought the next and said to him, "Bow down before the idol."

He said to him, "God forbid! I will not bow down before the idol."

"Why not?"

"Because it is written in the Torah, 'For the Lord your God is in the midst of you, a God great and awful' (Deut. 7:21)."

He forthwith had him taken off and killed.

Then he went and brought the youngest and said to him, "My child, bow down before the idol."

He said to him, "God forbid! I will not bow down before the idol."

"Why not?"

"Because it is written in the Torah, 'Know this day and lay it to your heart that the Lord, he is God in heaven above and on earth beneath, there is none else' (Deut. 4:39).

"Furthermore, we have taken an oath to our God that we will not exchange him for any other: 'You have sworn the Lord this day to be your God' (Deut. 26:17). And as we swore to him, so he swore to us not to exchange us for another people: 'And the Lord has sworn you this day to be his own treasure' (Deut. 26:18)."

He said to him, "Your brothers have had their fill of years and life and have had happiness, but you are young and have not. Bow down before the idol, and I will show you favor."

He said to him, "It is written in our Torah, 'The Lord shall reign forever and ever' (Exod. 15:18), 'The Lord is king forever, the nations have perished out of his land' (Ps. 10:16).

"You are nothing, and his enemies are nothing. A human being lives today and is gone tomorrow, rich today and poor tomorrow, but the Holy One, blessed be he, lives and endures for all eternity."

He said to him, "I will toss my ring to the earth in front of the idol. You just pick it up. Then people will know that you have obeyed Caesar."

He said to him, "Woe to you, Caesar, if you fear mortals, who are no different from you, shall I not fear the King of kings of kings, the Holy One, blessed be he, the God of the universe?"

He said to him, "And is there a divinity in the world?"

He said to him, "Woe to you, Caesar, and have you seen a world without rules?"

He said to him, "And does your God have a mouth?"

He said to him, "And concerning your idol it is written, 'They have a mouth but cannot speak' (Ps. 115:5). But in connection with our God: 'By the word of the Lord the heavens were made' (Ps. 33:6)."

He said to him, "And does your God have eyes?"

He said to him, "In regard to your idol it is written, 'They have eyes but do not see' (Ps. 115:5), but in connection with our God it is written, 'The eyes of the Lord that run to and fro through the whole earth' (Zech. 4:10)."

He said to him, "And does your God have ears?"

He said to him, "In regard to your idol it is written, 'They have ears but they do not hear' (Ps. 115:6), but in connection with our God it is written, 'And the Lord listened and heard' (Mal. 3:16)."

He said to him, "And does your God have a nose?"

He said to him, "In regard to your idol it is written, 'They have noses but do not smell' (Ps. 115:6), but in connection with our God it is written, 'And the Lord smelled the sweet odor' (Gen. 8:21)."

He said to him, "And does your God have hands?"

He said to him, "In regard to your idol it is written, 'They have handles but they do not handle' (Ps. 115:7), but in connection with our God it is written, 'Yes, my hand has laid the foundation of the earth' (Isa. 48:13)."

He said to him, "And does your God have feet?"

He said to him, "In regard to your idol it is written, 'They have feet but they do not walk' (Ps. 115:7), but in connection with our God it is written, 'And his feet shall stand in that day on the Mount of Olives' (Zech. 14:4)."

He said to him, "And does your God have a throat?"

He said to him, "In regard to your idol it is written, 'Neither do they speak with their throat' (Ps. 115:7), but in connection with our God it is written, 'And sound goes out of his mouth' (Job 37:2)."

He said to him, "If he has all of these traits, how come he does not save you from my power as he saved Hananiah, Mishael, and Azariah from the power of Nebuchadnezzar?"

He said to him, "Hananiah, Mishael, and Azariah were meritorious, and they fell into the hands of a meritorious king, while we are guilty and have fallen into the hands of a guilt-ridden and cruel king.

"And as for ourselves, our lives are forfeit to heaven. If you do not kill us, the Holy One, blessed be he, has many bears, wolves, snakes, leopards, and scorpions to kill us.

"But the Holy One, blessed be he, has given us over into your hand only so as to exact from you vengeance for our blood in the future."

He immediately gave the order to put him to death.

His mother said to him, "By your life, Caesar, give me my son, so I may hug and kiss him."

They gave her son to her, and she took out her breasts and gave him milk.

She said to him, "By your life, Caesar, kill me first, then him."

He said to her, "I cannot do that, for it is written in your Torah, 'And whether it be cow or ewe, you shall not kill it and its young in one day' (Lev. 22:28)."

"You wicked man! Now have you kept all of the commandments of the Torah except for this one alone?"

He immediately gave the order to put him to death.

His mother threw herself upon her child and hugged and kissed him, saying to him, "My son, go tell Abraham, our father, 'My mother says to you, "Do not take pride, claiming, I built an altar and offered up my son, Isaac."

"'Now see, my mother built seven altars and offered up seven sons in one day.

"'And yours was only a test, but I really had to do it.'"

While she was hugging him, the king gave the order, and they killed him in her arms.

When he was put to death, sages calculated the matter of the child's age and found that he was two years, six months, and six and a half hours old.

At that moment all the nations of the world cried out and said, "What kind of God do these people have, who does such things to them! 'No, but for your sake, we are killed all day long' (Ps. 44:23)."

They say that after some days the woman went mad and threw herself from the roof and died: "She who has borne seven languished" (Jer. 15:9).

An echo came forth: "A joyful mother of children" (Ps. 113:9).

And the Holy Spirit cried, "For these things I weep."

The tension is between the Caesar and the Israelite sons and their mother, the sons dying for theological truth, embodied in the capacity of the youngest to participate in the disputation.

Chapter 42

Song of Songs and
Song of Songs Rabbah

*T*he Song of Songs, known in some Christian Bibles as "the Song of Solomon" (both referring to the opening line, "The Song of Songs, which is Solomon's"), is a set of love poems. The poetry finds a place in the Torah because the songs in fact speak about the relationship between God and Israel. The intent of the compilers of *Song of Songs Rabbah* is to justify that reading.

The rabbinic sages' reading of the Song of Songs turns to everyday experience—the love of husband and wife—for a metaphor of God's love for Israel and Israel's love for God. Then, when Solomon's Song says, "O that you would kiss me with the kisses of your mouth! For your love is better than wine" (Song 1:2), sages of blessed memory think of how God kissed Israel. Reading the Song of Songs as a metaphor, the Judaic sages state in a systematic and orderly way their entire system.

This reading was debated by the ancient sages. Mishnah tractate *Yadayim* 3:5 defines the setting in which sages took up the Song of Songs. The issue was, which documents are regarded as holy, among the received canon of ancient Israel. The specific problem focuses upon Qohelet (Ecclesiastes) and the Song of Songs. The terms of the issue derive from the matter of uncleanness. If a document is holy, then it is held to be unclean, meaning, if one touches the document, the person has to undergo a process of purification before he can eat food in a certain status of sanctification or go to the Temple. What was the point? That meant in practice people would be quite cautious about handling such documents. So when sages declare that a parchment or hide on which certain words are written imparts uncleanness to hands, they mean to say, those words, and the object on which they are written, must be handled reverently and thoughtfully. Here is the relevant passage of the Mishnah:

Mishnah tractate *Yadayim* 3:5

All sacred Scriptures impart uncleanness to hands. The Song of Songs and Qohelet impart uncleanness to hands.

R. Judah says, "The Song of Songs imparts uncleanness to hands, but as to Qohelet there is dispute."

R. Yose says, "Qohelet does not impart uncleanness to hands, but as to Song of Songs there is dispute."

Rabbi Simeon says, "Qohelet is among the lenient rulings of the house of Shammai and strict rulings of the house of Hillel."

Said R. Simeon b. Azzai, "I have a tradition from the testimony of the seventy-two elders, on the day on which they seated R. Eleazar b. Azariah in the session, that the Song of Songs and Qohelet do impart uncleanness to hands."

Said R. Aqiba, "Heaven forbid! No Israelite man ever disputed concerning Song of Songs that it imparts uncleanness to hands. For the entire age is not so worthy as the day on which the Song of Songs was given to Israel. For all the Scriptures are holy, but the Song of Songs is holiest of all. And if they disputed, they disputed only concerning Qohelet."

Said R. Yohanan b. Joshua the son of R. Aqiba's father-in-law, according to the words of Ben Azzai, "Indeed did they dispute, and indeed did they come to a decision."

Clearly, the Mishnah passage, ca. 200, records a point at which the status of the Song of Songs is in doubt. By the time of the compilation of *Song of Songs Rabbah,* that question had been settled. Everybody took for granted that our document is holy for the reason given.

Song of Songs Rabbah XXIII:I.1–4 to Song of Songs 2:6
1. A. "O that his left hand were under my head":
   B. this refers to the first tablets.
   C. "and that his right hand embraced me":
   D. this refers to the second tablets.
2. A. Another interpretation of the verse, "O that his left hand were under my head":
   B. this refers to the show-fringes.
   C. "and that his right hand embraced me":
   D. this refers to the phylacteries.
3. A. Another interpretation of the verse, "O that his left hand were under my head":
   B. this refers to the recitation of the Shema.
   C. "and that his right hand embraced me":
   D. this refers to the prayer.

4. A. Another interpretation of the verse, "O that his left hand were under my head":

   B. this refers to the tabernacle.

   C. "and that his right hand embraced me":

   D. this refers to the cloud of the Presence of God in the world to come: "The sun shall no longer be your light by day nor for brightness will the moon give light to you" (Isa. 60:19). Then what gives light to you? "The Lord shall be your everlasting light" (Isa. 60:20).

What are the marks of God's love for Israel? The following items are listed: (1) the Ten Commandments; (2) the show-fringes and phylacteries; (3) the Shema and the prayer; (4) the tabernacle and the cloud of the Presence of God in the world to come. Why these items in particular? The reason becomes clear when they reach their climax. It is in the analogy between the home and the tabernacle, the embrace of God and the Presence of God. So the whole is meant to list those things that draw the Israelite near God and make the Israelite cleave to God, as the base verse says. So the right hand and the left stand for the most intimate components of the life of the individual and the home with God.

Chapter 43

Esther and *Esther Rabbah I*

*I*n *Esther Rabbah* Part One (covering the book of Esther's first two chapters), of no certain date but possibly ca. 500 C.E., we find only one message, and it is reworked in only a few ways. It is that the nations are swine, their rulers fools, and Israel is subjugated to them only because of its own sins. No other explanation serves to account for the paradox and anomaly that prevail. But just as God saved Israel in the past, so the salvation that Israel can attain will repeat the former ones.

Esther Rabbah II:I.1

    A. Samuel commenced by citing the following verse of Scripture: "Yet for all that, when they are in the land of their enemies, I will not spurn them, neither will I abhor them so as to destroy them utterly and break my covenant with them, for I am the Lord their God; but I will for their sake remember the covenant with their forefathers, whom I brought forth out of the land of Egypt in the sight of the nations, that I might be their God: I am the Lord" (Lev. 26:44–45):

    B. "'I will not spurn them': in Babylonia.

    C. "'neither will I abhor them': in Media.

    D. "'so as to destroy them utterly': under Greek rule.

    E. "'and break my covenant with them': under the wicked kingdom [Rome].

    F. "'for I am the Lord their God': in the age to come."

    G. Taught R. Hiyya, "'I will not spurn them': in the time of Vespasian.

    H. "'neither will I abhor them': in the time of Trajan.

    I. "'so as to destroy them utterly': in the time of Haman.

    J. "'and break my covenant with them': in the time of the Romans.

    K. "'for I am the Lord their God': in the time of Gog and Magog."

The two readings are complementary, the one invoking times of trouble in ages past, the other in the perceived present. What holds together the two readings, A-F, G-K, is that they comment on the same sequence of verses, and they make the same point through different cases.

Chapter 44

The Fathers ('Abot) and
The Fathers According to Rabbi Nathan

*I*n 250 C.E. tractate *'Abot* (*The Fathers*) delivered its message through wise sayings assigned to named sages. Attached to, but not part of, the Mishnah, tractate *'Abot,* also called *Pirqe 'Abot* ("sayings of the fathers"), is made up of five chapters of wisdom sayings for disciples of sages, especially those involved in administration of the law. These sayings, miscellaneous in character, are assigned to named authorities. The recurrent emphasis is on Torah study and the social, intellectual, and personal virtues required for Torah study.

A few centuries later—the date is indeterminate but it is possibly ca. 500 C.E.—the *Fathers According to Rabbi Nathan* set forth a vast secondary expansion of that same tractate. It took the names mentioned in the list of sages and their sayings in tractate *'Abot* and endowed those anonymous names with flesh-and-blood form.

The *Fathers According to Rabbi Nathan* presents two types of materials and sets them forth in a fixed order. The document contains amplifications of sayings in *'Abot* as well as materials not related to anything in the original document. The order is the same. First, the editor presents amplifications of tractate *'Abot,* and only second does he tack on its own message. This is accomplished through telling stories about sages in particular.

The upshot is simple. The sage in the *Fathers According to Rabbi Nathan* presents his Torah teachings through what he does, not only through what he says. Therefore telling stories about what sages did and the circumstances in which they made their sayings forms part of the Torah, in a way in which, in the earlier document, it clearly did not.

As we saw in part 4, the *Fathers According to Rabbi Nathan* contains stories not of the birth but of "the origins" of masters of the Torah. By "origins," the storytellers mean the beginnings of the Torah study of a famed authority. Life begins at birth, but when we wish to tell sage-stories, beginnings are measured differently. The sage begins life when he begins Torah study.

And the sages whose origins are found noteworthy began in mature years, not in childhood. The proposition implicit in origins-stories then is that any male may start his Torah study at any point in life and hope for true distinction in the Torah community.

The stories make essentially the same point, which is that one can begin Torah study in mature years and progress to the top. When one does so, one also goes from poverty to wealth through public recognition of one's mastery of the Torah. The supernatural relationship, which has superseded the natural ones to wife and father, generates glory and honor, riches and fame, for the sage, and, through reflection, for the natural family as well. That is the point of the stories of the origins of sages, which take up what is clearly a pressing question and answer it in a powerful way. We begin with the statement of 'Abot that is subject to amplification in the *Fathers According to Rabbi Nathan*.

'Abot 1:4

Yose b. Yoezer of Seredah and Yose b. Yohanan of Jerusalem received [it] from them.

Yose b. Yoezer says, (1) "Let your house be a gathering place for sages. (2) And wallow in the dust of their feet. (3) And drink in their words with gusto."

The Fathers According to Rabbi Nathan VI:IV.1

Another comment on the statement, **And wallow in the dust of their feet:** This refers to R. Eliezer.

. . . and drink in their words with gusto: This refers to R. Aqiba.

We concentrate on the story of R. Aqiba.

The Fathers According to Rabbi Nathan VI:V.1

How did R. Aqiba begin [his Torah study]?

They say: He was forty years old and had never repeated a tradition [that is, he was completely illiterate and had never studied the Torah or learned its traditions]. One time he was standing at the mouth of a well. He thought to himself, "Who carved out this stone?"

They told him, "It is the water that is perpetually falling on it every day."

They said to him, "Aqiba, do you not read Scripture, 'The water wears away stones' (Job 4:19)?"

On the spot R. Aqiba constructed in his own regard an argument a fortiori: now if something soft can wear down something hard, words of Torah, which are as hard as iron, how much the more so should wear down my heart, which is made of flesh and blood.

On the spot he repented [and undertook] to study the Torah.

Aqiba's conversion to Torah study led to his entering an elementary school with children—this at a mature age. But his brilliance swept all before him.

> He and his son went into study session before a children's teacher, saying to him, "My lord, teach me Torah."
>
> R. Aqiba took hold of one end of the tablet, and his son took hold of the other end. The teacher wrote out for him aleph bet [the first two letters of the Hebrew alphabet] and he learned it, aleph taw [the first and last letters of the alphabet] and he learned it, the Torah of the Priests [the books of Leviticus and Numbers] and he learned it. He went on learning until he had learned the entire Torah.
>
> He went and entered study sessions before R. Eliezer and before R. Joshua. He said to them, "My lords, open up for me the reasoning of the Mishnah."
>
> When they had stated one passage of law, he went and sat by himself and said, "Why is this aleph written? Why is this bet written? Why is this statement made?" He went and asked them and in point of fact reduced them to silence.

The Fathers According to Rabbi Nathan VI:V.2

> R. Simeon b. Eleazar says, "I shall make a parable for you. To what is the matter comparable? To a stonecutter who was cutting stone in a quarry. One time he took his chisel and went and sat down on the mountain and started to chip away little shards from it. People came by and said to him, 'What are you doing?'
>
> "He said to them, 'Lo, I am going to uproot the mountain and move it into the Jordan River.'"
>
> "They said to him, 'You will never be able to uproot the entire mountain.'
>
> "He continued chipping away at the mountain until he came to a huge boulder. He quarried underneath it and unearthed it and uprooted it and tossed it into the Jordan.'
>
> "He said to the boulder, 'This is not your place, but that is your place.'
>
> "Likewise this is what R. Aqiba did to R. Eliezer and to R. Joshua."

The point is the power of words of Torah to wear down the hard heart of a human being.

The Fathers According to Rabbi Nathan VI:V.4

> Every day he would bring a bundle of twigs, half of which he would sell in exchange for food, and half of which he would use for a garment.

His neighbors said to him, "Aqiba, you are killing us with the smoke. Sell them to us, buy oil with the money, and by the light of a lamp do your studying."

He said to them, "I fill many needs with that bundle, first, I repeat traditions [by the light of the fire] I kindle with them, second, I warm myself with them, third, I sleep on them."

The next statement draws a lesson from the record of Aqiba's remarkable mastery of the Torah, accomplished in mature years. He became the greatest sage of the Torah among the masters of the Mishnah. He shames all those who use poverty or family responsibility as excuses for not engaging in Torah study.

The Fathers According to Rabbi Nathan VI:V.5

In time to come R. Aqiba is going to impose guilt [for failing to study] on the poor [who use their poverty as an excuse not to study].

For if they say to them, "Why did you not study the Torah?" and they reply, "Because we were poor," they will say to them, "But was not R. Aqiba poorer and more poverty-stricken?"

If they say, "Because of our children [whom we had to work to support]," they will say to them, "Did not R. Aqiba have sons and daughters?"

So they will say to them, "Because Rachel, his wife, had the merit [of making it possible for him to study, and we have no equivalent helpmates; our wives do not have equivalent merit at their disposal]."

The inclusion of Aqiba's wife, Rachel, draws in its wake a story about the reward she received for her patience and support.

The Fathers According to Rabbi Nathan VI:V.6

It was at the age of forty that he went to study the Torah. Thirteen years later he taught the Torah in public.

They say that he did not leave this world before there were silver and golden tables in his possession,

and before he went up onto his bed on golden ladders.

His wife went about in golden sandals and wore a golden tiara of the silhouette of the city [Jerusalem].

His disciples said to him, "My lord, you have shamed us by what you have done for her [since we cannot do the same for our wives]."

He said to them, "She bore a great deal of pain on my account for [the study of] the Torah."

This item completes the foregoing, the narrative of how Rachel's devotion to Aqiba's study of the Torah produced a rich reward.

Glossary

Ab, Ninth of: Day of Mourning for destruction of Jerusalem Temple in 586 B.C.E. and 70 C.E.

'am ha'arets: literally, people of the land; rabbinic usage: boor, unlearned, not a disciple of the sages

B.C.E.: before the common era; used in place of B.C.

berakah (*plural* **Berakot**)**:** benediction, blessing, or praise

C.E.: common era; used instead of A.D.

cult: a system of religious worship, a mode of serving God, not to be confused with another use of the word "cult," a religious group that is unconventional

diaspora: dispersion, exile of Jews from the Land of Israel

dietary laws: pertaining to animal food; pious Jews may eat only fish that have fins and scales, animals that part the hoof and chew the cud (e.g., sheep, cows, but not camels, pigs). Animals must be ritually slaughtered (Hebrew: *shehi-tah*), humane method of slaughter accompanied by blessing of thanks. Jews may not eat shellfish, worms, snails, flesh torn from a living animal, etc. Any mixture of meat and milk is forbidden; after eating meat, one may not eat dairy products for a period of time (one to six hours, depending on custom). Fish are neutral (pareve). *See* kosher

El, Elohim: God, divinity

eschatology: theory of the end of time, death, judgment, world to come, messianic era, resurrection of the dead

exilarch: head of the exile; Aramaic: *Resh Galuta*; head of the Jewish community in Babylonia in talmudic and medieval times

Gemara: completion; comments and discussions of Mishnah. Mishnah + Gemara = Talmud

habdalah: the rite that at sundown at the end of the Sabbath or festival marks the separation of the holy time of the Sabbath or festival from the secular or profane time of the everyday week

haggadah: literally, telling, narration; generally: lore, theology, fable, biblical exegesis, ethics narrative, particularly the narrative read at the Passover banquet (Seder)

halakah: "the way things are done," from *halak*: go; more broadly, the prescriptive, legal tradition

Hillel: first-century Pharisaic leader; taught, "Do not unto others what you would not have them do unto you."

Jehovah: transliteration of divine name, based on misunderstanding of Hebrew letters YHWH. Jews did not pronounce name of God; referred to the name as *Adonai,* Lord. Translators took vowels of *Adonai* and added them to consonants JHVH; hence JeHoVaH. The J represents the Hebrew Y.

Judah the Patriarch: head of Palestinian Jewish community, 200 C.E.; promulgated Mishnah

Ketubim: writings; biblical books of Psalms, Proverbs, etc.

kosher: literally, fit, proper; applies to anything suitable for use according to Jewish law

Mekilta: Rabbinic commentary to Exodus

Messiah: eschatological king to raise the dead and restore Israel to the Land of Israel; to rule in end of time

mezuzah: parchment containing first two paragraphs of Shema, rolled tightly and placed in case, attached to doorposts of home

midrash: exegesis of Scripture; also applied to collection of such exegeses

Mishnah: code of law promulgated by Judah the Prince (ca. 200 C.E.); in six parts, concerning agricultural laws, festival and Sabbath law, family and personal status, torts, damages, and civil law, laws pertaining to the sanctuary and to rules of ritual cleanness

mitzvah: commandments; technical sense: scriptural or rabbinic injunctions; later on, also used in sense of good deed; every human activity may represent an act of obedience to divine will

Mosaic: what pertains to Moses or to the writings attributed to him, e.g., Mosaic law

myth: religious truth set forth in narrative form

nasi: prince, patriarch

Parashah: chapter

Passover: (Hebrew: *Pesah*) festival commemorating exodus from Egypt, in spring month of Nisan (generally April)

Pharisee: (from Hebrew: *Parush*) separatist; party in ancient Judaism teaching oral Torah revealed at Sinai along with written one, preserved among prophets and sages down to the Pharisaic party; espoused prophetic ideals and translated them to everyday life of Jewry through legislation. Distinctive beliefs according to Josephus, the Jewish historian of the first century: (1) immortality of the soul; (2) existence of angels; (3) divine providence; (4) freedom of will; (5) resurrection of the dead; (6) oral Torah

pisqa: chapter

profane: secular, not sanctified; not to be confused with "profane" as profanity

Purim: festival commemorating deliverance of Persian Jews from extermination in fifth century B.C.E., as related in Scroll of Esther; on 14th of Adar, generally in March

rabbi: Hebrew for "my lord, my master"; title for teacher of oral Torah

Reform: religious movement advocating change of tradition to conform to conditions of modern life. Holds halakah to be human creation, subject to human judgment; sees Judaism as historical religious experience of Jewish people

Rosh Hashanah: New Year, first day of Tishre (generally September)

Sadducees: sect of Temple priests and sympathizers; stressed written Torah and the right of the priesthood to interpret it against Pharisaic claim that oral tradition held by Pharisees was means of interpretation; rejected belief in resurrection of the dead, immortality of soul, angels, divine providence

Sanhedrin: Jewish legislative-administrative agency in Second Temple times

seder: order; Passover home service

Shammai: colleague of Hillel, first-century C.E. Pharisaic sage

Shavuot: feast of weeks; Pentecost; commemorates giving of Torah at Mt. Sinai

Shekinah: presence of God in world

Shema: proclamation of unity of God: Deut. 6:4–9; 11:13–21; Num. 15:37–41

Sifra: Rabbinic commentary on Leviticus

Sifre: Rabbinic commentary on Numbers and Deuteronomy

Sukkah: booth, tabernacle

Sukkot: autumn harvest festival, ending high holy day season

synagogue: Greek translation of Hebrew *bet hakeneset* (house of assembly). Place of Jewish prayer, study, assembly

Talmud: Mishnah (see above) plus commentary on the Mishnah produced in rabbinical academies from ca. 200 to 500 C.E. (called Gemara) form the Talmud. Two Talmuds were produced—one in Palestine, the other in Babylonia. From 500 C.E. onward, Babylonian Talmud was the primary source for Judaic law and theology

Tanak: Hebrew Bible; formed of Torah, Nebi'im, Ketubim, (Pentateuch, Prophets, Writings); hence, TaNaK.

Tannaim: those who study and teach; rabbinical masters mentioned in Mishnah

Tannaite: an authority of the Mishnah or of the same period as the Mishnah, up to ca. 200 C.E.

tefillin: phylacteries worn by adult males in morning service, based on Exod. 13:1, 11; Deut. 6:4–9; 11:13–21. These passages are written on parchment, placed in leather cases, and worn on left arm and forehead

Torah: literally, instruction. At first, the five books of Moses; then Scriptures as a whole; then the whole corpus of revelation, both written and oral, taught by Pharisaic Judaism. Standing by itself, Torah can mean "study," the act of learning and discussion of the tradition

Tosefta: supplements to the Mishnah

tractate: a subdivision of the Mishnah; the Mishnah is divided into six divisions, and these, in turn, are divided into tractates, each with its own topic. A tractate then is a topical exposition of the Mishnah. Commentaries to the Mishnah, the Tosefta and the two Talmuds, then select Mishnah tractates for close reading and amplification.

Tsaddik: righteous man

tsedakah: righteousness; used for charity, philanthropy

Yahweh: *see* Jehovah

Yom Kippur: Day of Atonement; fast day for penitence